ABOUT THE AUTHOR

STANLEY L. McMICHAEL was in the real estate business for more than 40 years, and a prominent writer in the realty field for 30 years. He wrote 21 books, including *McMichael's Appraising Manual, Selling Real Estate, How to Make Money in Real Estate,* and *Leases—Percentages, Short and Long Term.*

This latest edition of his widely-respected real estate book has been completely revised and updated by the Prentice-Hall Editorial Staff to make it as accurate and authoritative as possible, and includes the latest methods, techniques and practices in the operation of a modern real estate business.

How to Operate
a Real Estate
Business

REVISED EDITION

How to Operate a Real Estate Business

REVISED EDITION

by
STANLEY L. McMICHAEL

Author of SELLING REAL ESTATE,
CITY GROWTH ESSENTIALS,
McMICHAEL'S APPRAISING MANUAL,
HOW TO MAKE MONEY IN REAL
ESTATE, LEASES—PERCENTAGE,
SHORT AND LONG TERM

Prentice-Hall, Inc.   Englewood Cliffs, New Jersey

34134

A WORD FROM THE PUBLISHER

This new edition of How to Operate a Real Estate Business has been revised by the Prentice-Hall Editorial Staff in answer to many requests.

The emphasis in this revision has been to preserve the sound, basic techniques of the late author, Stanley L. McMichael, while up-dating the information to meet today's needs.

Extensive changes were necessary in the important area of financing real estate, and in the chapter on shopping centers. New codes of ethics for the real estate profession are illustrated. The book has been revised to reflect the relatively new "fair housing" developments. Costs and other data have been revised throughout the book to reflect the latest available figures. Where significant changes in practices of policies of real estate offices have occurred, these have been added.

In addition, care was taken to revise in the same simple and concise language favored by Mr. McMichael and which makes this book so easy and practical to use.

The ten printings of the original edition attest to the popularity and usefulness of the book. It is our hope that this new revised edition will prove just as valuable a tool as was its predecessor.

THE PUBLISHERS

CONTENTS

How to Operate
a Real Estate
Business

REVISED EDITION

CHAPTER 1

The Real Estate Business —
What It Embraces

REAL ESTATE IS A FASCINATING BUSINESS which offers numerous possibilities for making money. You can speculate in houses, buildings, and lands and let someone else do your selling; you can channel all your energies into developing an agency which makes money by selling properties for fees; or you can combine speculating with a building program and create your own agency for selling, not only your own properties, but others as well. The sky's the limit in real estate, in terms of the number of opportunities you can develop, and in terms of the amount of money you can make by working hard and working smart.

Sales of lands and habitations are recorded in the Bible and many other ancient historical documents and books, but there is no record in the Bible of a real estate broker functioning in the way he is known to operate today. Early transfers of land and buildings were made direct from owner to owner but, even in ancient times, those transactions were governed by rules and regulations which were very strict. The sanctity of private ownership was universally recognized, and through the

1

centuries the protection afforded such transfers constantly increased.

The appearance of the real estate broker as he is known today is not recorded in history, but it probably occurred not much more than a century ago. Prior to that time and even to some extent after the real estate broker had demonstrated his usefulness, most real estate deals continued to be made through principals, with the aid of their attorneys, who looked after legal details and acted somewhat in the capacity of present-day escrow officers. Titles to land ownership have been in existence for many hundreds of years, some being graven in hieroglyphics on tablets of stone in earliest times.

The real estate business throughout many parts of the world (but not in the United States) still is conducted chiefly between sellers and buyers without aid from salesmen or brokers, but with the assistance of legal advisers who investigate the validity of titles.

As in the case of brokerage, the marketing of subdivisions is still a relatively young business. The first man in America to popularize subdivision sales and to apply the installment selling idea to real estate was William E. Harmon. Subdivisions had been sold on a cash basis, the buyer making a substantial down payment and the seller taking back a straight mortgage for the balance. The down payment ranged from one-third to one-half of the purchase price. Only a customer with a substantial amount of money could thus hope to acquire a building lot, and he frequently felt that he had to pay for it in full before he could proceed to build his home. Harmon changed all this.

The real estate business as now conducted throughout America includes the activities of brokers, subdividers, rental agents, management experts, builders who work with subdividers or who purchase tracts of land which they themselves improve with dwellings, and other specialists such as those who engage in the mortgage loan business, investment companies which develop and manage their own properties, chain-store leasing experts, and others.

What Is a Broker?

A realty broker is one who buys and sells lands and their improvements for others on a commission basis. It is his business to be familiar with available listings of property in the territory in which he functions and to secure permission to offer such properties for sale, either through an exclusive contract or by means of a general listing in which he agrees with the owner as to the price and terms on which a property may be offered. If the owner consents, the agent secures an exclusive contract for 60, 90, 120 days, or longer, granting him the exclusive right to represent the owner in the sale of the listed property. During this period the owner forfeits the right to sell the property himself or through any other broker without paying the original listing broker a full fee for his services. The listing broker usually is glad to coöperate with other brokers if suitable clients are offered.

Having obtained a variety of exclusive or general listings, a broker proceeds to attract the attention of potential buyers, maintaining a suitable office as his headquarters, which is marked by signs of various kinds indicating that he has properties for sale. Advertisements are inserted in daily and weekly newspapers to attract the attention of buyers. Mail-order campaigns may be instituted wherein the broker addresses his advertising appeal in the form of letters and circulars to lists of potential purchasers. It is the broker's chief business to constitute himself a medium through which sellers and buyers are brought together to the end that a property transfer may take place.

Having displayed his listed property in such an attractive and attention-demanding manner that a prospective buyer has become interested in it, the broker proceeds by means of salesmanship to *secure a meeting of the minds* as evidenced in a written contract to sell and purchase, signed by the seller and the buyer, the latter depositing with the broker at the same time a cash deposit of suitable amount to guarantee that the buyer will in good faith go through with his commitment. Then follows the preparation of an abstract of title, or title insurance, which proves the seller has good title and can convey it to the prospective buyer. A deed, conveying ownership, and a mortgage from the buyer to the seller agreeing to pay the balance of the purchase price not covered in the initial payment, setting forth agreed terms, are then prepared and signed. Such proceedings may take place in the office of the real estate broker, at the office of an attorney representing either side, or in a regularly constituted escrow department of a title company or bank. Once the title has been proved to be properly vested in the seller, the abstract or title insurance policy is delivered to the buyer, the deed is filed with the county recorder, and the mortgage is likewise filed with the same officer, to be placed on the public records for all the world to see that a real estate transfer has been accomplished. Customarily the seller assumes the expense of preparing the statement of title, the real estate broker's commission, the federal revenue stamps, and a portion of the escrow expense if such is involved. The buyer stands the expense of recording his new title and other minor expenses. The foregoing, briefly, is the routine through which a real estate broker proceeds from the time he enters the business until he closes his first deal. Thereafter the same procedure takes place, with variations, every time another deal is consummated.

Subdivisions

The business of being a subdivider is radically different. The subdivider generally acts in the capacity of a principal, being the owner in most instances, although occasionally a subdivider may sell a tract of land for an owner on a commission basis. Most subdividers, however, operate as owners of tracts of land, which they purchase in a more or less raw state, proceed to improve and sell at retail. The real estate subdividing business has changed considerably in the years since it was first instituted in 1887. The earliest developer simply purchased a tract of land at a place served with suitable transportation facilities, cut streets through it, marked off vacant lots with stakes, ploughed ditches along the sides of the new streets, and proceeded to sell the lots, leaving to the purchasers the problems of getting pavements past their doors, sewers, gas, telephone, water, electric service, and such other conveniences as a modern home demands. Lot buyers had many problems to meet. Often they banded together to secure the necessary improvements by having costs assessed against their individual lots, which made them a good deal more expensive than the original price tags indicated.

William E. Harmon originated the now famous *purchase contract* plan whereby the subdivider gave a bond that, when a certain proportion of the sales price of a lot was paid, the buyer would be given his deed and permitted to pay the balance upon a regular installment basis. Friends told Harmon such a plan would land him in the poor house but he proceeded to demonstrate that it was a sound idea that was soon to sweep America and become the basis on which most subdividing operating was to be done for many years.

Subdividing up to that time had been a dull business and proceeded slowly. Other operators, witnessing what Harmon had accomplished, adopted his tactics, and soon subdivisions were booming throughout the country. Some of the early subdivisions were terrible affairs; no improvements were offered in most cases. Practices gradually improved throughout the years, Harmon being hailed as the father of the modern subdivision movement.

In later years subdivision developers began to install all necessary improvements, adding the costs to the selling prices of lots and producing much more satisfactory homesites for average buyers. Some developers even erected a few houses on their properties for the purpose of establishing the character and cost of other structures which they hoped to see erected in subsequent years.

A further step has been taken by the subdivider of the present day. Now all public service improvements, including pavement, water, gas, and electric service, are installed; and in addition, the subdivider does practically all of the building of new houses. In other words, the modern subdivider delivers to the buyer a completed home in every detail, sometimes even installing stoves, refrigerators, radios, and colored television. It seems probable that the trend will continue indefinitely.

Rentals

The business of conducting a rental department in connection with a real estate office depends a good deal upon the attitude of the head of the office. Some brokers believe that a rental bureau attracts persons who subsequently become buyers. To establish a rental business, it is necessary to canvass a territory and become familiar with owners so that, when vacancies occur, owners will list them with the real estate office. By means of advertising and signs, and by telephoning prospects, the vacancies are filled and commissions earned.

Important leasing departments develop in real estate offices that are aggressively managed. Stores and business and industrial properties are leased at substantial rentals for long periods of time. Chain-store merchandising has given real estate men an opportunity to specialize in the rental of retail stores in so-called "hot spots" where rentals are high and earnings of merchants run into large figures annually. This is a profitable type of rental business and well worth cultivating.

Management

In recent years there has developed a new and important branch of the real estate business involving the operation and management of properties of all kinds. There have been professional managers for many years for such properties as large skyscrapers, condominiums, and apartment houses. The newer phase of the business consists of streamlined organizations which manage large numbers of properties, on a scientific basis, in which the very latest methods are used and economies are effected through the mass buying of supplies, the shifting about of skilled labor from place to place as needed, and the maintenance of complete records of every phase of activity carried on.

Building

Many large real estate organizations throughout the country maintain building departments that work in conjunction with their subdivision departments in erecting dwellings in the various new tracts being opened from time to time. They also accept contracts to erect buildings on vacant lots sold through the brokerage department, and in addition may contract to erect various types of stores or industrial buildings. The department is usually headed by a practical building contractor who, in collaboration with an architect, plans the structures and supervises their erection. The building department also assists the management department, when necessary, in the repair and alteration of various properties under its control.

Financing

No large well-rounded real estate office is complete without its own mortgage loan department. This is in the charge of a man familiar with ways of securing money to lend from individuals, institutions, and others having cash reserves seeking conservative investment. First mortgage loans are arranged at current rates of interest. The broker may be paid a commission for obtaining the loan. However, since most state laws prohibit a broker from taking commissions from more than one party to a transaction without consent of the others, a broker who represents the seller should obtain the seller's permission if he is going to receive a commission for arranging a loan for the buyer.

Syndicates and Real Estate Investment Trusts

In times of great real estate activity, considerable sums of money appear in the market for investment from men com-

paratively unfamiliar with real estate activities. To afford an
outlet for the use of such funds, important real estate offices
maintain departments for the organization of syndicates of
investors who will contribute the necessary cash to swing
large and important transactions. A group of half a dozen
investors may be assembled, each of whom may advance, say,
$25,000, thus making a total of $150,000. This sum can be used
by the syndicate manager to buy an important property,
which, after being rehabilitated and allowed to "ripen" over
a few months' time, may be sold at a substantial profit. The
money then is reinvested until the speculative period appears
to be coming to an end; then the wise syndicate manager will
sell off all his properties and divide the profits among the investors, reserving reasonable fees for the office and himself for
having managed the operations. Sometimes such investments
are made through the medium of a real estate investment trust
(REIT) that gets favored tax treatment if it meets certain
qualifications set up by the federal tax laws. Indeed, an REIT
can go completely untaxed if it distributes all of its earnings.
(This applies to federal taxes only.)

The query occasionally arises: "Why a real estate broker?"
The answer may be found in the old saying: "Everybody's
business is nobody's business." Real estate brokers originate
and carry through a majority of all the real estate deals recorded from year to year. Their foresight, originality, keen-
ness of perception, and dogged persistence bring deals into
being, pilot them along rugged and perilous trails and finally
guide them into the home port, a credit to both buyers and
sellers and affording a profit to the brokers for their perseverance.

It is a curious but well-known fact that most owners have
difficulties in selling their own properties. Even real estate men
can't sell their individual holdings profitably in many instances.
The attitude that exists between buyer and seller changes the
minute they begin to bargain over the quality of the product
or its price. A buyer may believe what a broker tells him while
he might suspect the seller of the property who is earnestly

praising up his own property or justfying its price. When a buyer and a seller get together without a broker as mediator, it is often not long before they part at loggerheads over some minor detail that the broker, with his knowledge of real estate and salesmanship, could smooth over in a short time.

The ordinary seller of a parcel of real estate knows little about the elements of salesmanship. Most properties actually *must be sold;* that is, the buyer does not just see a place and buy it of his own free will. The clever broker knows just what features to play up, how to arouse interest, and how to carry the sale along until a buyer's name is on the dotted line.

To the man who contemplates becoming a real estate salesman or broker, let it be said that it is not easy to qualify as a successful operator. Very substantial monetary rewards await the man who prepares himself and has the necessary qualifications to graduate from the school of experience it is necessary to attend. Don't ever imagine that it doesn't mean hard work, and lots of it, because it does require incessant activity, intelligently applied. It demands courage and honesty and, above all, *infinite patience.* It calls for long preparatory work in qualifying oneself in the various branches of the business. One will succeed to just the extent that one studies and trains and through experience actually engages in the conducting and closing of real estate deals.

CHAPTER 2

Know Your

Home Town

ANYONE DESIRING TO ENGAGE IN THE
real estate business as a life calling should first of all seek to
obtain a complete knowledge of the community in which he
expects to carry on. This knowledge must be full and factual,
for a real estate broker should be an authority on matters pertaining to the city or town in which he decides to become
active.

Almost anyone has considerable information about the
community in which he resides. Using this as a foundation,
the student should first read all available historical material
about the city's origin and early growth. Who founded the
town and why? There is always a reason for a town or city
coming into being. It may have been the presence of a good
harbor; or it may be that an early trade route crossed a water-
course that later became a well-known river. Many a crossing of two early trails or trade routes has developed into an
important city in later years. Perhaps some early mining operation resulted in the mushrooming of a small town which
was later to achieve the status of a city. There is always a
reason. Find out what it is and what bearing it may have
on the activities of those who live there today.

Chicago grew great because it was not only a lake port but
also the center of a great network of railroads extending in

every direction. New York owes its early growth to a first class harbor, and one of the nearest ports of call to vessels hailing from Europe. It, too, later became the focal point for railroads extending north, west and south. Boston, Baltimore, New Orleans, and San Francisco all grew to be important because they, in early days, were busy seaports. Detroit grew great because the mass production of automobiles by Henry Ford first took place there. Cleveland is the natural meeting place of coal and ore. Los Angeles, originally a sleepy Spanish pueblo, became the center of an important agricultural development, then capitalized on its climate by attracting tourists, finally becoming an important manufacturing and export center. The sleeping giant that was Houston awakened to become a supergiant when the vast complex of the NASA space center became located near it.

Small towns as well as large cities all have their reasons for being and for the growth that has come to them or will come when proper conditions warrant it. These are the things that the real estate man must know if he is to merchandise his wares profitably.

Information about early real estate developments will be helpful. Find out who some of the early subdividers and builders were, just where the first subdivisions were located and what prices they sold for, what are the earliest buildings still in existence, and similar historical data which may be useful from time to time.

Until recent years most cities, like Topsy, "just grew." There may be plenty of evidence of that in the street layout in the sections which were developed in earliest years. There may be an entire absence of planning. When a town is small, additions come slowly and little effort is made to design them attractively. Dead-end streets may be found in many sections where developers of land farther out failed to connect their streets with those already in existence. At the edges of the city may be found modern subdivisions, with winding streets and every up-to-date improvement that city planning now affords.

Zoning practices must be thoroughly familiar to the alert

real estate student. Most modern communities now have zoning laws. These provide that land in certain areas must be used for specified purposes. Up to a few decades ago little effort was made to segregate different types of activity into definite sections. Factories were found in the center of minor home districts. Business places and apartments cropped up next to fine residential areas without any semblance of control. Then came a realization that zones of control must be established, and that each type of development must be segregated within its own borders.

In towns and cities most space is given over to the erection and maintenance of private homes. Consequently this is usually the first and most important activity to which zoning is applied. A typical zoning ordinance sets up the following classification of uses:

Zone R 1—Single-family homes only. Zoning does not attempt to specify anything regarding architecture, or costs.

Zone R 2—Two-family houses, doubles, and duplexes are permitted in this area. Height limit is two and one-half stories, with limit of one living unit to each 2,500 square feet of area.

Zone R 3—Buildings four stories high, unlimited as to living units.

Zone R 4—This is an area in which unlimited numbers of multiple residential units may be built to any height permitted under local ordinances and out of any materials allowed by the building ordinances.

Zone C 1—Restricted type of business and commercial use.

Zone C 2—Neighborhood types of business.

Zone C 3—General business and commercial uses.

Zone M 1—Manufacturing zone. Lighter types of industry permitted.

Zone M 2—Heavy manufacturing, including steel mills, foundries, and the like.

There has been a definite tendency in the past several decades to restrict more tightly the uses to which property may be put in cities. By the segregation of certain classes of industry to certain localities all other sections have been benefited. Likewise business activity has been kept within reasonable bounds so that it cannot encroach upon residential areas. The result has been to stabilize values in all zones of activity.

Zoning has been applied in suburban areas as well as in cities.

Large cities like Los Angeles have county zoning ordinances which prescribe the type of activities that may be carried on in all unincorporated sections of the county outside of its towns and cities.

In many cities where zoning was instituted some years ago, experience has taught that far too much frontage was originally allotted to business and to multiple-dwelling use. The tendency has been to re-zone and scale down such use so that more home areas may become available.

Perhaps no knowledge a real estate man may have about his own town is more important than how land in certain sections may be utilized, for it is use translated into income that really establishes the value of land.

A liberal knowledge of the requirements set forth in building-department ordinances is required by the real estate man. Some progress has been made in standardizing such ordinances in different cities, but almost every community of standing now has its own set of rules under which building operations may be safely conducted. In certain areas the use of fireproof or semi-fireproof materials is required. Walls of buildings must be of concrete or brick, although wooden floors and roofs are permitted in some areas. In others then entire structure must be fireproof. Those building ordinances define, also, the area of the lot that may be used for different types of structures. A corner building in a business district may use 100 per cent of the area of the lot while inside buildings can use only 60 or 80 per cent. In residential districts only 40 or 50 per cent of a lot may be covered with a dwelling and all buildings must stay at least four feet away from the lot sidelines. Many other rules and regulations of a similar nature exist with which the alert real estate agent should be fully familiar. Copies of the building ordinances can usually be obtained from departments in charge of such work, and these should be studied until a working knowledge of the provisions is obtained.

Fire departments likewise establish rules and regulations regarding certain types of buildings, particularly theaters and places of public assemblage. Locations where rubbish burners can be placed and used are also specified. In many cities rubbish can be burned only before 9 o'clock in the morning, special permits being required when fires of any kind are lighted after that time.

Property restrictions on subdivisions are imposed usually for periods of twenty, twenty-five, thirty, or forty years, although they have been extended as long as 99 years in some known instances. Such restrictions can be changed only by the action of a majority of the property owners in a general district. This may happen at the end of the term; by that time it may be found that a single-family home district has so changed that it is desirable that multiple units be erected there, or, in some instances, that a business district be created.

Subdivision restrictions differ in every part of a town or city, and that is why a broad knowledge of them is necessary. They sometimes provide that in certain areas all buildings erected must have an initial value of a certain sum, or that they shall be of a prescribed type of architecture, or that the buildings erected shall all be frame or of some specified material. Many residential restrictions provide that intoxicating liquor cannot be sold within a subdivision's boundaries. Provision may be made for the use of land for the erection of churches or schools or these may be barred, according to the notion of the original developer, but for the most part, complete residential communities are the order of the day.

When restrictions written for a definite number of years do expire, it is found that a great deal of valuable protection is afforded by city zoning ordinances that continue the particular use to which the land has been applied. Zoning *does not expire* and is subject to change only by the action of a majority of the property owners involved. So, in the case of a nice subdivision which has come to be twenty-five years of age and finds its land restrictions of no further use, the zoning law picks up and carries on from that time until a majority of the owners want the use of the land changed to some other purpose.

Restrictions such as the foregoing are matters of public

record at courthouses and are available for anyone to read and become familiar with. They affect every piece of property sold and can be verified at any time by a real estate broker.

All cities depend for their existence and development upon their retail and wholesale trade, which in turn are created for and serve those engaged in manufacturing and business enterprises of various kinds. Cities depend also on the agricultural interests in rural neighborhoods as well as on the needs of many persons who live in hamlets and small towns nearby and who come to the larger town or city periodically to shop. A broker or salesman must know more or less intimately a good deal about the manufacturing enterprises located in his community and the real estate needs of those employed in such places, from department heads who are able financially to live in fine residences to workmen who must occupy humble places of abode. Except in the larger cities, such neighborly interests must be kept track of and acted upon whenever possible.

It is the real estate man's business to extend his acquaintance so that his knowledge of his home town can be readily capitalized on. This may be done through civic and religious organizations, chambers of commerce, and service clubs of all kinds. One never knows when he is stirring up the makings of a profitable deal. An idle conversation while coming down the steps of a church after a Sunday service, the banter across the luncheon table of a service club, or a "hunch" the realty man may have got from something he has learned through his chamber of commerce affiliations may lead to a substantial real estate transaction later on.

A close study of newspapers and reports from various organizations will widen the knowledge a person has of his home town and its functionings. Always read the newspapers carefully, for they are constantly filled with tips on what is happening or what may develop later. Reports of public officials, chambers of commerce, and business club committees may be loaded with information that points the way to profitable real estate deals.

Advance information about an important street improvement, or the moving to town of a manufacturing concern, or the shifting of a business enterprise to a new location which may result in its becoming a "hot spot" of retail business, may often be gained through close and intimate contact with the powers that be and a thorough knowledge of your home town. Plans may be afloat for the creation or extension of a boulevard, which may result in the transfer of much property and the creation of new values in certain locations. The advance agent of a manufacturing enterprise may be glad to contact the real estate man in connection with the purchase of a factory site, which may lead in turn to the sale of much other property in the same area. The lusty new department store, which has been getting along so well under young and aggressive management, may be looking for a larger location and may want help in quietly securing a new site at a reasonable price. Adjoining property, naturally, will be in demand, and the advance knowledge which the realty broker has obtained may lead to the making of one or more commissions. A person engaged in the real estate business who is known generally to have a wide knowledge of his home town will be able to capitalize handsomely over the years.

It is a good idea also to know personally the bankers in your home town, or at least in your portion of it if the city is a large one. These men and their associates frequently receive inquiries from persons interested in purchasing and selling real estate, and they are glad to refer such inquiries to a real estate man of standing whom they know and respect for his knowledge of his own business and city. Many a substantial deal has sprung from such a source.

Visit the public library and read the books dealing with the history and development of your home town. Nearly every town or city has a local historian who records for the benefit of later generations the facts surrounding the community's origin. Such books are filled with interesting information about the locality in which you live. You will get inspiration from many things that you never knew existed.

One of the important things for a real estate man to know is the type of realty development in each part of his town or city. From the time of their inception, most cities *grow away from their point of origin.* What was originally the place from where a fine city has sprung up often degenerates into a factory district or a slum. What were fine home districts of a generation or two or three ago are now overrun with boarding houses and nondescript buildings where minor business enterprises have taken over. "Twilight zones" they are called, and they are to be found on the fringes of the business section of almost every city. A palatial mansion which may have cost $50,000 forty years ago has a fruit stand on one side and a saloon on the other. A little further out the infestation may not be quite so bad but the keen student of city growth can perceive what is coming. A definite knowledge of situations and conditions such as these must be a part of the education of every real estate man who is to guide his clients correctly.

The presence of factories, which may make a neighborhood unpleasant to live in, nuisances such as stockyards, rendering plants, and glue factories, and the directions of prevailing winds which may blow smoke and fumes towards an area which someone has planned to develop into a pleasant home district, must all be known to the real estate man who would advise buyers intelligently.

One excellent definitions of *value* is: "the present worth of *future benefits.*" How necessary it is, therefore, for the real estate man who is to be successful and a credit to his community to know in great detail all of the influences that are likely to affect the future value of a property he is seeking to sell!

Cities on harbors usually expand fanwise. The same may be said of cities that grow up on one bank of a wide river. If the river can be bridged, the city usually grows to a substantial size on one side before it leaps to the other. The newer section often becomes the location for high-grade residential developments. Cities that develop at the intersection of main highways or trade routes usually grow in the shape of a star. This was particularly so in earlier years when transportation was by street car lines extending out main arteries like the points of a star. With the advent of the automobile, the spaces between the points began to be filled.

But the real estate man must keep abreast of the most modern trends. Frontage on major highways will not always retain its present value. Properties on frontage roads of multilaned freeways have, in many instances, degenerated in value because the traffic has been shifted away from them. Stay alert to the most current changes.

The automobile, in the past several decades, has made many changes in the growth of American towns and cities. Distance today *is measured in minutes and not in miles!* Because one could, by automobile, proceed out ten, fifteen, or twenty miles within a half-hour, the natural inclination was to pass over high-priced land on the edge of the community. As a result, in some cities are seen sections of comparatively vacant land out beyond the business district which has never been needed for business use and which is not particularly desirable for homes, at the prices asked for it. The alert real estate man will be able to find many uses for this land, such as multiple-dwelling projects or new business uses. Study your town and become familiar with the vicissitudes through which its real estate has gone in the past twenty-five or fifty years, and opportunities may reveal themselves for profitable developments.

Study your city in relation to the possibilities of creating new sub-centers of business development. These have sprung up on the edges of every city of any size in America, and substantial values have been created in business frontage in such neighborhoods. Highest real estate values always attach to business frontage. Then comes land for multiple-dwelling development, industrial purposes, and homes. The range in prices for dwelling purposes may extend from $25 per foot front to several hundred dollars, according to the advantages offered and the character of the developments.

The crossing of any two main outlying thoroughfares may possibly develop into a new business sub-center a few years hence. The corners first fill up with a gas station, a small repair shop, a roadside restaurant, and a market. Five years later these have disappeared and substantial buildings have replaced them. More such buildings appear close by each year, and in a decade there blossoms out a full-fledged business sub-center where land values may reach $500 to $1,000 or more a foot front. This has happened many times and it will happen again and again. Actually, this type of property has become so expensive that prices are now being quoted as so much per square feet. A dollar per square feet sounds much less prohibitive than, say, $43,560 per acre or $800 per front foot. Watch for these *crossroads of opportunity* and make yourself and your clients some money.

Study your city and visualize, if you can, what can be done with tracts of attractive land now lying idle but suitable for subdivision development. These lands may now be used for gardens or large estates, or may just be lying idle and waiting for someone to transfer them into high-grade home areas or multiple-dwelling developments.

It is the real estate man's business as well as his duty to help his town grow and be a pleasant place in which to live. Always boost—never knock your home town. It was Thomas Gibbons who wrote:

> The man may last but never lives,
> Who much receives and little gives,
> Whom none can love, whom none can thank,
> Creation's blot, creation's blank!

Finally, make it a steady and consistent policy to read everything that may give you new and interesting information about your home town. Every scrap of information may prove useful to you in some argument in some emergency later on. Memorize it or make a record of it and keep it always ready at hand as ammunition to be used in prosecuting your plans to be a successful broker or salesman.

CHAPTER 3

What Is Real Estate?

A NEWCOMER PLANNING TO ENGAGE IN the real estate business should develop a fundamental conception of just what real estate is, of its uses, and of its peculiar characteristics.

Volumes have been written about the nature of real and personal property; consequently, the subject can be touched on but lightly here, and the student is advised to carry on a course of reading on varied phrases of this vast subject.

Property, in the broad sense, is anything capable of being owned. It is what has been termed a *bundle of rights,* guaranteed and protected by precedent and government decrees, which have grown up over the centuries. All property has an owner, whether it be the state, where an established government is in control, or an individual to whom the rights of ownership have been conveyed.

Real estate consists of *real or immovable property*, including land and buildings and other "improvements" thereon. Personal or movable property embraces all other things which are not real property.

Broadly speaking, all property may be divided into three types—investment, non-investment, and service.[1] Investment

---

[1] For amplification see Chapter 10 of *McMichael's Appraising Manual,* Englewood Cliffs, Prentice-Hall, Inc.

properties are those capable of earning the owner an income. They comprise the majority of non-residential buildings in a town or city. Non-investment properties are almost exclusively of the home class and the sites on which dwellings are erected. Houses that are rented should be included in the investment class. Service properties include all publicly owned structures, whether controlled by the community, the state, or the nation. Investment properties are created and owned by investors, for the most part, who seek to earn incomes on the money invested. Non-investment properties include homes, mostly owned individually by those who occupy them. Service properties are created and owned by cities, states, and the federal government.

ALL PROPERTY

Investment	Non-Investment	Service
Office buildings	Residences	Churches
Hotels	Home sites	Hospitals
Stores	Estates	Museums
Flats	Condominiums	City halls
Two-family dwellings		State capitols
Apartments		Libraries
Banks		Schools
Theaters		Post offices
Factories		Auditoriums
Garages		Custom houses
Freight terminals		Streets, roads
Resorts		Dams
Parking yards		Government buildings
Gas stations		Army and Navy camps
Railroads		Navy yards
Airports		Airports
Piers, docks		Space installations
Amusement centers		
Bridges, toll roads		
Oil wells		
Mines, deposits		
Farms, ranches		
Orchards, groves		
Irrigation systems		
Radio and television stations		

Real estate men have little to do with service properties but much to do with those of the investment and non-investment types. The methods of valuing the three kinds of real estate are radically different. Non-investment holdings are valued on a comparative value basis. Investment properties have their value determined by their ability to produce a fixed net income which is suitably capitalized at a current rate of interest. Service properties are valued on a cost-replacement basis.

There is never any question about land itself being considered real property. Appurtenant thereto are many kinds of property, however, some of which are considered real and others personal property.

Alfred Marshall, English economist, gives the following definition of land: "By land is meant the material and forces which nature gives freely for man's aid in land and water, air, light and heat."

Kent, in his *Commentaries* (III) has another definition: "Land, according to Lord Coke, includes not only the ground and soil but everything which is attached to the earth, whether by the course of nature as trees, herbage and water, or by the hand of man as houses and other buildings; and which has an indefinite extent, upward as well as downward, so as to include everything terrestrial, under or over it."

The term *real estate* came into use ages ago because it relates to real property such as land and buildings, which in themselves are estates and are considered such by their owners.

Land, the great imperishable product which is found everywhere and which originally was free to whomever sought it, has three primary functions to perform in behalf of its owners.

1. Its productive surfaces can be used for raising food and agricultural products of all kinds.

2. From its subsurfaces there may be developed mines from which many rich and useful metals and mineral substances, including oil, may be taken.

3. Land provides the sites on which homes, villages, towns, and cities may grow and develop.

Under all human activity rests land. Railroads have most of

their value represented in their rights of way through the open country and through the towns and cities they serve. Large manufacturing enterprises listed as being worth millions of dollars invariably have large holdings of land which they utilize in their operations. Banks, public service companies, educational institutions, all control large land holdings without which they could not operate. Land is a great human need, and man could not for a moment exist without access to it.

While little difficulty exists in identifying what real property is, a great many perplexing problems develop when one attempts to ascertain just what *personal property* consists of. Innumerable court decisions might be quoted to show the efforts which have been made to do so. Property of the same kind may be real estate in one place and personal property elsewhere. For example, window screens offered for sale in a hardware store are personal property; attached to a house which is offered for sale, they become real property.

Real property was at one time generally supposed to include everything under the earth and also the air and sky above it. Today, however, private rights to ownership are often retained when land is sold which has oil or mineral deposits below the surface. Furthermore, with the development of aviation, there is considerable doubt as to just how high in the air a property owner's rights actually go, as demonstrated in suits unsuccessfully maintained by property owners near airports who have attempted to prevent airplanes from passing over their holdings when engaged in landing.

It has been held that gases and oils in their natural states are part of the land and are real property unless a definite agreement exists to show they do not go with the surface rights to use. (Recent lawsuits charging slanted drilling techniques have been rendered in favor of the landowners under whose land the oil deposits lay.) Oil and gas separated from the land and held in storage are personal property.

Growing things such as vines, herbage, and trees are real property, unless reserved and sold separately. Removed from the land, they become personal property.

A mineral such as copper is real property while in the ground; when refined and made into plumbing fixtures, it is personal property. When those fixtures are built into a house, they again become real property. Removed from the property and sold as junk, they once again become personal property!

Fruits growing on trees or vines are considered real property but become personal property when they ripen and become salable. Crops, including grains growing in the fields, are usually considered personal property.

State laws differ as to the classifications into which many articles may be placed. If in doubt, look up your state laws governing the matter.

Taxation authorities have been compelled to set standards of their own. One of the clearest expositions as to the differences between real and personal properties has been set up by the Illinois Department of Revenue, as outlined in its *Assessors' Manual*, which states that the following is a partial list of property legally defined as real estate for taxation purposes:

Land; buildings, structures, and improvements and "other permanent fixtures"; interstate toll bridges; trees growing on land; mines, quarries, gas and oil wells; rights pertaining to mining, oil, or gas production; leasehold estates; buildings on leased ground; fixtures in a building that cannot be removed without physical injury either to the building or to the fixtures (*Cross v. Weare Commission Co.,* 153 Ill. 499); fixtures in a building that can be removed without substantial injury but which are attached to the building by screws, nails, and so forth, are real estate if owned by the owner of the building (*Fifield v. Farmers Nat. Bank,* 148 Ill. 163); fixtures in a building that can be removed without substantial injury to the building but which are attached to the building by screws, nails, and so forth, are real estate even if owned by the tenant, if the lease provides that such fixtures shall remain with the building (*Fifield v. Farmers Nat. Bank,* 148 Ill. 163; *Baker v. McClurg,* 198 Ill. 28).

To indicate what the same authorities consider property, here are some of the items required to be reported on an Illinois personal property tax return: passenger automobiles, aeroplanes and boats, trucks, busses and trailers, livestock and poultry, grain, hay, etc.

Household furniture and furnishings, including: air-conditioners, art objects, dishes and glassware, musical instruments, pool and ping-pong tables, radios and TV sets, sewing machines, and stoves.

Personal effects, including: athletic equipment, clothing and jewelry.

Machinery and equipment, including: farm equipment, electric motors, printing presses, shop and garage equipment, tractors and X-ray, surgical and dental equipment.

Merchandise, goods on hand and in process.

Money on hand or on deposit.

Taxable stocks and bonds.

There may be a distinct title to the surface of the earth and its use, and other titles to different strata underneath it. One person may own iron ore, another may own lead, and a third party may own a stratum of coal, if all three should happen to exist under the same piece of land.

Growing crops planted by a land owner are part of the real estate. If a tenant plants them, however, they are the personal property of the tenant and may be removed by him. Whether he has a right to crops unharvested before a lease has expired depends upon the certainty of its duration. This is termed the right of emblements. If termination is uncertain, the tenant will have the right of entry to work crops until they can be harvested.

Trees are a part of real estate, being a product of the soil. If a tree is on one owner's lot but the limbs extend over the line and trespass on another owner's property, the latter has the right to trim them back to the lot line, even to shearing off the roots themselves as well as the branches. A tree on a boundary line becomes the joint property of the two owners, and neither can remove or injure it without the other's consent.

If a person, by mistake, erects a building on a tract of land not owned by him, the actual owner of the land can claim it and demand compensation before it can be removed. The land may be sold outright to the builder of the structure. In transferring land, most deeds merely recite the conveyance of the lot, as defined by a legal description, improvements being mentioned only in exceptional instances.

It is held by eminent legal authorities that there cannot be an *absolute* ownership in land. Laws dealing with the transfer and ownership of real property in America are based largely on English common law. They were first created under the ancient feudal system of England and were revised in many ways in later years. The fact that there can be no absolute ownership is based on the contention that absolute ownership is first vested in the state, from which all comers receive their rights, known as *estates*. Three elements are present in an estate: (1) the right of possession, (2) the right of enjoyment, and (3) the right of disposition, subject to the state's right to defeat it and condemn it for public use. This right to condemn is covered in state laws and differs among various commonwealths.

Associated with the ownership of real estate, which may be in fee simple or in some lesser estate, is the practice of placing encumbrances on land when it is purchased or sold. The most common type of encumbrance is the straight mortgage, which is an interest in lands given to secure payment of money or its equivalent. The rights of a mortgage holder are considered by law to be almost as sacred as those surrounding the ownership of land itself. Mortgages are written for terms of years with stipulated interest rates payable monthly, semi-annually, or yearly. In some sections of the United States the use of mortgages has been replaced largely by trust deeds, which are similar in their general intent and nature insofar as they secure a debt, but are entirely different from mortgages in the manner in which they may be redeemed if the debtor defaults. A trust deed names a trustee to whom the property is conveyed until such a time as the owner has met all obligations noted in the trust deed. The instrument also provides that, if the property owner fails to meet all interest payments and other obligations for a period of *three months,* the trustee may convey the property, with but brief legal procedure, to the person who has lent the money. Redemption may take place, usually, up to a full year in the case of a straight mortgage, and title is vested in the owner until court action separates him from it.

No effort has been made here to cover, other than sketchily, the voluminous procedures and problems which surround the ownership and transfer of real estate. The real estate broker will do well to familiarize himself with real estate law, but when he gets into difficulty he had better consult a lawyer versed in that subject. Moreover, most communities now have escrow departments where the legal features of consummating real estate transfers are intelligently taken care of, leaving the broker or salesman free to go on making deals. The broker would do better to center his studying on the subject of salesmanship and various branches of the real estate business itself and leave to persons better qualified than himself the solving of legal problems as they come up.

CHAPTER 4

Preparations for Entry

Into Business

HAVING SURVEYED THE FIELD AND studied some of the problems connected with the conduct of the real estate business, the newcomer who is eager to get started either as a salesman or as a broker will want to know what he must do to qualify himself for entry into the real estate field. Times have changed and the requirements now are more exacting than they were for the first half of the century.

The first thing necessary is to ascertain whether the law in the state in which he resides requires that all persons engaged in real estate activities be licensed. Most states have real estate license laws, enacted for the protection of both the real estate interests themselves and the public at large. Some state license laws have been in effect for many years and with excellent results. Inquiry among real estate men, or addressed to the real estate commissioner at the state capital, will reveal if a license bureau does exist and the kind of examination that must be passed to obtain permission to engage in business.

Some states require persons selling business property, cemetery lots, oil and mineral lands, and other types of property to qualify by passing required examinations. The examination for a salesman is, naturally, less difficult than that for a broker. In many states schools exist where newcomers may take courses of lectures and lessons at which the various requirements of the examinations are discussed, and salesmen or brokers are tutored to the end that they may pass the tests successfully.

California, for example, has had a license law for several decades. It was found necessary to regulate and control the business because of repeated booms and depressions during which tremendous activity would occur for several years, to be followed by a gloomy depression. In both of these periods, the activities of unscrupulous persons made it necessary to establish state control over real estate transactions.

California has perhaps as advanced a procedure for conducting its examinations and policing the real estate and subdividing business as any state, so reference to its methods may be useful.

The applicant for a real estate *salesman's* license must have a sponsoring broker who will sign the application and certify that the applicant is "honest, truthful, and of good reputation." Upon receipt of the application and the examination fee of $10, the State Division of Real Estate will notify the applicant to appear for examination at a specified time in the District Office closest to the applicant's place of residence. The applicant can purchase a *Reference Book*, published by the Division, which contains a vast amount of information relating to real estate practice and the responsibilities of licensees. The book also contains examination items, some with answers, or, in the case of forms, examples of correct completion.

The applicant for a real estate *broker's* license must possess prerequisite experience or educational qualifications to be eligible for the license examination. Most candidates qualify on the basis of two years' full-time experience as licensed real estate salesmen. Others depend on equivalent experience in the general field of real estate, and still others qualify by having completed a four-year college or university course which included specialization in real estate.

Examinations for broker's and salesman's licenses are similar in structure, although the test for the broker's license is much more comprehensive. The two examinations are weighted in exactly the same way:

1. Weight assigned to legal aspects, including the writing of listing and deposit receipts 50%
2. Weight assigned to matters of public control 10%
3. Weight assigned to evaluation 15%
4. Weight assigned to finance 10%
5. Weight assigned to miscellaneous special fields 15%

Each examination runs not more than six and a half hours and includes essay and multiple-choice items. The broker's license candidate, in addition to passing the basic or all-day test, is required to pass special tests; one on the subject of the legal aspects of real estate, and the other on real estate practice. If, however, he has completed satisfactorily, at an institution of higher learning, courses in one or both of these subjects, he is excused from the necessity of taking one or both of the special tests.

The examination fee for the real estate salesman's license is $10; the same fee is required for each reexamination. The fee for the real estate broker's license examination is $25, and if reexamination is necessary, the same fee is payable. After qualifying by examination, the candidate for a real estate salesman's license pays a $40 fee for a four-year license; the candidate for real estate broker's license pays a $65 fee for a four-year license.

All examinations place great emphasis on the applicant's knowledge of the state Real Estate License Law and the Regulations of the Real Estate Commissioner. These are published in full text in the *Reference Book* previously mentioned. They are also contained in a smaller publication entitled *The Real Estate Law and the Regulations of the Real Estate Commissioner,* which sells for $1.00, plus sales tax when applicable.

Many other states in which license laws exist do not afford applicants the information needed to pass examinations in as ready a form. It therefore is necessary for the applicant to read extensively on all phases of the real estate business in order to qualify. To become a salesman or broker, one should begin at the outset to accumulate a library on real estate subjects for use in passing his examination as well as for collateral reading and reference later on. One's library can never be too large. It is wise also to subscribe for the best real estate magazine available as well as one devoted to architectural and building developments.

Merely to pass an examination for the right to operate as a salesman or broker is not all that is necessary. Only by assiduously studying lessons and reading books and engaging in the business itself can one expect to be successful. One must have a clear understanding of the principles of agency and the relationships that exist between a broker and his principal and the buyer who becomes involved in a sale.

One cannot simply go into the real estate business without any qualifications or training whatsoever. It takes a good plumber several years of apprenticeship to become a master craftsman. A doctor, psychologist, or dentist takes a course of several years at a college to permit him to engage in his chosen profession, and then he must serve an internship of one or more years. The real estate broker, too, must toil and study and learn through experience many of the complicated ramifications of the real estate business before he is qualified to engage in it and make money.

Most persons seeking to engage in the real estate business begin by taking an examination for a salesman's license. Having obtained this, they become qualified to engage in some branch of the business. In periods of great real estate activity there is always a demand for subdivision salesmen. Selling subdivisions is perhaps the easiest way to get experience. The fundamentals of selling lots are quickly learned. The salesman of general real estate on a brokerage basis faces vastly more involved and intricate problems than the subdivision salesman. Subdividers have trained salesmanagers who drill into their salesmen the facts about a single tract, the advantages of every lot in the tract, its price, the terms of payment, and other information a salesman should have. In a few days he may become an excellent lot salesman, if he is destined to become a salesman at all. The principles of salesmanship applied are fundamentally the same in selling a lot as in disposing of a house or a small business property. The knowledge a salesman needs, however, is different and much more extensive in the case of a brokerage proposition than for selling a vacant home site. After breaking into the real estate business by getting a job selling vacant lots, the salesman can, studying all the while, advance until, in time, he is able to handle the more complicated types of properties.

In most states an applicant for a salesman's license must have a sponsor, who may be a broker or a firm that agrees to employ him in the event he is successful in obtaining a license. Thus the salesman has a place to go immediately upon qualifying himself as one who has passed the necessary examination.

The following represents typical statutory definitions of a broker and a salesman:

A *real estate broker* is a person who, for, or in expectation of, compensation, does or negotiates to do one or more of the following acts for another or others:

(a) Sells or offers to sell, buys or offers to buy, solicits prospective sellers or purchasers of, solicits or obtains listings of, or negotiates the purchase, sale or exchange of real property.

(b) Leases or rents, or offers to lease or rent, or negotiates the sale, purchase or exchanges of leases on real property, or collects rents from real property, or improvements thereon.

(c) Solicits borrowers or lenders for, or negotiates loans or collects payments or performs services for borrowers or lenders or note owners in connection with loans secured directly or collaterally by liens on real property.

(d) Sells or offers to sell, buys or offers to buy, or exchanges or offers to exchange a real property sales contract, or a promissory note secured directly or collaterally by a lien on real property, and performs services for the holders thereof.

A *real estate salesman* is a person who, for, or in expectation of compensation, is employed by a licensed real estate broker to do one or more of the acts set forth in the definition of a broker, above.

A person seeking to take a real estate license examination may obtain information in various ways. One way is to become acquainted with a practicing broker who is willing to explain matters or to lend books, magazines, or articles dealing with different phases of the business. Another way is to go through the available reading matter at the nearest public library. A third way is to buy the best current books on real estate salesmanship, leasing, selling, and appraising. The state real estate licensing board will doubtless have some printed matter about the examination to be taken and possibly a list of questions similar to those that will be asked at the examination.

A matter with which the student must become familiar is land titles. Title is the right to or ownership of property—or the means by which an estate is acquired. The right of ownership may be acquired (1) by descent, (2) by purchase, (3) by act of the parties concerned, or (4) by an operation of law. Nearly every title company of any considerable size has pamphlets and books on the subject of land titles and title insurance. The latter is an arrangement by which the title company will, for a consideration, absolutely insure the title to any property that it issues. Insurance is for the full value of the property. Title insurance prevails very extensively in California and in some other states where the early land grants were cut up rather haphazardly and little authoritative evidence is left of former ownerships. In many of the older sections of the country titles are passed entirely by deeds accompanied by abstracts, which are histories of properties taken directly from official records showing their transfer from earliest days. Apply to the larger title companies in the district and see whether booklets on this subject are available.

A knowledge of the legal forms used in the transfer and renting of real estate is essential to the newcomer. Study the manner in which a deed, lease, or contract of purchase is made out and used, as well as many other real estate legal documents. Real estate men do not engage in the practice of law, but it is necessary for them to use the customary legal forms in the conduct of their business, going to an attorney when involved legal documents are required. Ordinary legal forms can be acquired at stationery stores or may be found in real estate textbooks.

Every real estate examination is certain to have some questions dealing with ethics. Codes of ethics are obtainable from the National Association of Real Estate Boards, Chicago, the state associations of real estate boards, and the local exchanges in the various cities and towns of the country, there being over 1,500 such boards in the United States alone. The codes prescribe the proper conduct to be followed in practically all kinds of real estate activities. For example see Chapter 36.

In many cities the general practice is for real estate deals to be placed in escrow with departments conducted by title companies, banks, and concerns which simply engage in the escrow business as such. An escrow officer takes charge of a deal, accepts the payment of money from a buyer and a signed deed by the seller, and makes the transfer in escrow when a clear title has been recorded in the name of the buyer. The escrow officer acts as a referee and relieves the broker or salesman of the many small, irritating details that surround many deals. Escrow service is paid for by the seller and buyer, the former usually paying about double what the buyer is required to pay. Escrow companies have reading matter on this subject which should be read by the student seeking to become proficient in the real estate business. See also Chapter 34.

CHAPTER 5

How to Get Started

In Business

REAL ESTATE SELLING IS ONE OF THE few occupations in which one may engage which does not require a great outlay of capital to begin operations. Consequently, the newcomer in the field may start work immediately after qualifying as a licensed salesman or broker or, in states in which license laws do not exist, directly after a course of study and reading that qualifies him to operate.

The salesman will want to affiliate himself with some office or organization where he may engage in selling and also learn further about the business problems he will encounter. Let no salesman think he has learned the real estate business simply because he has passed an examination that has earned him a license. He will learn quickly enough that he must never cease to be a student. The older he grows, he will realize the less he knows about real estate and the tremendous field it covers. As in law, or in medicine, he can never hope to know more than a relatively small part of it, and then only after years of experience and practice. Nevertheless he may from the very start be successful if he is willing to work hard, accept advice, and conduct himself properly.

"He profits most who serves best" is the motto of Rotary, a world-wide service organization. The activity of a real estate man is, basically, service. He seeks to serve the seller by disposing advantageously of his property; he serves the buyer by securing real estate, properly priced, which the buyer can use for a home, in his business, or as an investment to produce income. The salesman's personality should dominate the deal. Otherwise no sale will result; the salesman fails to earn his way and soon departs from that field. Don't think that a salesman sells every property he presents to a prospect. Far from it. Some offices have maintained careful records of the number of prospects to whom properties have been submitted, and the ratio of sales is about one in twenty-five in fairly good times and much less during unstable periods. The manner in which the salesman injects genuine service into his dealings will assure his success or failure.

What office shall the new salesman join? If the question has not already been settled by having some established office vouch for him and promise him employment, it will have to be settled now. There are always offices seeking new salesmen, that will accept them with any kind of qualifications, employ them, send them out "on their own" to sink or swim, with but little support in the way of good listings, advice, or advertising to obtain qualified buyers. The "turnover" of salesmen in an office of this type is high. They expect the salesman to go out and canvass his friends and his relatives—especially prosperous relatives—and sell them some real estate, on which the office gets half the commission. Failing to do this, the salesman gropes in the dark for a few days, gets discouraged, and quits.

Then there is the conservative type of office which seldom seeks new salesmen and which gives little help in the way of education, advice, or support. This office is composed of men who made their way in the business world, who have clients who do business with the office all the time, or who have personal holdings of a remunerative type which make it unnecessary for them to go out and hustle for deals. A new salesman in such an environment gets little assistance and soon dries up on the vine and drifts away.

Another office may be made up of virile young men and

others who have not lost their eager desires for success and who are constantly on their toes, seeking out good listings and presenting them to inquiring clients. It is in an office of this kind, with a capable sales manager, that the new salesman should display his abilities. He will be directed through a course of activities that will strengthen his ability to perform the functions for which he has trained himself. He will learn a lot of things about selling techniques he never imagined existed, and slowly but surely will be developed into a master salesman, qualified to set out on the pathway of life as head of his own office, with independence as his goal.

The newcomer who has qualified himself as a broker and who purposes to go into business immediately as his own master will have different problems to solve. First of all will be the question of just what kind of business to engage in. Shall he become a lease expert; a salesman of houses, of industrial properties, of business properties or high-rise condominiums; or enter any other branch of the field that appeals to him? It is usually simplest to start selling houses and vacant home sites, graduating into other branches of the business later. Being a good house salesman will tax his abilities to the utmost and allow plenty of scope for whatever undeveloped talents of salesmanship he may possess. It is usually the easiest field in which to secure listings and to learn a restricted territory in which to operate. And it will become necessary to work in such a restricted territory if one is to be successful. The average buyer is critical and wants to know a great deal about the neighborhood in which a dwelling is being offered for sale. He wants to know about the way the building is constructed, who the neighbors are, at what prices adjoining properties have been sold, about transportation and shopping facilities, and a host of other matters relating to the property being shown him.

Having decided the kind of property he will handle, the new broker must then select the neighborhood where he will work. Shall it be downtown or in one of the outlying sections of a growing city? Shall it be in a district which has filled up and grown old? Or shall it be on the fringe, where there is still room for expansion and where new building is going on much of the time? Here the mature judgment of the broker must manifest itself, as there will be other things to consider, not the least of which will be the current period of the business cycle in which the real estate business finds itself. In most instances the newcomer can break in more rapidly in an outlying office. Operations in large downtown offices in the larger cities are complicated; the newcomer is at sea for a long time and learns but slowly of the intricate operations being pursued. If he is of exceptional business caliber, he may learn quickly and qualify, but generally he will be more successful in a smaller outlying office, unless the town itself in which he is operating is rather small. Later, he can move downtown and compete with the big offices as much as he desires.

Selecting the office from which he will function presents more problems. Naturally he will not want to be associated with another real estate man who may dominate the picture or who may capture the best customers. Some newcomers secure desk space in an office, operating in this way for a time until they get themselves established. The most obvious way, of course, is to rent a suitable office, equip it, and then go to work.

Furnishing an office is not difficult. Whether it is done simply or elaborately will depend upon the funds at the disposal of the new broker. It is wise not to splurge unnecessarily but to set up an establishment in good taste. The most necessary piece of equipment is a good flat-top desk with plenty of drawer space. It is usually well to have a typewriter desk and a typewriter of standard make. A good letter file is essential, as well as several 4 x 6 inch card files. Record books will be necessary. Listing cards may be printed or purchased from stationery concerns which supply them. The listing cards should cover the following types of property: vacant lots, houses, apartments and multiple dwellings, industrial property, leases, farms, business property, and, if such a department is conducted, rentals of different kinds. A small photocopying machine, while reasonably expensive, is apt to pay for itself shortly in terms of the time and effort saved.

A real estate office must be properly equipped with maps and an atlas of the territory in which business is solicited. Most of the larger cities have firms which issue and maintain and correct atlases covering an entire city or a portion of it as the broker desires. Smaller cities nearly always have comprehensive maps showing subdivisions and other tracts. The county tax offices can usually supply maps which are duplicates of those used in assessing and taxing real estate throughout the area. Copying machines are becoming standard equipment, and are invaluable for duplicating maps, plats, etc.

A large, clearly designed and well executed sign is necessary for a progressive real estate office. Likewise there should be a supply of signs for use on houses offered for sale, vacant lots, and other types of properties. These can be purchased from sign manufacturing companies in lots of fifty or more, designed to suit the name, slogan, and address of the broker. Striking signs will prove valuable in selling many types of property, and they are much cheaper in the long run than newspaper advertising. This does not mean that no advertising should be done. It should be employed cautiously at the outset, however. Most brokers just entering business rush in and do a lot of advertising the first few months but get comparatively few results. Talk with other brokers, learn what the best real estate newspaper medium is, and then use it, rather than rushing into a variety of publications which bring no results. Do not buy calendars, specialties in the way of pocketbooks, ballpoint pens, and such things. They never pay out in a manner proportionate to their cost. Be conservative about your advertising until you learn more about the kinds that bring results, and you will save considerable money.

It is a good idea to have an announcement printed and sent to a selected list of persons whom you would like to have as your clientele. This may be a brief announcement simply stating that you are entering the real estate field, establishing an office at a certain address, where you would be glad to greet them, list their properties, and offer them listings from which they may select some type of real estate they desire to own. The announcement may be quite elaborate, dwelling on the history and qualifications of the new broker.

"Every business is the lengthened shadow of a man," said Emerson. I used this phrase when I first went into business many years ago. It applies particularly to real estate brokers. Divorce the mainspring from an office and it seldom continues to function. That is why it is difficult to sell a real estate business as such. The motivating force, once removed, leaves the furniture and fixtures the only things of value, and they can be sold only at current values for such equipment. Give a good deal of thought to the preparation, printing, and distribution of attractive notices when you plan to go into business.

As you will probably become a good customer in the course of time, it is only right that the newspapers should give the public notice of the fact that you are engaging in business. Write out as completely as possible a story about your entering the realty business, dressing it up with as much actual information as possible and giving complete details as to the location and the type of business you plan to conduct. Either take your story or mail it to the city editors of the newspapers where you plan to advertise your wares, saying that you believe you are entitled to such an announcement in their news columns. If the story is printed, the publicity resulting will prove useful and valuable by establishing in the public's mind that you are a going concern.

If you do not have a car, plan to get one. A real estate broker without a car is like a cowboy without a horse. It does not need to be a de luxe model but it should not be a worn-out jalopy that stalls when you need it most. Keep it clean and attractive, for women are likely to be your main customers and they notice such things. In warm climates, you will find air conditioning a must for your car.

In planning a campaign to build up your office, do not go too far afield for listings. Select the territory in which you want to work and then cultivate it. Do not go running all over town looking at listings, for you cannot thus conserve your time. On the proper use of your time depends the success that is to reward your efforts. Consequently, when listings at distant points are offered, make a note of them but don't go racing all over creation looking at them. Concentrate at first on a few square miles around your office until you get going and perhaps have someone else to help you.

It will not take the new broker long to realize that he must concentrate on favorite listings which show the best promise of being disposed of. "Keep on the tails of the hot ones." Get yourself thoroughly sold on a property, and you can go out and sell it.

"A property rightly listed is half sold" is another axiom of real estate which is absolutely true. Don't let the owner of a property come into your office and dictate a price beyond reason. Make it a practice to go out and look at a property directly after listing it and before submitting it to a client. It will require some genuine appraising ability to ascertain in your own mind whether the property is within shooting distance of the price asked. If it isn't, then discard it and work on something *that will sell.* Select listings carefully, culling them out when you find that they have no appeal or the prices are too high. Being sold on a property he is submitting will do more to bring the new broker success than anything else. He works with an enthusiasm that communicates itself to the client, whose mind is then made up so that he makes an offer that may bring a sale.

Having set up an office, keep that office for a reasonable time, at least, or until you can move to a much better location. The new broker who goes into business and then for a period of months bobs around from one place to another "gathers no moss" and creates doubt in the minds of both buyers and sellers. Every month you remain in a location will win you new friends and clients. You should at least become enough of a fixture so that people think you are a success, even if it happens that you are not.

Don't be a "moocher," trying to do business with the listings of other brokers. They may tolerate your coming around and trying to help them sell properties which they would find no difficulty in selling themselves, but after a while they tire of this and will refuse to work with you. Go out and get your own listings and conduct your own business deals. If you find this impossible, fold up your tent and silently steal away, like the Arab, for you are not destined to remain long in the real estate business.

Throw yourself heart and soul into your business. This does not mean that you have to work all night or every Sunday. But you must be really interested in selling real estate as your life's work if you intend to become a success at it. Study the methods of your competitors and read over and over again the books on real estate which deal with salesmanship, leasing, and appraising. You will find opportunities every day to utilize the information in actual conduct of deals.

Master appraising technique. Nothing will make you a good salesman quicker than knowing how to value property. Value is the basis of all real estate, and if you can develop your judgment of values, you will avoid a great deal of trouble caused by owners insisting on prices which you as a broker can never obtain.

It is suggested once again that the new broker specialize in a particular kind of property. If it is houses, see that you know about every house listed in your territory, how it compares with other offerings, and its special advantages. With houses, you can very well also handle vacant lots. With a pent-up demand for new houses, there will be a tremendous demand for new building sites. While the total amount of money realized from lots is not so great as that from the sale of houses, the commissions are adequate, and lots are often easier to sell than houses. After you have mastered the selling of one kind of property, you can study the techniques required for selling another kind, thus gradually mastering the broad field which is real estate. Later you may decide to specialize in business property, or income or industrial property, or to try to sell all kinds as the occasion permits.

At the outset the broker should seek to sell himself to the owner of every worthwhile property to the extent that he is given an exclusive contract, by the owner, to sell the property over a period of sixty or ninety days. (An exclusive contract isn't worthwhile unless it is for at least ninety days.) Such a contract gives a listing broker the sole and exclusive right to sell the property for a stated period. He may permit some other broker to join him in a sale, but the owner cannot sell direct without paying the listing broker a commission. This arrangement is just as advantageous to the owner as it is to the broker, as it protects him from irresponsible brokers and curbstoners who will not spend money advertising the property and any two of whom may present a prospect at the same time and cause the property owner a headache in trying to avoid the payment of two commissions.

A new broker should begin the day he enters business to build up a great mass of information which can be used from time to time. When you list a property, get every possible detail at the *first* call. Check it with maps and other data at the office. If you sell the property, put the card in a "sold" file, for two or three years later it may be on the market again and the old card will provide full information about it. By filing away old listing cards for future reference, you will in a few years have a tremendous amount of useful and valuable information about properties in your area.

In real estate activities your time, energy, and skill are your main assets. Don't waste your time. Don't spend the afternoon at a movie when you might be showing property. Your time represents money. Your time is what you have to sell. Don't let others waste it, if you can help it. Be industrious. Be active.

Read the newspaper ads daily and on Sunday for new listings, and news about properties which have been sold or are to be built. Some owners think they can save a commission by trying to sell their properties themselves. Their ads tip off the fact that their properties are on the market. Contact them and you may obtain new, live listings. The ability of an owner to sell his own property is constantly questioned by buyers who try to do business with him. Usually an argument ensues about the price and terms, or some other feature, and the owner finds it impossible to act as broker and owner at the same time.

The new broker will find immediately that he will be required to refinance some of the properties he is handling. It will be necessary to become acquainted with mortgage loan officers at banks and at mortgage and building and loan companies. Here a knowledge of appraising will prove most useful in getting adequate loans. Many properties offered for sale have low or inadequate loans. New ones must be negotiated. The broker should know what sources are available and where the best terms can be arranged. This financial area is one with which a broker must become familiar and proficient, for he will be called on from time to time to refinance properties which he is selling.

A new broker should also establish contact with a good builder or a firm engaged in building different kinds of structures. Many sales of vacant lots are immediately followed by building operations. Before such lots can be sold it is often necessary to obtain estimates and sketches of what can be done. It is sometimes quite feasible for a broker to have a builder occupy a part of his office, for the two occupations go hand in hand.

A broker starting business will learn at the outset, in answering persons inquiring about advertisements, first to secure the name, telephone number, and address of the person calling so he may have a record for later reference. If the person declines to give this information, the broker may make an appointment to convey the information direct. If this fails, the call may be one of mere curiosity on the part of the person calling, or it may be a curbstone broker seeking an opportunity to "horn in" on a good listing not held on an exclusive contract basis. In this connection, a broker should have printed and use a "prospect" card on which the name, address, and kind of property wanted is written. Below will be written the properties and the dates shown. Following up those prospect cards is part of the routine of a real estate office and one that brings many sales to a successful conclusion.

Before a broker can expect to do much business, he must have made a careful canvass of the territory in which he plans to operate. In many cases, this means door-to-door canvassing, something that is not always pleasant. It must be done, if the broker is to become familiar with the class of property on different streets, its ownership, advantages, and disadvantages. *CIRCULATE!* Keep moving around. Keep in touch with your neighborhoods. You will learn much and run into many promising listings. Swivel-chair salesmen never sell much property. Even if it means shutting up your office once in a while, keep circulating around from time to time, gradually widening the scope of your investigations until you know your territory like a book.

A useful adjunct of a new brokerage office is a contact with the county recorder's office whereby information about property ownership may be obtained. This service is sometimes given by the map department of a real estate board, a title company, or a concern which specializes in this work. Knowing the street number and legal description of a property, you can telephone and in a brief space of time secure the name and address of the owner, whom you can then contact by telephone or by calling personally. This information, as it is collected, should be carefully preserved on cards in the listing files, as it may prove most useful later on.

One way for a new salesman or broker to break into the real estate business and get valuable experience without the expense of conducting an office is to join a real estate subdivision office and learn the techniques of selling vacant home sites. A live subdivider usually hires a clever salesmanager who drills his salesmen in the ordinary rules of realty salesmanship, which are virtually the same in all branches of the business. Having a specific commodity for sale on which delivery is certain and sure, the salesman can learn the lessons as they are given him, become thoroughly familiar with the property to be sold, and then go into the field and sell within a very few days. It may take him weeks to make his first sale in a regular brokerage office, particularly if it is his own and he is new at the business. After picking up commissions from the sale of subdivisions for a few months, the salesman may shift to a brokerage office, and the new broker may open his own office, somewhat richer in income and experience than if he started directly with his own business and spent his own time gaining the experience which must come to those who would succeed.

Completion of several deals affords an opportunity to get some publicity, particularly if one or more of the local papers conduct Sunday real estate pages. Write up in detail all of the facts concerning the sales you have made and mail or take them to the real estate editor or the city editor of your local papers. In all probability they will be used as news stories. These will prove very useful while you are new in the business and seeking to build up a clientele. "Nothing succeeds like success," and people seeking real estate naturally gravitate to the live offices where business is being done. Likewise, property owners, noting that you are active and making sales, will drop in with listings of their holdings instead of you having to beat the brush and go out after them.

The critical time in the life of a real estate business is the first three or four months it is in existence, particularly if the broker has few financial reserves to fall back on. If it is necessary to make expenses as he goes along, he is eager to make a deal and collect a commission. This seldom happens in the first few weeks. One must first get property listings, which takes time. Then the prospect appears and negotiations begin, which takes more time. Finally an offer is secured and it is accepted. Then the transaction goes to escrow and the title report or abstract must be prepared, which takes additional time. Finally the deal goes to record and the commission is earned and paid to the broker. The whole transaction may take as much as three months to complete. So the final lesson is: *patience*. One needs *infinite patience* to engage in the real estate business. Because the commissions are sometimes large and occasionally easily earned, don't think that it is always that way. Many deals drag and test one's soul while difficulties are being ironed out and adjusted. So one must learn to be patient as well as earnest and honest and persevering in the real estate business.

CHAPTER 6

Establishing an Office

THE NEWCOMER MAY ESTABLISH AN office in one of the following ways:

1. By opening his own complete office.
2. By renting desk space in some desirable office and expanding from that beginning.
3. By associating himself with another broker, either as a salesman or as an associate broker.
4. By joining an office with a number of well established departments, in which he can specialize on one kind of property after another until he is qualified to work in all branches.

Assuming that you make up your mind at the outset to open your own office, the first consideration is to determine just where you want to engage in business. This may require much study and careful survey of the entire community in which you live. Don't choose a decadent district, with old buildings and few vacant lots on which to build, which has reached its peak and may be on its way downward. Remember that you are planning to be in business for a good many years and you want to operate in an area that promises definite growth and expansion. Most buyers of real estate like to settle in fairly new neighborhoods, and women, who actually do the buying of most of the houses, almost invariably want to acquire new dwellings whether they can afford them or not.

Don't start in business in an old district simply because you live there and know a good many people. It may be better to begin in a fairly new section, even if you have to move your home there to be reasonably near your office. Give a good deal of thought to the subject of picking a district. Consult other active real estate men, who can judge the relative merits of available locations, who know whether there are too many real estate brokers in a given area and who, because they have been longer in the real estate business, may be able to steer you clear of many pitfalls.

Once having selected the section in which you want to operate, the next problem is to find a suitable office. Remember, its location and appearance are of vital importance. Although you may need to start out modestly, never forget that nothing speaks so eloquently to the public as the office you keep.

Your office should be located in an action center. Prominent locations in shopping centers are very good. Obtain a location where many people walk by so that the public relations aspect of your place of business may be used adequately. Be sure adequate parking space is available.

If you are fortunate enough to have window space, be sure to display photographs of your properties in an attractive manner. And, above all, place the name of your agency prominently so that it may be seen for several blocks.

If you have the means to do so, and you think the district worthwhile, you may even purchase a small business property and establish yourself permanently in the locality. You can use one unit of your building as your real estate office and rent the others to pay for the overhead. Going into a district early and picking up a strategic location of this kind often proves later to have been wise, when the property has increased in value owing to normal growth or to other influences which have made the district expand rapidly.

If you are specializing in a kind of property not confined to one district, such as, for instance, industrial sites, you may not want a ground-floor office at all but will want to establish yourself in a well-located office building. Some brokers who specialize in chain-store promotions, or in gas stations, or who coöperate with builders in erecting small business structures, will want to establish offices downtown rather than in neighborhood offices on the ground level.

Surveys made to determine the relative value of ground-floor offices in contrast with those located on the upper floors of office buildings have shown that brokers engaged in a general real estate business almost unanimously favor ground-floor locations, where displays in windows and easy access from the street usually tempt customers to enter and seek properties who would never have been influenced to go into an office building and ascend to an upper floor to consult a broker.

Having arranged for the exact location for your office, your next step is to furnish it adequately. You will need a large flat-top desk for yourself and a similar desk, with a typewriter compartment for your stenographer. You may want a large map of your community, and if one is available you should have an atlas showing all property in your territory. Such atlases are published in most towns and cities. If not available, detailed blue or white prints can probably be secured from your county recorder or assessor, showing tracts and lots in detail.

At this point the question will arise as to the type of records you are going to require to keep track of your property listings. This subject will be discussed in another chapter, but at the very outset you will have to make up your mind whether you are going to use 4 x 6 inch cards or loose-leaf books. Both are available from stationery stores. An enterprising real estate man who has decided to use cards will have his own printed, having plates made of the type so they can be readily reprinted when needed.

Display signs are a very necessary adjunct of a real estate office. You will need attractive signs to bring customers to your place of business, and you will need a supply of signs to erect on vacant lots and attach to buildings you have for sale. These should be, preferably, of metal or some tough pressed board which will stand the weather and exposure. Signs 2 x 4 feet in size or larger can be purchased in lots of fifty or more from professional sign-manufacturing concerns. It is a good idea for a broker to have a distinctive sign showing his name and his business, and possibly a slogan to go with it. Think up something new and novel if you can, and it will bring you excellent returns once you have begun to capitalize on it.

The question often arises as to whether a real estate man starting in business should use his own name or should incorporate a company under the laws of the state in which he is located. In most cases it is probably wiser to just use your own name. Later, if you get into big operations, you can incorporate under your own or a company name. Incidentally, some customers are skeptical about doing business with a broker who is ashamed to use his own name but hides his identity behind a general company name such as the Atlas Realty Co. You have a good name, don't be ashamed of it! *Use it!*

It will be necessary at the outset to secure a supply of stationery, including letterheads and envelopes. Shop around and get several bids every time you want printing done, until you are satisfied you are dealing with a printer who is giving you fair prices as well as good work. In addition to letterheads, you will require business calling cards to leave with customers whom you have interviewed. You will also require contract of sale forms. A typewriter will be used for correspondence and for preparing contracts, records, and so forth.

When you get your desks you will at the same time buy chairs, one being a swivel chair to go with your own desk, and a typist's chair for the desk at which your stenographer will work. Half a dozen chairs will be required at the outset. These should match the desks. If suitable closet space is not available, you will need one or more hat racks.

You will need a car. Make sure the customers ride with you—not in their own car following you. You will often pick up information from their conversation that will help you find the right spot for them. And the ride home may give you just the time you need to close the deal. Your car needn't be luxurious, but it must be clean and comfortable. Air-conditioning can be very helpful in the summer months.

Whether you, as a new broker, can afford to hire a stenographer will depend upon your resources. You may be able to get along without one if you can operate a typewriter yourself. It is doubtful if at the outset you will have enough work to keep a stenographer busy. The problem presents itself at this point as to who will look after your office if you are out in the field with customers. You may be able to get someone who can share your office with you while you are establishing your business, and such a person can take your telephone calls and answer queries of customers who call in your absence. On the other hand, you may prefer not to leave anyone in your office to take business away from you. The most profitable customers may call when you are not in. You may miss them or your associate may get the first crack at selling them something that should have fallen to your lot.

If you prefer not to hire a secretary to take your calls, you can subscribe to an answering service. These services will make every effort to get in touch with you should something rather urgent arise, and the personnel of the answering services are adroit at getting information from callers to pass onto you.

On the other hand, perhaps one of the message recorders available from your telephone company may be just the thing for you. Callers may leave recorded messages which you can play back when you return to the office.

You may want to consider the advantages of sharing your office with another broker, either as a partner or as an associate. Frankly, in my forty years of experience I have found that partnerships in real estate do not often turn out very well. One partner always works a little harder than another. It is difficult to stifle petty jealousies which arise in businesss life, despite the fact that each may have something to contribute that the other does not possess. However, think long and earnestly before you tie up with someone as a partner and leave the way open to dissolve the arrangement should you become dissatisfied with it.

Having an associate broker in your office is another matter. Arrange for yourself to own the office outright, with all of its equipment. Give your associate broker a desk, and work out an arrangement for the rental he is to pay or for the division of commissions, as the case may be. It is usually better for the other broker to work in the office as a salesman, with a definite arrangement for splitting commissions and an understanding that you, as owner of the office, will pay the usual expenses of conducting it. These include rent, newspaper advertising, signs, cards, contract forms, and such help as you can give in the closing of transactions. Brokerage salesmen usually work on a 50-50 arrangement, but a fully qualified license broker with experience sometimes gets 60 per cent of the total commission for his part of a deal when he handles it himself.

If an associate broker is acting in the capacity of a straight salesman in your office, do not forget that you are responsible for the actions of your agents. If an associate broker works for you, it is likely that a similar responsibility exists. If the associate broker is working "on his own" as a broker, you will probably not be responsible for his acts.

When you open your office, you will promptly find at your desk the advertising representatives of the local newspapers who will all want to sign you up to contracts in their respective media. By making a contract for space you will save possibly 25 per cent of the cost of your advertising. At this point, decide to move slowly. Don't be hurried into signing up for advertising until you have canvassed the field and have found out from other brokers which are the desirable papers in which to advertise. There is always one paper in a community that is the favorite real estate medium. No one knows just why it is so, but in every city there is one popular paper which handles more real estate advertising than any of the others. That is the one in which to advertise, for you will reach a wider field at less expense. Do a good deal of investigating before you rush into print with a lot of advertising. There is always the temptation for the new man to make a "splurge" for the first two or three months. This definitely costs money. If you have it to spend, well and good. If you have to watch your cash reserves, go slowly and advertise cautiously until you know more about the matter and decide which medium gives you the best coverage. In any event, don't sign noncancellable contracts until you have carefully investigated the entire question of advertising.

The new broker in the average city will have to decide whether to join the organized real estate interests of his community and become a member of the local real estate board. Joining is strongly advised, for the contacts you will establish will be extremely useful. The new man is able to seek advice about many problems from men who know the right answers. Membership in your local board usually carries with it similar membership in your state and the national organization, the latter now having over 1,500 boards in different cities throughout the country. Join your real estate board, attend its meetings, keep your ears and eyes open, and you will gain much of value from reliable sources. You will benefit by being able to display the "Realtor" emblem, which right is afforded to members of the board.

It is a commonly accepted belief that a man going into the real estate business requires no capital. From the foregoing it must be very evident that such is not entirely the case. To be a salesman requires no great outlay of capital, but to engage in the real estate business itself, even conducting just a one-man office, *does require capital!* So do not get the idea that you can take a "flyer" at the business and drop out of it any time you want to without making a substantial cash investment on top of a lot of time spent preparing yourself to become a competent broker.

The following is a rough estimate of the capital required to open and equip a small one-man brokerage office on the most modest of scales:

Your desk	$150
Stenographer's desk	140
Chairs	140
Typewriter, used (minimum)	75
Table(s)	100
Lamps	100
File cabinet (minimum)	60
Index boxes	10
Listing cards, forms, letterhead envelopes, business cards, etc.	200
Maps and atlas (minimum)	50

Office sign and window lettering 100
Metal signs for use on properties 75
Miscellaneous (waste baskets, ash trays, desk supplies, coat
racks, etc.) 100
                                                                      —————

    Total initial outlay $1,300

From the foregoing, it may be seen that a broker can expect to spend at least $1,300 to launch a very small real estate office in even the most modest manner, exclusive of the cost of his automobile. But don't let that worry you! You may earn a $1,000 commission the first week and almost pay for the whole outfit! More elaborately equipped offices will cost more in proportion.

Among the things you will probably want to add as soon as possible are a photocopying machine and a camera. A Polaroid camera can be especially useful in giving you pictures that are immediately available to show prospective purchasers.

In selecting a spot for your office, seek a location that will leave you some room to expand without having to move. (A new building is often a good choice since it is apt to take some time to rent it and other space is apt to be available.) Of course, the location should be in an up-and-coming part of town. Some place in the fringe area along the main artery is best—but try to avoid a spot where a number of other real estate firms are already established.

Two or more brokers may join in fitting up an office, but this involves problems that sometimes make the venture a questionable one. One should be very sure indeed that the parties involved will get along pleasantly as well as profitably in the proposed arrangement.

The new broker or salesman may find a haven in an office already well established. While commissions must be divided, the benefits to be derived by the salesman or broker are usually worthwhile, particularly while the newcomer is learning some of the details of a very involved business. The larger offices can assist materially in helping the new salesman develop his prospects and close deals when it becomes necessary to do so.

It is occasionally possible for a new broker to buy the office of an etablished broker who is about to retire or move to another city. The value of such an office is largely represented in the value of the furniture and equipment it contains. "Good will" in a realty office as such can seldom be shown to have much value. The man who is leaving takes with him the dynamic force that has been behind the office, and that, once removed, leaves little but the chattels for sale. Such an office may be quite complete, however, and ready to be used, and it may have a slight additional value because it can actually be considered a going concern in most respects.

A large office is not necessary for the new broker to begin in, but neither should it be a mere cubbyhole that lacks character and fails to afford sufficient space in which to operate. Occasionally several customers may arrive almost together, and to have them piled one on the other is not good business.

Sometimes it is a good idea for a new broker opening an office to have a salesman on his staff right from the beginning. The two can work together advantageously, relieving each other at lunch time and when one or the other has to be out in the field.

Time will be well spent in carefully considering the problems associated with the establishment of any real estate office. The ultimate success of the broker may definitely depend upon the location of the office itself, the manner in which it is equipped, the way in which it impresses the public, and the way in which business is conducted. Weigh very carefully the merits of the associates you select to work with and the relationship they bear to your main effort. Having finally made up your mind concerning all details, go ahead earnestly and enthusiastically and you will, without doubt, meet with the success your efforts deserve.

CHAPTER 7

Pitfalls to Avoid

IN HIS EAGERNESS TO GET STARTED AND TO earn commissions, the newcomer to the real estate field, be he salesman or broker, would do well to proceed cautiously. If you have chosen your office location well, it will be in a section near new home construction. Your first thought must be toward the securing of listings on newly built homes, since a large part of the modern real estate business is for such homes, and this is what almost all of the newcomers will be looking for. You must contact the builders; you must secure listings. If you can't get exclusives, obtain the right to sell anyway.

But you will need all types of properties. Many of the settled citizens will be seeking bigger houses and they won't always be able to afford new construction.

Take a map. Draw a circle around your office location. Travel up one street and down another, looking every property over carefully. Note the kind of unit it is, how it is constructed, and everything about it that you may want to know later. Call at several houses in every block and find out whether listings can be obtained there.

"No, this house isn't for sale," the first owner may say, "but I understand my neighbor in the third house from here has his place up for sale."

A new listing is in sight! Interview the owner of that house and try to get a listing. Here is where your knowledge of real estate valuation will come in handy. Every owner fondly believes that his or her piece of property is the best on the street; that it is endowed with some extraordinary value, and that no difficulty should be found in selling it. The owner will begin to recite all of the unusual advantages of the house and wind up by telling you the price, which is about 50 per cent more than it is actually worth. Wise judgment on the part of a broker who knows valuation procedure will indicate instantly that the asking price is too high and that he will have a mighty difficult time finding a buyer for it.

Get down to cases right away. Measure off the house to ascertain its total area in square feet. Apply a cost factor of so much per square foot that the house could be built for, new. Learn from the owner or estimate how old the house is. Then depreciate it for age, using a standard table for this purpose. This will give you the cost new, less depreciated value of the building. Then apply a factor of value to the lot; add this to the value of the house, and you should have a reasonable idea of the market value of the property. You may check your estimate by seeking out in your own mind a comparative property of approximately the same size and character. The value of such a comparative property should check reasonably well with your reproduction figure. You are then in a position to show the owner that his price of $23,000 for an old three-bedroom house is altogether too high and that it should sell for $17,000 or $18,000 instead. In this manner the real estate salesman can avoid listing property at far higher sales prices than he can hope to sell it for.

To get property listed correctly at the outset is most important, and will prevent a tremendous amount of trouble.

After a few days spent canvassing your territory, you will come to a realization of several things:

1. You will know how much real estate is for sale.
2. You will begin to recognize the standard of values that exists and the prices that must be obtained for average listings.
3. You will have obtained a number of listings, without which you could not hope to engage in business.

4. You will be in a position to quote comparative sales prices on properties, knowledge of which will be convincing to both sellers and buyers.

5. You will have brought to the attention of a number of owners in your neighborhood the fact that you have gone into business and want their patronage.

After you have been in the field for a few days, have canvassed your restricted territory quite faithfully, and have established some stock in trade in the way of listings, you will realize that you should, for the time being at least, engage in the sale of one particular type of property (assuming that you are working as a broker who has his own established office). You will doubtless have found several kinds of property in your area, including dwellings, two-family houses, four-flats, large multiple-unit buildings, and possibly some business structures. While you may later become proficient enough to include the sale of all those kinds of real estate, it will be well to specialize, at the outset at least, on residential units. The listings you have obtained, for the most part, will be houses, and the general fund of information you will have accumulated will mostly concern houses. Make up your mind, then, to sell houses exclusively for a time, and do it faithfully until you have made some sales and gained more experience.

Understand, at this juncture, the value of an exclusive listing. Such a listing makes you, in writing, the exclusive agent with the "sole and exclusive right" to sell a property within a stipulated period of time at a specified sum and upon certain terms and conditions. This right holds good "whether the property is sold by you as said agent, by the owner, or by another agent or through any source whatever, or whether the property is transferred or conveyed during the time set forth in the exclusive listing."

Do not take an exclusive listing on a property if the price asked seems too high. Some brokers will seek such listings, hoping to convince owners that the price should later be reduced. This is a questionable practice and should be avoided.

If you have an exclusive listing, you can place a sign on the property or advertise it openly without fear of having other brokers interfere with your sale of it. The wise broker always carries exclusive contract forms with him to use whenever necessary.

A very definite pitfall to avoid is the request of someone who comes into your office who asks for a certain type of property in another part of the city with which you are not acquainted and where you have no listings. The prospect will indicate the exact kind of a property he wants, the price he will pay for it, and the location where he wants to go. If you are inexperienced or over-enthusiastic, you will dash out into the area mentioned and try to dig up a listing of the kind of property wanted. You may be two or three days doing this, in all probability, and when you get back to the prospective buyer—if you are able to find him again—you will find that he has decided that he wants to get a place in another district, or in the meantime has bought a property and is entirely out of the market.

Stick to your own district! Don't waste your time traipsing all over the city looking for property. If you know a broker in another district who may have such a listing, it might be well to contact him and try to make a joint deal; but, if not, stick to your own territory and sell someone the property you have on hand! The seasoned broker knows that more time and effort are wasted in this way than most people realize.

Another pitfall lies in the way you get your listings. When canvassing, get all of the information about a property on the *first call* if at all possible. Know what facts you must have and then insist on getting them. Don't let the owner tell you that he "thinks" the lot is 50 feet wide and that he doesn't know the depth; that the taxes are "about" $300 when they are actually $365; that the age of the house is "in the neighborhood" of ten years when it is actually eighteen years old; that the mortgage is "about" $5,000 when it is actually $6,500; that the mortgage can be paid off when actually a bonus must be paid if the new buyer wants to negotiate a new loan. Mis-

information poured into the ears of a gullible real estate salesman or broker and then retailed to a prospective buyer causes
a vast amount of trouble in the proper consummation of a
sale. Get your information correct and get all of it *on the first
call.*

Have definite understandings with owners about the prices
and terms on which properties can be sold. A telephone conversation does not appoint a broker as an owner's agent, and
usually a broker cannot collect any compensation for his services from the owner of a property if the place is sold, even
if the broker may have submitted it to someone who eventually
buys it. Listing by telephone and getting and making offers
over the same medium are risky and unnecessary practices.
If you get a firm offer on a listing, don't rush to a phone and
communicate it to an owner. Make the prospective buyer sign
up a written offer and give you a check as a good-faith deposit.
Even then don't talk over the telephone to the owner but go
to see him personally. Explain all of the circumstances of the
deal, show him the check you have received, and get him to
sign a written acceptance on the contract form.

Of all of the things that prevent men from getting along
successfully, lack of real and concrete information is perhaps
the most baffling bar to success in the real estate business.
Too many salesmen and brokers are willing to enter business
with but little actual knowledge or experience. The fact that
they have passed an examination or have read a few books is
no reason to suppose that they are fully qualified to conduct
important and involved negotiations dealing with the transfer
of valuable property. Get a thorough grounding on the general
practices followed by successful real estate brokers, then fully
learn the facts about the properties you are submitting to
prospects, and you will have a much better chance of closing
your deals. Whether an offer and deposit check will be forthcoming from a buyer depends largely on an appreciation of
details in listing property and the manner in which they are
relayed to the interested but canny buyer.

Perhaps the primary advantage of a salesman or broker

associating himself with a well-established real estate office is the fact that much necessary information is usually on tap from members of the firm or from other salesmen. When you haven't the information, you at least have a source where you can go and get it. A man who holds a broker's license is often wiser at the outset to associate himself with a representative office. He may feel that he will have to work on a division of commissions, but he seldom realizes the overhead expense that is entailed in the conduct of an office of his own. In the long run he is often better off financially working for the larger office, because he is then free to concentrate on making deals instead of looking after the annoying details which often come with conducting an office of your own.

A broker working alone must do his own appraising of properties. Unless he is skillful, it will take him quite a while to become proficient to the point where he can convince a seller that the price asked is right. Many large offices make a regular practice of having all properties appraised before listings are accepted. A salesman, when listing, may get all of the information, including even the seller's idea of a fair price for a property, but the office will not confirm the acceptance of such a listing or agree to work on it until an official appraisal has been made. This is usually done by members of the firm, accompanied by the sales manager and the more experienced salesmen. At an appointed time each listed property is visited. The value is carefully established and a selling price agreed upon. If the owner's price is too high, it must be adjusted downwards, within reason, or the office will not proceed further. In this way the salesman knows that when a listing is confirmed the price is right and that the property should, within a reasonable time and upon proper exposure to the public, find a buyer. In this way the salesman conserves his time and eventually makes more deals. In some offices every salesman is required to make a personal trip of inspection to all the properties he offers for sale. He must learn all about the listing and the neighborhood in which it is located. He is thus in a position to act intelligently when offering it.

If a salesman tells a buyer that he can keep roomers in a single-family residence district, he may leave himself open to a charge of misrepresentation. He must not tell a dentist that he can maintain his office in his home if the district is zoned for residential use only. The salesman must be aware of the provisions of the zoning law in effect in his home town, if there is such a law. In listing property, careful inquiry should always be made as to the character of the zoning. If the owner does not know, it is possible, in most instances, to obtain the information from the zoning commission at the city hall.

In some cities much damage is caused by termites, dry rot, and fungus. Termites attack houses at any stage of their lives, and dry rot may appear quite suddenly. A good many buyers will stipulate that a property must be free and clear of infestation when delivered to them. Misrepresentation on the part of the broker may get him into serious difficulty and possibly void a sale that might otherwise go through without question.

A difficulty sometimes encountered by a salesman is the insertion of a wrong description in a sales contract. Such contracts call for the use of a legal description as well as an accurate designation of the property by street and number. Vacant properties usually have no street number to identify them, and the legal description is the only one that can be used. If for some reason a buyer wants to worm his way out of a contract, he may do so if the legal description is not exactly right, on the ground that he did not agree to purchase the property described in the contract. A careful salesman will go to extremes to see that the legal description is absolutely correct.

Another pitfall is to get involved with lawyers representing the buyer or the seller in a deal. Most lawyers are glad to work with brokers and to help them with their deals. On the other hand, some lawyers feel it necessary to find something wrong so that they can impress their clients with the fact that they are accomplishing something in their behalf. Many, many deals have been wrecked by such officious lawyers. A clever salesman will dominate the transaction to the extent that the buyer and the seller will feel confident that he is representing them fairly and that a lawyer is not necessary when a sale is being conducted through an escrow office. Unless the salesman takes full charge, the principals may fairly require that their lawyers look over and approve papers in the deal. When an escrow is being used, the broker can draw attention to the knowledge and experience of the escrow officer in handling real estate deals.

Occasionally great skill is necessary to sell a house where there is a tenant, for the tenant may "knock" the property to the prospective buyer because the tenant will have to move if the place is sold. During critical housing shortages, when tenants find it difficult to secure other accommodations, they go to extreme measures to keep properties from being sold and tell the prospective buyer weird stories about the place. The wise broker will see to it that the buyer visits the property never alone but always when the broker is along. Some buyers seem to delight in sneaking around and having private conferences with the tenant, hoping to find out things about a property that have not been divulged. The broker must be on his guard constantly in this respect.

Generally speaking it is not good practice to bring a seller and a buyer together until a firm offer in writing has been made and accepted, unless the seller occupies the property. Even then it is sometimes wise to take the buyer into escrow alone, to be followed by the seller. Some personalities clash upon the slightest provocation, and once the buyer and seller have a chance to meet they may dig up some unimportant matter on which they cannot agree. This may result in wrecking the entire deal, one or the other refusing to sign escrow instructions and the necessary deed and the mortgage. Study your clients and, if you think it wise to keep them apart, do so. Little is gained by having them meet, anyway.

Be very careful in selecting the kind of offer-to-purchase contract you will use in making deals. There are many forms; some are got out by escrow concerns, or prepared by attorneys for publishing houses that print legal papers. See to it that the contract, in proper language, covers the matters on which you seek to have the parties agree. A form used by the author for several decades, and refined from time to time, has passed the scrutiny of many lawyers. One unique feature of this form, which was developed by the author from his experiences, is a sentence which reads: "It is mutually agreed between purchaser and seller that this agency contract shall become an integral part of the escrow proceedings in which the transfer of this property is consummated and that all agreements herein contained shall be binding upon both parties *even if such are not specifically recorded or mentioned in escrow proceedings set up by the escrow agent named here.*" This paragraph was inserted because escrow officers, when a dispute arises between buyer and seller, simply sit back and mark time until it is settled, holding the money the buyer may have deposited until the parties agree. Furthermore escrow officers will not accept many provisions of a broker's contract and in many instances will not even permit the contract itself to become a part of the escrow proceedings. The above wording prevents the broker from being frozen out when certain kinds of disputes occur.

A broker eager to live up to the ethical standards of the real estate business will not make a practice of accepting a net listing, that is, a listing wherein the seller agrees to sell the property at a certain sum to go to him intact, the broker to get his compensation by adding to the net listing price such additional sum for commission as he chooses. Such a net listing is somewhat in the nature of an option. Brokers who utilize either or both are usually headed for trouble. When a seller wants a certain sum net, the broker should add the commission and consider the total as the selling price of the property and have the owner so agree. Net listings are a fertile source of disagreement and should be avoided. A broker, if he intends to buy a property himself, should reveal the fact to the owner and then proceed with that condition fully known.

The retention of a money deposit made by a buyer in connection with an offer to purchase should receive careful consideration. Sometimes the deposit is placed in escrow. Sometimes a broker retains the deposit in a separate trustee bank account and, upon conclusion of the deal and the passage of title, retains whatever amount represents the commission due him and pays over the balance to the seller of the property. The practice for handling this matter differs in various parts of the country but the agreement, whatever it is, should be lived up to religiously by the broker. On general principle, the broker should not commingle his sales deposits with his regular banking account.

Hidden easements and restrictions on a property may get a broker into trouble unless he specifies in his sales contract that they are not guaranteed against. (An easement is some right, such as the right to walk across a part of the land, which a person other than the owner has.) Such easements are seldom revealed before a thorough search of the official records is made. They show up in the abstract of title when it is finally prepared. Most easements and restrictions go with the land and are a part of it, and the buyer must accept them if he wants the property. The broker should be very careful, however, not to say that there are *no* easements and restrictions when actually such may exist.

Another difficulty occasionally arises in the settlement of an estate. A broker may have a property for sale in which an estate has not been completely settled in probate, and only by going into court and having an offer approved can a sale be made. It is well to inquire whether the property being listed is subject to such a settlement, if for any reason the broker thinks it may be so.

There is a definite difference between an exclusive agency or exclusive listing and *the exclusive right to sell*. An exclusive agency or exclusive listing is a written instrument giving the agent the right to sell property for a specified time but reserving the right of the owner to sell the property himself without the payment of a commission. The *exclusive right to sell*, on the other hand, is a written agreement between owner and agent giving the agent the right to collect a commission if a property is sold by anyone during the term of his agreement. Always arrange to get the latter, if possible, and have it definitely in writing to avoid trouble. If the property is held in the names of husband and wife or of several people, always get the signatures of all interested parties. Though the husband signs, a wife who hasn't signed may refuse legally to go through with a deal.

It often happens that, before buying, a prospect wants to sound out the market and get an idea what listings are available. He may take up a considerable amount of the salesman's time by running around and looking over other real estate offerings before calmly announcing that he isn't ready to buy until he sells a property he is living in. It is difficult for the salesman to know just how to handle such a prospect who may eventually become a customer. If the salesman knows definitely, however, that a sale is dependent upon the disposal of another property which the prospect already owns, a great deal of time and effort can be saved. The prospect can without much trouble on the part of the salesman, be given a cross-section of available listings. Later, when the prospect is actually prepared to buy, much greater attention can be paid to him. Time is one of the most valuable assets a salesman has, and time wasted can never be regained. Consequently steps should be taken at an early point in the interview to ascertain the fact that the prospect is ready to proceed before making a sale of his own property.

CHAPTER 8

Essential Things to Know
About Property

THE BUYER OF REAL ESTATE OFTEN IS EN-tirely uninformed of the things he should look for in securing for himself a sound piece of property. He knows whether he likes the outward appearance of a property, and he can study the neighborhood and its apparent advantages without much help. There are, however, many things about property with which the average buyer is unfamiliar, and it is about them that the broker or salesman is called upon to inform him. By the same token, the salesman should thoroughly investigate every property he lists and attempts to sell, for in doing so he may be called upon for information about a wide variety of matters, without which it would be difficult to influence a buyer to act and thus complete a sale.

Many problems concern neighborhood influences, such as the presence of adequate business centers and transportation, and the possibility of undesirable persons moving into the neighborhood. Others have to do with the property itself—both the land and the buildings on it. A salesman thoroughly familiar with a neighborhood will know instantly the answer to questions about the district itself, but he may not know the condition of the buildings themselves until he has studied them.

Nothing purchased during one's lifetime requires more careful investigation than does real estate. Such a purchase usually involves the largest single outlay of money ever spent by an individual, and one must know fully all the particulars about a property before money is invested and ownership assumed. Nevertheless many buyers proceed to acquire real estate without advice. It is here that the broker or salesman can save the buyer money.

Real estate is unique! Of all the things in the world that possess individuality, a piece of real estate may be considered a primary one. No two pieces of real estate are exactly alike. If in nothing else, they differ in exact location. One is nearer a corner than another, a little higher, or a little lower. Every parcel of land possesses certain advantages of soil, location, and convenience that are absolutely unique and can never be exactly duplicated.

Because real estate is unique, it cannot be standardized like automobiles, colored television or loaves of bread. Thousands of automobiles of one pattern can be turned out under given specifications and they are alike in every particular. They can be relied upon to give certain mileage for given amounts of fuel and to perform service on a standardized basis. No two houses, however, can be exactly alike. Their locations are different. They have been built piecemeal by different groups of mechanics, and they differ in many particulars. Neighborhoods all vary from each other, each having certain advantages over the others as well as disadvantages. In selecting a piece of real estate such as a home, therefore, no exact rules or standards can be followed, and a wise choice can be made only through someone who has had years of training and study in real estate and in the selection and management of it.

Is a property under consideration subject to special hazards, such as floods, tornadoes, droughts, brush fires, or other unusual catastrophes, which may wipe out improvements, or even land itself, suddenly, at some future time? Hundreds of people, in periods of booming real estate markets, have bought home sites in river washes and on and under mountain sides. Came great floods, vast damage resulted, sometimes with serious loss of life. Alaskan earthquakes can hardly be anticipated, but

California mud slides are easily predicted. Probe keenly into the subject of site hazards in listing a home. Don't take any chances because you can sell a place cheaply as of the moment, for some owner may pay dearly for it later on.

Is a property you propose to list and sell subject to nuisances such as disagreeable odors from stock yards, smoke from factories, noise from huge jet aircraft, odors from sewage disposal plants, and similar hazards? These are extremely important considerations and require careful investigation. Many an otherwise attractive home has been a tremendous disappointment and loss because of some condition that was not known before the purchase was made. And the broker was always blamed!

Always find out whether all necessary public utilities are installed and paid for before listing and selling property. Pioneering in a new residential tract where there are no sewers, gas mains, telephones, or electricity is neither pleasant nor profitable. Check carefully to see that all necessary public-service facilities are installed. Check on television reception. Is cable TV available where reception is poor? Determine, too, whether there are postal service and fire and police protection. Many subdivisions in outlying areas have no modern public-service facilities. Lots can be bought cheaply there, but they are often dear at any price.

In buying a home site, determine whether an adequate supply of good drinking water is available. Pure water is absolutely essential to human life, and property values suffer keenly if it is not readily and cheaply available.

When listing an improved property, ascertain if possible whether buildings have been erected on filled land. Sound, solid foundations are essential to lasting construction, and care should be taken to see that they have not been hurriedly placed on filled ground which may later settle and cause slippage or collapse.

Is there a garage in connection with the dwelling? If not, is there a place where it may be built? An automobile is essential in almost every home. There should be at least one garage and preferably accommodations for two cars.

In listing and selling real estate, see that adequate transportation exists within a reasonable distance of the property. There should be regular service by car, train, or bus. Although a buyer may own a car, friends who want to visit him may not have one. Accessibility of adequate schools, libraries, churches, and parks is apparent, but the buyer should investigate them thoroughly.

In inspecting a dwelling, be careful to determine whether the roof is in good shape, whether the heating and air-conditioning system is adequate and sound, whether the plumbing is modern, adequate, and in good repair, and whether floors and walls of a building show the presence of dampness, decay, or insect infestation, such as termites, dry rot, or fungus growth.

A home site should be within reasonable walking distance of an adequate shopping center where one may purchase a number of articles. Are coin operated washaterias available? If an owner can buy foods, clothing, shoes, drugs, and hardware in one shopping center, he probably is being served by a fairly adequate business district.

A farm buyer should become interested in the character of the soil. Note whether it is tilled and properly fertilized, whether it is underlaid with shale, clay, or rock, and whether the territory has an adequate supply of water. Also ascertain whether the land is subject to overflow from creek bottoms in the rainy season, and whether there are hazards from brush fires or hillside erosion.

The selection of a piece of real estate is not the simple thing some persons believe it to be. True, anyone can go out and buy a house or a ranch or a business property. To purchase with the knowledge and reasonable certainty that one is getting his money's worth and that his new possession will bring happiness, comfort, profit, and satisfaction is something else again. There are, indeed, many hazards that will be encountered, and the broker or salesman must train himself to foresee them if he is to select and list properties intelligently.

CHAPTER 9

Records and Forms

IN LAUNCHING A REAL ESTATE OFFICE IT will be found that adequate and accurate records must be kept of all data encountered in connection with the business. A vast amount of valuable information costing a great deal of money to gather is accumulated over the months and years an office continues in operation, and these data must be filed and segregated for future use. Inability to resurrect a listing or important information at the proper time has lost many a sale!

Much of the information that comes to hand cannot be used immediately. This must be retained in some permanent form, preferably on cards, and filed away so that it can be brought to notice immediately when wanted.

The first thing that must be created is a complete set of listing cards. The most practicable size for such cards has been found to be 4 x 6 inches. For a general real estate business it will be found that cards of different colors must be provided for the following types of property:

1. Single-dwelling houses.
2. Double, two-family, and duplex houses.
3. Multiple dwellings, from 4 units up.
4. Business property, improved.
5. Industrial property.
6. Leases of stores and of business and industrial sites.

71

  7. Farms and suburban properties.
  8. Vacant property, lots, business and apartment sites, etc.
  9. Rentals of dwellings and apartments.
 10. Sales and leases of condominiums.

In most offices the cards are developed from samples used by other brokers or from stereotyped cards sold by printers for the purpose. A distinctive color will serve to make each type of card easily identifiable. The kind of information to be found on most listing cards is fairly uniform, although in some parts of the country certain unusual items may have to be inserted.

Make a practice of filling out the cards on a typewriter or *in ink* as completely as possible *at the first interview*. Then is the time you can get the information most easily. Insist that your informer give you the exact facts and not make mere guesses. If you give a prospective buyer information that has been given you by an owner and it is found to be wrong, you share the responsibility for misrepresenting the property and may get into serious difficulty. If your informant is not sure of his facts, don't enter them on the card but check them later on.

Listing cards represent your stock in trade. They are the goods on your shelves, and if you haven't written listings you won't sell very much real estate. Don't just pile up a lot of listings just for the sake of having them. Pick your listings and choose only those you think you can sell. Better to have a dozen good salable listings than a hundred that represent overpriced properties and a lot of miscellaneous trash that no seasoned broker would accept.

Some offices maintain a *master listing file* for use in the office only. This may be kept in a locked-drawer file from which cards cannot be easily removed. Salesmen may copy the cards for their own use. As soon as a listing is sold or withdrawn, it should be promptly removed from the master file and all salesmen asked to turn in their duplicate cards.

It is important that a copy of every "sold" listing be maintained in a "dead" listing file. Here will accumulate a vast amount of useful information which can be dug up later when a property again appears on the market for sale. From this file a complete history of the place can later be found which makes it unnecessary in many cases to go through a long routine of getting the same information from another owner who now wants to sell it.

A system for the identification of listings is necessary so that you can locate them readily when wanted. One way is to segregate them according to price; that is, to start a house file with all dwellings under $15,000, then have special guide cards for the $15,000 to $20,000 houses, then from $20,000 to $25,000 and up. The same system may be followed for other types of property as well.

Another and more common system is to identify listings by neighborhoods. Start with the district in the immediate area where your office is located and set up arbitrary districts around it so that you will be able to put your hands immediately upon the listings in any specific district. Guide cards will tell you instantly where to go if your prospect indicates the area in which he is interested.

Whenever you pick up some interesting data or find that a property has been sold, make a practice of jotting down the information on a card and inserting it in your files in such a way that you can refer to it later if the occasion offers. Make it your business to fill in all cards neatly and completely from the beginning. It will soon become a very useful habit.

Some salesmen use loose-leaf listing books that may be obtained from book stores in some sections of the country. Information is listed about individual properties arranged according to their street addresses or by price or area. Different systems are preferred in different places, and it would be well to find out what the local practice is.

You will then need to adopt some kind of a "contract to purchase" form, to be used when you obtain offers which you must submit to owners. Never take verbal offers from buyers and transmit them by word of mouth to owners, for to do so will speedily get you into trouble. Verbal offers and acceptances can be easily repudiated, and you have little means of enforcing your rights if a bona fide offer is accepted by an owner who later refuses to go through with the deal. It is only good business to use a formal, printed offer-to-purchase form. Your local stationer may have such printed forms. Banks or title and trust companies that maintain escrow departments may have pads of contracts which you may obtain and use. In any event, be sure to get a good offer-to-purchase form and use it at all times. Refuse to take an offer without a written contract and a check equal in amount, usually, to 5 per cent of the purchase price, as an earnest-money deposit. With this you can go to a buyer assured that its acceptance means that you have your parties tied together legally as well as morally. In using such a contract make three copies in all, the original for your own use and the other two copies for the buyer and the seller. This is a workmanlike way to conduct a sale that will indicate to both buyer and seller that you know your business and leave nothing to the mere chance that verbal commitments will be lived up to.

Every broker should use some kind of prospect card, to keep track of the people with whom he hopes to do business. The minute you make a contact with a prospective buyer, get out a card and fill it in as completely as possible. Use a 5 × 8 inch white card. It will be found invaluable in going back over prospects and properties you have submitted to them and then forgotten about or neglected to follow up. Many a deal has been made through persistent following-up of prospects. The prospect card should contain a list of every property submitted and the prospect's reaction, whether favorable or otherwise.

Many forms of legal papers are used in the real estate business; the broker should become familiar with these forms even if he does not use many of them. In some states lawyers have caused laws to be enacted that prevent real estate brokers as such from executing real estate documents other than contracts of sale and some of the simpler forms, such as options, rentals, and short leases. In cities, where brokers handle their deals through escrow offices—a practice highly recommended —it is not necessary for them to make out deeds, mortgages, deeds of trust, and many other more or less complicated legal documents. That is all a part of the escrow service, paid for jointly by the buyer and the seller, which leaves the broker free to go about his business and sell real estate.

In smaller cities where escrows are not conducted by title companies or banks, the buyer or the seller or both may want to be represented by their lawyers in the making out and checking of abstracts, deeds, and mortgage or trust-deed papers. In any event a broker new in the business will do well to avoid taking on too much responsibility in the handling of legal documents until he has had adequate experience.

In large real estate offices, where many legal matters are being handled continuously, it is often the practice to maintain on the payroll a lawyer who is familiar with such matters and to whom the salesman may go for information as he needs it. A broker may likewise avail himself of the services of his own lawyer in handling puzzling problems beyond the scope of his experience. In any event the newcomer especially should be extremely careful not to get too far beyond his depth in handling legal matters, but should let an experienced escrow officer or an attorney handle the legal details attendant upon the sale and leasing of real estate.

In these days of involved income tax returns, withholding taxes from employees' earnings, social security and unemployment insurance reports, and similar governmental documents, it will be necessary for the new real estate broker to set up a simple set of books for the purpose of keeping track of his receipts and disbursements. This record may be very simple or complex, according to the desires of the person maintaining it. It should, however, be provided from the outset, merely as a good business practice.

One of the records of a live real estate office is a prospect mailing list, maintained for the purpose of mailing out notices, or for reference when seeking individual prospects for a property. One broker in an eastern city maintains a prospect file of some 2,000 names, to which he adds constantly as new names come to his attention. The list is divided into five groups. The first is an operator's list, for active buyers of real estate who specialize in reselling at a profit without large investments of their own. The second is a list of lawyers who represent certain investors who are in the market for real estate purchases. Group three includes persons who have bought or sold through this broker's office and who are expected to repeat. Group four is a list of brokers with whom there are prospects of operating on joint sales. The fifth and last list is for builders who are in the market for new sites or who want to sell their properties after completing them. If one is always on the lookout for new prospects, the mailing list may be added to continually until it becomes a most valuable adjunct in any real estate office.

One approach to compiling mailing lists that will increase the probability of reaching ready prospects is through the use of telephone and city directories. First, determine in which areas of the city you are likely to find reasonable prospects,[1] in terms of socio-economic status. Next, find out which telephone exchanges serve these sections. Then, make a list—checking against the city directory—in an effort to isolate those persons who are gainfully employed, who do not own the type of property you are trying to sell, and who have families whose needs are likely to be satisfied by the qualities of the properties you are presenting.

Other records may be found useful in an office as it grows into a sizable establishment, just as more elaborate filing systems may follow the simple ones which serve any office at the time it is first opened. Time and experience will dictate which of these should be adopted and incorporated into office routine.

[1] From: Leslie E. Moser, *How to Find, Qualify and Induce Real Estate Prospects to Buy* (Englewood Cliffs, N. J.: Prentice-Hall, Inc.)

CHAPTER **10**

Prospects—Securing and Qualifying Them

A PROSPECT IS SOMEONE WHO IS INTER-
ested in buying real estate. To secure, classify, and qualify him
is a task that never ends but is not nearly so difficult as it may
appear, for the world is full of prospects. Real estate has a
universal appeal. Everyone must use it. Nearly everyone wants
to own it. To convert mere prospects into actual buyers is the
substance of the real estate business. Broadly speaking, prospects may be obtained in five ways:

1. Through personal contact.
2. By advertising for them.
3. By indulging in the process of constructive thinking.
4. By going out and beating the brush for them—leg work!
5. Through liaisons with other people (agents, friends, etc.).

Personal contact turns up prospects every day. On the street
corner, at the lunch table, at social functions of all kinds, conversation drifts along until you, the intelligent salesman, mention real estate. Real estate is a topic of genuine interest to a
great many people, and it is not long before opinions are expressed that reveal the fact that pay dirt has been struck—a
prospect has been revealed! By unostentatiously revealing your
business, you will at once open up an avenue of conversation

that almost everyone will engage in. Many opinions, competent and otherwise, will be expressed in a thoroughly free and unreserved manner. Out of it all will come a number of ideas to the salesman who can later contact his friends privately and develop them into prospects. *Keep circulating!* Let your friends know you are in the real estate business. Don't be a bore. Do it cleverly and interestingly, and you will find wide interest on the part of many people who may later be developed into customers.

Advertising for prospects is one of the commonest ways of obtaining them. There are hundreds of persons in every community who are seeking real estate of one kind or another. They watch the newspapers, read your signs on lots and buildings, come marching into your office or call you by telephone. Advertising and how to use it to obtain prospects will be treated in a later chapter.

Engaging in some hard and constructive thinking will develop some of the finest prospects you will ever want to meet. Few people like to be bothered with thinking. They read newspapers or listen to the radio or to sermons and addresses rather than use their minds to think up original thoughts through which they may expand and extend their interests. Learn to think your problems out. When you have listed a piece of real estate that looks promising, sit down and go over the possible uses and users of such a property. Keep it on your mind constantly until a likely prospect comes to mind. Constructive salesmanship is salesmanship of the highest order, and it may be practiced successfully only *with the aid of hard thinking!*

Going out and canvassing for prospects by ringing doorbells or by visiting places of business and interviewing proprietors is not so pleasant as having people come to you as a result of advertising, but it is usually quite productive. Few if any competitors will have contacted your prospects previously. You find your prospects in their natural environment and can learn much about them by observing their homes, their house furnishings and the manner in which they are displayed and maintained, and the apparent needs of their families. Some types of merchandisers get all of their prospects through door-to-door canvassing. This type of order-taking is not essential in the real estate business, but some occasional "cold turkey" canvassing is good for the soul and will turn up nuggets in the way of valuable customers.

Telephone canvassing for real estate customers is not recommended. It is perfectly all right to use the telephone to make appointments, but most people seriously object to being sold things over the wire. You are more likely to arouse resentment than interest if you try it, except when someone answers your ad or calls for information. It is then quite permissible to try a little salesmanship over the telephone.

Real estate prospects may be found or developed through the following sources: [1]

Daily transfers of real estate.
Membership rosters of women's clubs.
Publicity stories in daily newspapers.
Business firms whose leases are expiring.
Selling talks given to clubs and organizations.
Hotel clerks who know of guests wanting homes.
Lists from companies who compile them for sale.
Radio programs that pull in interested listeners.
Contests that provide names of interested persons.
New arrivals in the city as noted in daily newspapers.
Lot owners who may want to trade in holdings on new homes.
Managers of apartment houses whose tenants want new homes.
Tourists who register for sightseeing trips to new subdivisions.
Concerns whose business makes it imperative that they expand.
Architects, contractors and builders who have clients wanting new home
    sites.

Real estate offices on ground-floor locations may invite many prospects by means of attractive window displays—photographs of homes and business buildings listed for sale. Much ingenuity can be applied to ways of dressing windows. A modern electronic device which flashes colored slides on a

[1] From Stanley McMichael's *Selling Real Estate* (Englewood Cliffs, N. J.: Prentice-Hall, Inc.)

ground glass screen, changing the picture every half minute, is a genuine asset. A temptation, after a time, however, is to grow lax and let a decrepit geranium be the only thing exhibited! Avoid dirty, unattractive display windows. Better to paint the glass with attractive signs than not to show bright and interesting displays.

Study of your prospects will reveal a strange assortment of persons any of whom may speedily develop into a good customer if handled rightly. Each one may require a different approach and a different kind of selling technique. Among the types you will encounter are the following:

> The timid.
> The silent.
> The serious.
> The bluffer.
> The skeptic.
> The curious.
> The "kidder."
> The cautious.
> The practical.
> The "know-all."
> The speculator.
> The "smart guy."
> The talkative type.
> The bargain hunter.
> The "too easy" buyer.
> The one easily swayed.
> The seasoned "shopper."
> The well-informed man.
> The hard-headed fellow.
> The man without money.
> The "clinging vine" type.
> The one who lacks vision.
> The one who has a "friend" who wants to buy.

The list might be continued, but the foregoing types are the most common. It is the salesman's business to study every prospect and try to ascertain in his own mind just how to classify him or her, and then to apply such treatment as the type suggests.

It is important to qualify every prospect as to just what kind of property he wants and his ability to pay for what may be offered. It is senseless to try to sell a $35,000 house to someone who should live in a $15,000 dwelling. Little is gained by offering a property requiring a down payment of $5,000 when all the prospect can muster is $2,000. Quietly and without seeming to pry into the life and circumstances of the prospect, the following information should be obtained and then, or later, recorded in writing on a prospect card provided for the purpose:

His name.
His business.
Business rating.
How long married.
His earning capacity.
Does he have hobbies?
Is he an ambitious type?
Other members of family employed?
If he rents, what rental is he paying?
Amount of investment funds available.
What amount can he save each month?
Have other properties been submitted to him?
The kind of property in which he is interested.
Has he courage to assume a sizable obligation?
Does he own property? If so, is it for sale now?
Does he seem particularly devoted to his family?
The general locality in which he would prefer to live.
The kind of building he would like to have on his property.
Why is a change in location advisable at this time? Has his past owner-
    ship been pleasant?
If a house or lot buyer, learn the name of the church the prospect's family
    attends.
Has the prospect alone authortiy to make a final decision? If not, who
    does have? Who are his advisers?
If the prospect has children, ascertain whether they attend grade or
    high school or both; also the age and sex of children.
Any additional information you are able to obtain at this stage of the
    interview, when the prospect is still willing to reveal intimate matters
    that he may later refuse to divulge. Visualize a prospect from his
    point of view and his needs. *Get all the information you can at the
    first interview!*

Having obtained every possible bit of information about a prospect, the salesman is then in a position to do a little analyzing. He may want to make further inquiries:

Can he be approached through a hobby? If he likes dogs or chickens, or likes to go fishing, or plant a garden, or make furniture in his garage, the type of property that will suit him may be different in each case.

How can he be pressed into action? Does he act quickly or does he take his own sweet time in reacting to your suggestions about types of property you may want to submit? If he is of the rapid-fire type, he will have to be dealt with accordingly—quickly, decisively, without loss of motion. If he is a slow mover, he will have to be coaxed along, given time to reflect and make up his mind. Don't try to rush him into a decision, for he may rebel and walk out on you.

Does he have strong likes or dislikes? Does he dislike certain kinds of architecture? Does he express an objection to living in certain kinds of neighborhoods? This type of prospect must be handled carefully or he will blow up in your face and you may lose him after considerable time spent in cultivating him.

Has he the funds to go ahead and buy? This question requires probing into the financial status of the prospect and is a very important one. No use wasting time on customers who can't buy. Do it carefully, but definitely qualify him as to how much he can pay down on a deal.

Does the prospect, if a woman, have the backing of her husband in her plan to buy? This kind of prospect is met continually. Many women who know their husbands are not in a position to buy, or who are not interested in doing so, shop around among real estate offices, look at houses, discuss terms, and so on, and finally wind up by confiding that they can't go ahead because their husbands do not see eye to eye with them. They will want to have you see the husband some time and go all over the deal selling *him,* which frequently cannot be done. Try to discover this type before you waste too much time on her.

Who dominates the family, husband or wife? In other words, who wears the pants? Who is going to be the one to make up his or her own mind to go ahead? In almost every family the husband or the wife makes decisions. Cultivate the one who does but be careful not to alienate the other or you won't make a deal. Try to keep them together and let the leader bring the other along to the closing point.

Is the prospect a mere shopper? This matter should be found out as soon as possible. The seasoned salesman will quickly detect whether the propect is really sincere or just coming along for the ride. It takes what seems to be an extra sense to know the answer, but it can be done with a little experience. Show your best property but try to get a decision as rapidly as possible. In other words, try and force a showdown before you waste a lot of time on an insincere prospect.

Is the prospect a speculator? If he is, he may need a different sales technique from that required for a straight buyer. The speculator is looking for a bargain, something he can resell at a profit. At certain stages in the real estate market he can be readily accommodated; at other times you may be wasting a lot of time trying to fulfill his requirements and finally not make a sale. Study your market and your listings and make up your mind whether you can be of any service to a speculator before spending too much time on him.

Can he be sold because of his social or religious needs? Careful investigation into the needs of a prospect frequently reveals that he would like to live in a certain neighborhood because he has friends there, or because it is close to his golf or social club, or because his family attends a certain church. Try to satisfy this need and a sale will come much easier.

Is the prospect seeking to buy beyond his means? Some buyers like to put on a lot of front and look at properties which their means or incomes do not justify. Careful qualification of their financial status will reveal this weakness, and the salesman can get them down to earth by calmly discussing the price and terms required for the more expensive property.

In trying to meet the needs of the prospect with available listings, the salesman will have to keep in his mind the many factors that characterize a house. The following alphabetical arrangement compiled by the sales manager of a brokerage concern will be helpful:

1. Age.
2. Beauty.
3. Churches available.
4. Convenience.
5. Distance to places.
6. Environment.
7. Financial encumbrances.
8. Gardening.
9. Heating plant.
10. Institutions nearby (schools, lodges, libraries, parks, resorts).
11. Joinery (of structure).
12. Lines of transportation.
13. Measurement of rooms.
14. Neighbors.
15. Occupants (former).
16. Television reception
17. Possibility of enhancement
18. Traffic streets.
19. Resale values.
20. Structure.
21. Taxes.
22. Up-to-dateness.
23. View.
24. What standing will house give?
25. Extra features.
26. Yard.
27. Zoning.

Another sales manager with a subdivision company has compiled the following interesting analysis of different types of prospects and the way to handle them:

Type	Characteristics	Tactics to Employ
1. Overcautious	Will reason but decide slowly.	Be logical and patient.
2. Clever	Firm, not easily influenced.	Lead—don't drive him.
3. Argumentative	Hard to convince.	Know your line.
4. Conceited	Overbearing— unreasonable.	Appeal to his vanity.
5. Irritable	Discourteous— bluffer.	Be courteous and firm.
6. Flighty	Poor reasoner— illogical.	Use indirect suggestions.
7. Aggressive	Tries to boss the interview.	Be positive.

Where do you find prospects? One former sales counsellor for the National Association of Real Estate Boards lists the following thirty-seven sources:

1. The man next door.
2. Your friends and acquaintances.

3. Those who have listed their homes with you.
4. Those who have recently sold property.
5. The columns of your local newspapers.
6. Arrivals in the city.
7. Directories.
8. Apartment dwellers.
9. Former customers.
10. Lists of those paying income taxes.
11. Lists of large property owners.
12. Investors.
13. Other real estate dealers.
14. Visitors at own-your-home expositions.
15. Canvassing.
16. Courthouse and municipal records.
17. Belong to one or more business clubs or social organizations.
18. Prospects from other prospects.
19. Window displays.
20. Signs on the property.
21. Clipping bureau service for business deals.
22. Model homes.
23. The telephone.
24. Concerns which may wish to expand or establish branches.
25. "Foreign" chains.
26. Business firms whose leases expire.
27. Ambitious employees of established firms.
28. Names supplied by other salesmen in your firm.
29. New employees coming into the firm.
30. Distribution of literature with cards to be returned.
31. Contests.
32. Your prospect file.
33. Lists from companies specializing in the building of lists; addressing companies, list brokers, and clipping bureaus.
34. Direct mail.
35. Payrolls and successful men.
36. Christmas savings clubs.
37. Advertising.

It is always worth while, before dashing out with a prospect to look at properties, to sit down quietly and talk for a while. What you find out may make you do something entirely different from what you would do on the spur of the moment, without having investigated the requirements of the prospect and his ability to pay for what you show him.

Every well-ordered real estate office has prospect cards on which to record data. It is well to fill out a master card for the use of the office itself and to keep a copy for your own information. Make a careful note of how a prospect can be reached at his home or office. Every time a property is submitted it should be recorded on the card. Later, in going back over your dealings with the prospect, you will know exactly what kind of real estate you have shown him. As a follow-up device the prospect card is invaluable.

Lodge, social club, and church affiliations are productive of many contacts that may develop into business for real estate salesmen. Don't go to extremes in this respect, however, and waste time which should be devoted to more direct prosecution of your business.

Many a salesman has secured a liberal education from contacting clever prospects who have proceeded to tell him a lot of things about real estate he never knew. Don't get the notion that prospects as a class don't know anything about real estate and that you have to preach to them and tell them what it is all about. After a prospect has studied the newspapers and magazines for months, talked with architects, had interviews with a number of real estate men, investigated the merits of forty or fifty listings, as they sometimes do, he may be credited with having a rather liberal education on the subject of values and what he wants and does not want in the way of a piece of real estate.

In some cities model homes are erected and displayed for sale by enterprising builders and real estate companies. These are well advertised and, because of their attractiveness, they draw many visitors, many of whom are excellent prospects for homes. Realtors who display such houses arrange to have visitors enter at one door, and then ask them to write their names and addresses on a register before proceeding, over a well-defined route, through the house. Later the addresses are divided among salesmen and personal contacts established. Some visitors naturally are attracted out of curiosity. Others earnestly hope to find the kind of home they want. Such model homes are frequently furnished in great detail by leading furniture and equipment firms in the city where the house is displayed. It is good advertising for the furniture house and at the same time makes the model home more interesting to inspect.

Merely getting prospects is not much of a task for an intelligent and aggressive salesman. What counts more is how the prospects are handled and eventually converted into actual buyers.

CHAPTER 11

The Art of Selling

SELLING IS AN ART IF THE MEANING OF the word holds true according to its dictionary definition: "The skillful and systematic arrangement or adaptation of means for the attainment of some end." If there is one activity that requires systematic arrangement of means to attain an end, it is the selling of real estate. In no other calling can the art of selling be developed to a greater degree. Here is a subject that possesses charm, glamour, and allurement as well as plain common-sense interest, profit, and personal advantage.

Anything favorable one can say about almost anything one sells can be said about real estate. There are so many good things inherent in real estate that all the emotions of the mind and heart can be worked on. Love, safety, protection, profit, shelter, and security in old age are only a few of the many many themes that the real estate salesman dwells upon when disposing of his product.

While it is true that almost anyone with proper training and application can succeed in selling real estate, there is one attribute that really distinguishes all successful salesmen; for want of a better word, it is called *personality*. It is that rare gift that some men have for swaying the minds of others, of winning them to their way of thinking, of *getting favorable results* from people and eventually getting their signatures on the dotted line!

In a study made under the auspices of the Carnegie Founda-

tion, it was found that the success that comes to most men is
due 15 per cent to intimate and technical knowledge of one's
own business and 85 per cent to the presence of those qualities
that have to do chiefly with successfully influencing people.

Everyone has personality in some degree. In some it is constantly displayed while in others it has to be forced to perform.
Detailed knowledge of real estate alone will not make you a
successful salesman. It is only by discovering and developing
the other qualities that constitute personality that one can hope
to be genuinely successful.

What are the elements that enter into personality? Among
them are:

> Poise.
> Charm.
> Courtesy.
> Decision.
> Initiative.
> Confidence.
> Knowledge.
> Enthusiasm.
> Observation.
> Thoroughness.
> Concentration.
> Impressiveness.
> Organizing ability.
> Personal magnetism.
> Constructive imagination.
> Moral and physical courage.

Study the list carefully, line by line, again and again! Ponder
each item and ask yourself to what degree you possess it. If you
feel you are particularly weak in some of the attributes of personality, make up your mind to do something about it and
strengthen your will to act in a way that will help you to become better equipped to display more phases of genuine personality in your dealings with others. Some possess those traits
to a much greater degree than others, but anyone can improve
himself if he really desires to do so. A whole chapter could be
written about each one and its part in the selling of real estate—
or any other commodity for that matter.

Leaders of men are what they are because they strike forth and exhibit those qualities that attract other men who follow and are content to do so. Anyone can follow, but it takes a man with brains, aggressiveness, and *personality* to be a leader. And one who successfully engages in selling must assume the position of a leader and teacher, bending the propect's will to his.

The successful salesman is the man who has the capacity for successfully influencing the minds of others, and he gets that way by developing his personality, beginning with charm and ending with moral and physical courage. Charm is a pleasing fascinating manner that attracts and puts a spell on those with whom one comes in contact. It is no more important however than the moral and physical courage the salesman must have to face issues, to tell the truth, and to go on doggedly ringing doorbells until he overcomes his natural timidity and a desire to quit when the going gets tough.

The rewards for good salesmanship are great. Analyze any of the great business corporations of the country and discover who are the real leaders and the men who are making the biggest salaries. Are they the technicians working in factories and laboratories? No. Are they the skilled accountants in the office? No. Are they the designers and the artists, or the superintendents? No. Who are they, then? They are the salesmen who became salesmanagers, then vice-presidents, then heads of whole concerns. The men who sell receive the biggest salaries and wield the greatest power in almost every corporation.

The late Paul Stark, a master salesman of Madison, Wisc., and a former president of the National Association of Real Estate Boards, during his lifetime hired and trained many men to sell real estate. Before doing so he qualified them as to their capacity to develop their personalities. Mr. Stark said:

Personality is a quality difficult to define. It is a composite of many qualities. One feels its presence and responds to it quickly, but rarely do we stop to analyze it or separate it into its component parts. The successful sales manager must recognize the qualities which make for a good personality, for while there are undoubtedly good men with poor personalities, few of them ever make good salesmen. We lose money by training men of poor personalities, and, not being philanthropists, perhaps we had better develop a few tests which will help us to recognize those at least whose personalities are distinctly bad.

Cleanliness and neatness are prerequisites of sales personalities, and here is a test which we can easily apply. A purchaser may not be conscious of clean linen or shining boots, but untidiness attracts attention and immediately raises a barrier which salesmen find it difficult to penetrate. Let us not waste time teaching this class.

A good physique is undoubtedly a part of a good sales personality. Those without it can succeed in spite of this handicap, but they must draw heavily upon their other powers. A good physique is a large part of what we call a fine presence and helps to cover many minor faults. It helps to create confidence because it suggests power and endurance and ability to do.

Clean speech and good articulation is a part of a good salesman's personality. Profanity in its mildest form should totally disqualify an applicant. The salesman will be our personal representative, and his qualifications should be such as to make him welcome into every group with which we, his employers, have contacts.

A good salesman must have mental leadership. He must have a dominant personality. After we have taught him something, he must be able to get it across. He must guide the interview; and the man without the mental power to do this is useless in business. Trying to teach him would be a futile task.

Lastly, a good sales personality is unselfish. There radiates from it something which creates confidence and good will. Such a personality is born of a real love for humanity and a desire to serve. It cannot be assumed; it must be real and genuine. When the employer knows that this wonderful confidence-winning quality is present, he has at hand a great asset because his commodity, the home, is not only of large value but it is one in which confidence plays a large part. Complaints do not arise from the work of salesmen who have this quality. After we have them trained they will be better institutional advertising than our advertising department can buy.

The man who develops his personality will not be guilty of many of those offensive traits that sometimes make salesmen obnoxious to customers. He will unconsciously conduct himself in a gentlemanly manner and avoid the five cardinal sins of a salesman:

1. Never talk slow to a fast thinker.
2. Never talk fast to a slow thinker.
3. Never do all of the talking.
4. Never misrepresent or exaggerate.
5. Never argue and become belligerent.

Look in upon any outstanding real estate office in any city throughout the country and you will find, among its salesmen, one or more men who are the star producers. These are the men who have discovered that they possess rare elements of personality and who have been wise in developing those traits by close study and application. Such a man wins a customer with an irresistible smile. He proceeds to display a thorough knowledge of his subject, together with constructive imagination, enthusiasm, personal magnetism, charm, and all of the other elements which go into the unique quality called personality.

Alexander Graham Bell made a wonderful invention when he produced the first telephone, but it might have been lost to the world had it not been for the fine salesmanship of Theodore N. Vail, whose organizing ability developed the telephone into one of the world's most useful appliances. Inventors and producers are invariably poor businessmen. It is not until they link up their endeavors with the brilliant salesmanship of someone who has personality and who is able to carry the torch out into the waiting world that their efforts really count.

Personality alone will not make a man a master salesman. The world is full of bright minds who have failed to stabilize their efforts and who go through life lacking a full measure of success. Personality without an application of a full and complete knowledge of the product is of little practical use. The two together, if properly merged and balanced, will spell great and genuine success.

A survey was made among the members of the Chicago Sales Executive Club to find out what they thought were the most important traits of a successful salesman, and these were found to be:

1. Courtesy
2. Integrity.
3. Sincerity.
4. Judgment.
5. Initiative.
6. Sales ethics
7. Friendliness.
8. Dependability.
9. Determination.

   10. Persuasiveness.
   11. Aggressiveness.
   12. Care of health.
   13. Industriousness.
   14. Self-management.
   15. Resourcefulness.
   16. Work organization.
   17. Knowledge of product.
   18. Acceptance of responsibility.
   19. Understanding of buying motives.
   20. Appreciation of selling as road to success.

Valuable advice may be gleaned by salesmen from oldtimers in the business who have for years been students of the psychology of salesmanship. The former head of a very large real estate development firm offers these gems of wisdom to the aspiring salesman:

Understatement is more effective than exaggeration.
I'd rather have a salesman with a smile than with a college degree.
Present disadvantages along with advantages. If too many of the former, don't show it.
Don't neglect the small customer. He may develop into your best one.
Garrulity ruins many sales. Learn to be silent and you are on the way to success.
Don't ever argue with a client. You lose if you win.
Look right at your prospect when driving home a crucial point.
Good will originates from you and not your client.
Never talk loudly. The prospect hears your voice, not your selling talk.
Don't tell your troubles to the sales force. See the boss.
Never rattle money in your pocket. It's distracting.
In a trade-in deal, don't make adverse comments about the other fellow's property.
Never sit or stand on the opposite side of the desk of your client.
Prospects are interested in new things. Present your offering in a new way if possible.
Don't drop a client like a hot cake once you have made a sale. Cultivate him.
Boost your competitor. Favorable things reach his ears. Reciprocity builds business.
Don't ignore strangers. They may be good friends tomorrow.
Don't knock your city, your government, or your own or any other business.
Get your client to talk and let him express himself.

What are the attributes of a salesman? An experienced West Coast broker says that it is a hard question to answer but, in his opinion a *real* salesman is:

One who has a steady eye, a steady nerve, steady habits, and steady tongue.

One who understands men and who can make himself understood by men.

One who turns up with a smile, and who still smiles if he is turned down.

One who strives to out-think rather than out-talk the prospect.

One who is silent when he has nothing to say and also when the prospect has something to say.

One who takes a firm interest in the firm's interest.

One who knows that he looks after his own best interests when he looks out for the customer's best interests.

One who keeps his word, his temper, and his friends.

One who wins respect by being respectable, respectful, and respected.

One who can be courteous in the face of discourtesy.

One who has self-confidence, but who shows no ego.

One who is loved by his fellow men, his customers, and even his competitors.

Here are ten commandments for selling real estate as offered by a former president of the Florida Association of Real Estate Boards:

1. *Be agreeable.* If your voice is disagreeable and your manner of speech indistinct, see specialists. And remember, I like to be sunny, but I don't want to get freckles.

2. *Know your goods.* And when you tell me anything, talk plainly. Most salesmen lack imagination. They cannot conceive of the extent of my ignorance.

3. *Don't argue.* When you argue with a man, you are trying to push him. He may be weak and pretend to be convinced. Overnight he will change.

4. *Make it plain.* Get a grasp on the fellow with whom you are talking. Do not get out that little book that will only puzzle him. Answer his questions without looking at your books, charts, and tables.

5. *Tell the truth.* By the law of averages, honesty gives the greatest profits. If you are working for a concern where you cannot tell the truth, quit and go elsewhere.

6. *Be dependable.* If you tell a man you are going to do a thing, do it if it costs a leg.

7. *Remember names and faces.* Don't call me Green when my name is Crane. I am sensitive about my name. Don't call me Mister if my title is Doctor. Don't call me Major if I'm a Colonel.

8. *Don't be egotistical.* I am. You must not be. Don't show off. You came to sell me something, not to make a good impression. Magnify my ego, not yours.

9. *Think success. Radiate prosperity.* Do not mention calamities, dirges, operations, funerals. Be a Pollyanna—without, however, being a bore.

10. *Be human.* If the company merely wanted to disseminate information, it would use a catalogue—not you.

Here are ways to spot a good salesman as listed by George J. Frederick in *Forbes Magazine:*

1. **Posture.** The good salesman is springy of step, balanced and mobile of carriage. Chin, chest, and shoulders have thrust.

2. **Eyes.** Gaze is good, open, concentrative; not shifty, scowling, staring, narrow-slitted, dreamy.

3. **Interest.** The world is interesting. He enjoys new people, points of view, problems, facts.

4. **Humor.** Humor is a balance wheel, but it must be delicately adjusted; it can't be made of coarse material.

5. **Temper.** The more the provocation, the more he bridles his temper.

6. **"Grasp."** Alert people won't spend effort making a woolly-minded salesman grasp a problem or situation.

7. **Energy.** Plenty of steam up. You see it in his walk, talk, habits, ideas, plans.

8. **Ego-control.** Too many salesmen "I" themselves right out of an order. A sale is pulled to its goal by the prospect's ego, the seller's ego apparently pulling no load whatever.

9. **Friendliness.** Selling is human relationship; basic, sincere friendliness is worth more than shrewd tricks.

10. **Brains.** *The test for brains is not how much you know, but how you use them.*

11. **Scrupulousness.** A prospect must feel that a salesman will handle the buyer's interests scrupulously. Any sign of neglect is icewater on the transaction.

12. **Communicability.** The good salesman is a born communicator, a natural talker, teacher, teller. It shows in his voice, flow of words, believability, power of graphic expression and clear delineation, urge to convert others to his way of thinking.

13. **Wholesomeness.** He is a rounded, wholesome person, naturally liked by others.

14. Character. The core of character consists of endurance and non-yielding stamina; ability to hold to a line, work to a plan, stand up to punishment.

15. Resourcefulness. He jumps hurdles with resources within himself: quick thinking, originality, daring, adaptability, judgment.

16. Practicality. Business is practical; the buyer must have confidence in the salesman's practicality.

17. Self-starter. He needs no crank; he presses the self-starter button on himself, thereby avoids slumps.

18. Logic. Selling is debating; logic, a key to both, means orderly analysis and speech, clarified presentation, and persuasive reasoning which lead directly to admitted fact, truth, conviction, inevitable conclusion.

19. Liking for selling. The good salesman likes his work, likes to induce another to buy.

20. Manners. Salesmanship is nine-tenths relationship; so manners matter almost as much as argument or logic.

21. Self-discipline. He must get out promptly in all weather; plan his work; work his plan; make enough calls; toe the line under difficulties—all without urging from others.

22. Friends. The good salesman is a mixer, has many real friends on his own or higher levels.

No occupation is more profitable, interesting, and fascinating than that of selling. Columbus was as great a salesman as he was an explorer, for he became the latter only after he excelled in selling an idea. Napoleon was constantly selling himself and his ideas to his armies, which helped him to win great victories. Franklin D. Roosevelt sold himself and his ideas to enough people to elect him four times president of the United States. Everyone spends part of the time selling an idea or himself or some product in which he is interested. It is the individual who prepares himself, who studies the manner in which the impressionable instincts of human beings are influenced and controlled, who *develops his personality,* who eventually becomes preëminently successful as a salesman.

CHAPTER 12

Impelling Reasons for

Buying and Selling

IT IS JUST AS IMPORTANT TO KNOW WHAT prompts a buyer to buy a property as it is to know why the owner wants to sell it.

One might suppose that the imperative need for shelter, for having a roof over one's head, was a primary motive for buying real estate, but that is not always the case. There are many reasons, among which are the following:

1. Pride.
2. Profit.
3. Caution.
4. Shelter.
5. Ambition.
6. Necessity.
7. Imitation.
8. Desire to excel.
9. Love of luxury.
10. Companionship.
11. Physical comfort.
12. Desire for power.
13. Self preservation.
14. Income for old age.
15. Pride of possession.
16. Desire for affection.
17. Income for posterity.
18. Utility or usefulness.

19. Security for the future.
20. Desire for social prestige.
21. Enhancement of reputation.
22. Seeking esteem *after* death.
23. Desire for commercial leadership.

Why does the buyer buy? What impels him to take action? If the salesman can discover this secret while he is attempting to get the prospect's name on the dotted line, he will have advanced his cause immeasurably and leaped many hurdles which appear in almost every sale.

Buying real estate is unlike the purchase of many other commodities. It is *much more important* to the buyer than buying a shirt, a suit of clothes, or even an automobile. Real estate is a subject about which he knows comparatively little, and his natural caution compels him to set up barriers which the salesman must surmount. The average man is familiar enough with shirts or clothes to know what he wants, and he usually knows where to go to get it. A salesman in a shirt store does not have to know much about sales procedure to make a sale. If the buyer likes the color, design, and texture of a fabric, he promptly buys. The same is true, to some extent, with an automobile. He has driven a car that he likes and wants to duplicate it, or he has seen and ridden in one owned by a friend. He has been sold by its performance or its looks or its price, and he wants one like it. So, when he comes to the automobile salesman, about all he requires is a demonstration and he buys.

Not so with real estate. A lot or a house that he has never seen before is new to him. He wants to know all about it. He must be convinced that the price is right. Since the dawn of time men have haggled over the price of real estate. There has been no absolute standard of value because every piece of real estate is different from every other in some respect, even if the only difference is that it is one lot nearer the corner than a similarly priced one alongside of it. So, it may be seen, the real estate salesman has problems to solve and resistance to overcome that the purveyor of other types of commodities does not encounter. If, while searching the prospect's mind for some point on which to dwell, the salesman can discover some break in the customer's armor that can be penetrated, he has a distinct advantage. That is why the salesman should find out just what the prospect's motive is for buying. Satisfy that motive and a large measure of resistance may be overcome.

Motives may be real or imaginary, just as objections are sincere or insincere. The buyer may set up some motive that he wants satisfied just so that he can avoid committing himself. One old salesman put it right when he said, "Give the buyer plenty of opportunities to buy!" To do so the salesman from time to time should try to commit the customer on some given point; for example:

"Isn't that a marvelous view from here?"

"Don't you think these sliding glass doors add dignity to the house?"

"Don't you believe that being only three blocks from a school will be a great advantage for your children?"

Motives differ with different people and with different kinds of properties. One man wants to own a home as security against the future. Another desires to acquire real estate to realize a profit from its resale later on. Both are appealed to in entirely different ways. A manufacturer buys an industrial site to accommodate his business. An investor acquires business real estate to enjoy a steady income. A speculator thinks entirely of the chance he has to resell at a profit. All of these motives must become known to the salesman as early in the negotiations as possible. He must *qualify the prospect*. This is usually done before property is even submitted, and while the parties are on a free and easy basis. No pressure has been exerted by the salesman, and the prospect, not on the defensive against the salesman's appeal to buy, is still in a friendly mood and willing to tell a good deal about himself and his reasons for being interested in real estate.

Early in any interview, try to ascertain whether the prospect has a hobby—a penchant for photography, chicken or rabbit raising, carpentry, gardening, fishing, raising dogs, golf or tennis, or any one of a host of things that human beings become addicted to besides drink. Matching the needs of a hobby by pointing out the advantages of a property that can be used for its furtherance has led quickly to the closing of many a sale.

Here are some more or less well-known hobbies.[1]

Fishing.	Swimming.	Antiques.
Golf.	Midget trains.	Bridge.
Firearms.	Manuscripts.	Painting.
Boy Scout work.	Old bells.	Music.
Carpentry.	Cats, foxes, chin-	Musical instruments.
Weaving.	chillas.	Collecting match
Horse racing.	Poker games.	books.
Photography.	Old coins.	Butterflies.
Old books.	Camping.	Sports, all kinds.
Charitable work.	Old maps.	Postage stamps.
First editions.	Antique furniture.	Walking, hiking.
Horseback riding.	Collecting prints.	Chickens.
Flowers and plants.	Public speaking.	Old vehicles.
Dog raising.	Old glassware.	Automobiling.

Get a man to talk about his hobby, evince unusual interest in it, and you have made a friend for life. To him it is one of the important things in his existence. Sometimes, after trying unsuccessfully to clinch a sale, a salesman may casually refer back to a conversation about a prospect's hobby, and break down a barrier that can be surmounted in no other way. If there is a single thing about a property that will advance the hobby of a prospect, it should be dwelt upon, for this is a thoroughly legitimate matter, which may later prove useful or entertaining to the buyer.

You may note in a newspaper that someone has a particular hobby. To use this information as a means of getting an interview with such a person may result in a definite rebuff. It is only after a contact has been made that it is wise to attempt to capitalize on the knowledge one may have of a prospect's hobby. Don't make the hobby a single peg on which to seek or make a demonstration, for to do so may appear ridiculous even to an enthusiastic hobbyist. It all must be

[1] From *Selling Real Estate*, by Stanley L. McMichael (Englewood Cliffs, N. J.: Prentice-Hall, Inc.)

done skillfully and without the knowledge of the buyer that his hobby is being used as a means to an end.

Your knowledge of a customer's hobby may often be used as a means for a "come-back call" or second interview. One salesman took occasion to take with him on a second call an old and rare book, which promptly secured the attention of the prospect, who thawed out enough to take a renewed interest in a property which he subsequently purchased. Knowledge and use of information concerning hobbies must be cleverly utilized.

The average buyer of a property is usually interested in knowing why the owner wants to sell it.

"What's the matter with it?" asks the buyer. "If all that you say about this place is true, why does the owner want to get rid of it?"

This is a perfectly natural inquiry and one that the salesman must be prepared to answer. To do so, he should have asked the seller that same question and have obtained a satisfactory answer. Every property owner has a reason for selling, but he does not always reveal it. His reason may be a perfectly legitimate one. He may be required to move away to take another job. The place may have become too small for the use of his family. The owner's position in life may have improved to the extent that he can live in a better and more expensive neighborhood. His children, growing up, may need a place closer to the college or university they will attend. These and many others like them are quite understandable reasons for a man to want to sell his home, and they should be known to the salesman who seeks to sell the place.

However, the owner's reason for selling may be a discredit to the property; if so, he will not readily divulge it and the salesman may be heading for trouble if, during negotiations with the prospect, it turns out that:

1. Undesirable neighbors have moved next door.
2. Jet aircraft at a nearby airport make sleep well-nigh impossible.

3. Obnoxious odors, dirt, or noise have begun to make themselves felt, as the result of a factory development not too far away.

4. The whole neighborhood is slipping rapidly, due to a change to a type of tenancy not in keeping with the district's former standards.

5. The dwelling offered for sale has become infected with dry rot, fungus, or termites.

6. Transportation facilities have been curtailed by the abandonment of facilities such as railroad or bus lines.

7. A new highway has been projected that will come too near for comfort, with its traffic noise, fumes, and so on.

8. Zoning has broken down and neighboring property owners are stealthily installing extra apartments in parts of their residential quarters.

These conditions and others like them tend to depreciate the value of real estate of a residential character and are reasons for promptly selling and moving elsewhere. If the salesman discovers a real reason of this character, he will do well to do one of two things: (1) Promptly tell it to a prospect or (2) refuse to submit the property for sale.

Knowing why an owner wants to sell, therefore, is important to the salesman, and he should make it his business in every listing to ascertain this important fact. His general knowledge of a district will often reveal the reason why an owner seeks to sell, but if it is not apparent the salesman should continue to investigate until he finds out the actual conditions. Then he can decide whether the real reason will prevent him from honestly merchandizing the property to a new and uninformed buyer.

A salesman, determined to act honestly and in the interests of both the seller and the buyer, is in the position of a referee. He must see that neither the buyer nor the seller takes advantage of the other, and he himself must treat each of them in a thoroughly fair and upright manner. He must demonstrate to the buyer that he has a knowledge of the property's market value and that the seller is not seeking to get more than it is reasonably worth. At the same time he cannot let the buyer take advantage of the owner and secure the property for less than it is worth. It may be seen that the position of the salesman is loaded with genuine responsibility and that to act in the interests of both parties requires his highest ability as a negotiator and judge.

A wise salesman will seldom attempt to bring a buyer and seller together during the negotiations leading up to the making of an offer by the prospective purchaser. In showing a property the salesman should gently caution the seller to stay out of the picture, even to permitting the salesman and his prospect to go through the premises unaccompanied. Many a talkative owner has ruined a sale. A buyer feels uncomfortable in the presence of an owner and will not ask questions or make a proper investigation of the premises. Keep the buyer and the seller apart until an offer has been made and accepted. Even then it is sometimes wise to take the two parties into escrow at different times, especially if both have strong and unbending personalities that may clash.

If, as Edgar Guest says, "It takes a heap o' livin 'to make a house a home," it also takes a lot of clever maneuvering on the part of a salesman to sell that same home to a new occupant!

CHAPTER 13

Mental Stepping Stones
To a Sale

SELLING REAL ESTATE REACHES ITS climax as a sale is closed. This is the goal for which all study and preparation have been carried on. To have brought a buyer and a seller together in a state of mind where they mutually agree to a transfer of property is a reward worthwhile.

A sale occurs as the result of a receptive state of mind which comes to the buyer some time before he actually announces that he is ready to act. Up to this time he probably has exercised every effort to sidestep conviction. He has projected objections into discussions for the purpose of delaying action or to avoid reaching a decision. Then, gradually—very gradually—his mind begins to unbend and he realizes that he is about to succumb and say, *"Yes."*

The mental maneuvering that takes place is nearly always of the same pattern. Some people are sold more easily than others. It depends a good deal upon the character of the buyer how much resistance he will exert, or whether he will refuse to go through with the deal altogether.

If a salesman understands what is going on in the mind of the prospect, he naturally is in a better position to offer those facts and arguments most necessary to influence the buyer's mind favorably. If he does not understand, he may blunder along and never know how near he may come to making a sale—and then muff it because he did not take advantage of information that was written all over the prospect's face or buried in his utterances and defenses.

Many born salesmen, who have grown up in the business and have shrewd insight into the manner in which their customers' minds are working, may be entirely ignorant of the accepted processes of a sale and still be successful in securing action. How much easier, however, is the task of the new salesman if he is aware of the pattern of thoughts and emotions that are found in the mind of the average buyer of real estate!

Not every sale passes through all the theoretical steps of a sale. In fact, many sales are made in which only an occasional action can be recognized as part of the stereotyped pattern. A close analysis of any sale, however, will show that the ground work is there and that to a greater or lesser degree the same approach and treatment are necessary. The salesman, therefore, should be familiar with the way a sales presentation is built up. Make the process so much a part of your selling technique that you will unconsciously react properly when the occasion demands.

Broadly speaking, there are seven steps in a sale of a parcel of real estate:

1. Preparation.
2. Approach.
3. Attention.
4. Interest.
5. Desire.
6. Action.
7. Closing the sale.

Preparation

No man has ever qualified himself as a real estate salesman who has not prepared himself to some degree for the work. The broader and more complete the preparation, the better and more successful the salesman. Mere order takers do not last long in the real estate business. Occasionally a sale comes easy, but most sales are accomplished only after a hard and vigorous fight.

The day will never come when you will know it all! The older you grow the more you will realize how little you know! No one ever learns all there is to know about real estate any more than anyone ever knows everything about the law, chemistry, or medicine.

So, a good motto is: *Study incessantly!*

Approach

Before attempting an actual approach to a customer for the purpose of making a sale, it might be well for you to sit down quietly and do some sober thinking, and, possibly, some investigating about the prospect you are about to meet. Determine the most interesting way in which you can submit a property, and be sure you have all pertinent facts about the offering. If there is any way of learning something about the prospect's life, position, and methods of thinking, secure the information now, before the actual interview.

The way a prospect greets a salesman depends largely on the way the salesman makes his approach. The prospect is naturally on the defensive, for he feels that you are trying to sell him something, and to most persons this very fact is distasteful—they like to buy, *not be sold!*

Let a smile light up your face. Don't dash into the subject of your call without some generalities which will help to pave the way. Be friendly but not obsequious, reserved rather than jovial. Remember that your ultimate purpose is to sway the mind of the prospect to your way of thinking. Knowledge of the mental laws involved here may make it easy for you to break the ice and get on a friendly footing with your prospect.

No trite set of words or expressions can be suggested for the best way to greet a prospective customer. It is your business to be friendly and to win the interest and respect of the buyer. Never say or do anything that will in any way antagonize him.

Treat him as you would any of your friends under similar circumstances.

"Good morning, Mr. Doe," you might say. "My name is Charles Roe, and I want to talk with you about something that I think will interest you."

"What's that?" asks the prospect, curiously.

"I understand you are interested in securing a home. You have a family growing up, you need more room, and I believe you have been studying the real estate market rather closely lately."

"Yes," admits Doe, "I have been looking into real estate lately . . ." and he proceeds to tell the salesman some of the things *he* knows about real estate. This is a good way to get a customer's interest and encourage him to air opinions that may later indicate methods for completing the approach.

Developing the "self-interest" approach is one of the easiest ways in most instances. Everyone thinks his own ideas and opinions are best and that he understands most of the subjects he attempts to discuss. If you can draw out the prospect and secure his confidence by flattering his bump of "self interest," it may be helpful. Infinitely more people begin a sentence with "I . . ." than with "You. . . ." Everyone wants to succeed. There is a strain of selfishness in everyone that can be capitalized on by the salesman

Attention

There are many ways of centering attention on real estate after you have made an agreeable approach. One is by means of photographs. Another may be a written statement about a property, or an elaborate property brief that includes a statement, maps, and pictures.

"A picture is worth ten thousand words." A few photographs may do more in one minute to win the interest of a prospect than fifteen minutes of rapid conversation, most of which rolls off the prospect like water from a duck's back.

Failure to secure proper attention is fatal in any real estate interview, for attention creates desire which in turn stimulates understanding.

One device that can be used successfully is an appeal to the profit motive. One does not buy a home, ordinarily, for profit, but there are many ways in which one may profit by owning a home. Everyone is interested in making a profit, and nearly everyone knows that money can be made in real estate. The profit motive is particularly appropriate when used in connection with income business and investment properties.

Pride of possession or ownership is another peg on which the interview may be hung. Nearly everyone has a desire to own real estate of some kind. If you can show a man how that can be accomplished within his means and with profit, you will have his attention.

Don't use bizarre or startling ways to attract attention. Most prospects resent them. Circus methods are all right for circuses but not many other kinds of business.

Always remember that interest and desire cannot be aroused if the prospect's attention is not properly centered on your offering.

Interest

Interest ripens out of sustained attention. Human emotions must be analyzed skillfully here. Enlarge upon the merits of your offering. Interest has been aroused if the prospect asks questions. Taciturn and critical prospects here begin to thaw out, or go off the beam entirely and fall into the total-loss category. If the prospect evinces curiosity about the offering, pour forth more information as it is needed, holding in reserve, if possible, some features that may later be used in clinching the sale.

Five considerations occupy the mind of the prospect as the salesman tries to create a desire to buy, and on those five strings the salesman may lightly strum his message:

1. Profit.
2. Protection.
3. Pride.

4. Utility.

5. Pleasure.

Each of these can be dwelt upon at length and in many ways, and out of it all will begin to appear in a lively form the element of desire.

Desire

Interest properly promoted and maintained ripens into desire. Desire is closely enveloped in self-interest. Dwell upon the benefits the prospect himself would obtain through the purchase of your offering, the joy it would bring to his loved ones, and the admiration it will receive from his friends. Interest gradually develops into definite desire. The salesman's own enthusiasm will help the matter along by breaking down and by-passing some of the objections the customer will continue to inject into the proceedings.

The next task is to stimulate awakening desire into positive action. You have developed in the prospect's mind some motive of self-interest that will eventually prompt him to act. The self-interest chord in his heart *must be touched* if action is to ensue. If a salesman does not understand the prime impelling motives of human life, he will not be able to influence the prospect's heart and mind; nor will he become a successful salesman.

Desire is what really rules human actions. If the prospect's interest is not advanced to this point, the sale may be lost. A customer may be very much interested in a real estate offering; but, if he does not develop a keen desire to own it, the work of the salesman goes for naught. You may be going along a street and see a new automobile and become very much interested in looking at it. But if your interest does not ripen into desire for ownership, no salesman could sell you one. The point is that you can become interested in many things but only those for which you develop a desire are you likely ever to buy.

Gentle but intense persuasion intensifies desire. Here is where a salesman's personality enters into his sales demonstration. If he has personality, he will certainly use it at this point of the interview. Definitely the salesman will now seek strongly to secure action.

Action

Intensified desire leads directly to affirmative action. The signal is out that tells the salesman *to go ahead and close!* Here the pathway of sales resistance must be trod lightly. Avoid the barriers which, at the very last moment, may be set up to avoid taking action. Give the prospect plenty of opportunities to close! Take out a contract form and start filling it out, asking the customer how he wants the property taken, in his own name or with that of his wife added. Act as if the sale had actually been made, unless objections are again brought up. If they are they must be calmly yet skillfully classified as either sincere or insincere and dealt with accordingly. Try at this point to dominate the prospect's mind. Don't let him deviate from the main purpose, which is that of actually signing an offer to purchase and writing a deposit check. If, after bringing the prospect this far along the way, he does not willingly sign, then *he hasn't been sold,* and it is the salesman's business to continue his selling pressure until the propect becomes a customer and actually signs a contract to purchase.

Closing the sale

The different steps in a sale do not necessarily take place in one interview. Real estate is seldom sold after one call by the salesman. It often becomes necessary to pick up the thread of sales procedure at different points, to refresh the mind of the prospect, and to prepare him for an orderly demonstration.

The stepping stones to a sale, as outlined here, must become ingrained in the very mind and heart of the salesman. He must recognize the conflicting emotions that are going on in the mind of the customer, and must manipulate those emotions to the end that they will eventually lead to the closing stage.

CHAPTER 14

Objections—How to Meet
and Overcome Them

SALESMEN WOULD REQUIRE LITTLE SKILL and training if customers did not offer objections to buying. Order takers, such as are found in department stores, could sign up all customers and true salesmanship would become a lost art.

The scores of different objections that can be offered by the prospective purchaser of real estate can all be classified under three headings:

1. *Honest* or sincere objections

2. *Insincere* objections—usually in the form of excuses advanced in the hope that better terms may be made available.

3. *Trivial* objections advanced in the hope of stalling off an immediate decision.

Honest objections are based on features of a property that actually exist. The sliding glass doors stick, the built-in electronic oven needs a light bulb within, the carpet bulges here and there, or an extra TV jack is needed in the bedroom. Often the objection is to a matter that is comparatively unimportant yet should be corrected. In other instances the objection is a more serious one that might prevent the property from being sold and that should be corrected by the owner before the place is even offered for sale.

Sincere objections can be allowed for in the price asked for the property or be made a point of issue wherein the customer will agree to purchase if the cause of the objection is removed. Elimination of many things that are objectionable is often the easiest course of action. Don't mistake requests for information as objections. Give the prospect every atom of information he seeks; give it freely, promptly, and pleasantly.

There is a time in any sales demonstration when a prospect will present insincere objections while he is trying to satisfy himself that he desires to commit himself to a purchase. The time is during or just after a property has been looked over. The eagle-eyed prospect points out every crack, every defect, every wall smudge that may be apparent. Such things are often not important to him, but he is sparring for time, trying to prevent himself from being sold. Be aware of this state of mind, and don't magnify the objections or let them perturb you unnecessarily. Maintain a calm and confident attitude, as if you knew the customer was actually going to buy. Nearly every deal will witness the injection of insincere objections while the customer is trying to make up his mind whether to buy or not. Occasionally a type will be found that will blandly agree with everything you tell him and thus prevent you from knowing what impression you have created. In such cases you should openly seek to commit the prospect.

"Don't you think this place is attractive and well priced?" is a question to lead the prospect into a commitment.

"Isn't this just the kind of property that will meet your needs and one that you can handle?" is another probe that may stir the prospect to action.

Trivial objections are offered by the prospect while he is still stalling for time. He has made all the sincere objections that are possible and has added a few insincere ones. Then comes a time when he is still not ready to act, so he starts to offer more objections. They are seldom of a serious nature and are offered to test the salesman's ability or actually to bait him.

The easiest way to meet trivial objections is to consider them as simply that—and to dismiss them blandly with a few words calculated to get the ideas out of the prospect's mind:

"Yes, I agree with you that is so, but did you ever consider that . . ." and here go back over some of the good points about the property. If the objections are really trivial ones, the prospect will promptly forget them.

Or, "Yes, that is so, and I'll come to that in a moment. . . ."

Or, "Yes indeed, I see how you feel, but have you ever thought of it this way . . ." diverting the prospect's mind to some other feature of the property.

Don't let the prospect dominate the interview. Don't talk too much, and *never argue with a customer* or assume an attitude in direct opposition to the customer's expressed opinion.

Try to anticipate a prospect's objections, no matter of what type they may be. If possible, never let a prospect *discover* a serious defect, but point it out to him. If the prospect finds it out for himself, he is likely to over-emphasize it; if you point it out, the defect will not seem so bad as it might otherwise appear.

Don't imagine that only the important objections of a sincere nature are dangerous. Often a very minor matter, not handled properly, will kill a sale. Try to meet and answer *every* sincere objection without equivocation, while gently brushing aside the trivial and the insincere ones.

Don't assume a contradictory attitude when a prospect voices objections of any kind. A prospect who is asked to buy adopts a somewhat superior attitude, and to have a salesman dispute some opinion he may express comes as a rude shock. Sales resistance will immediately stiffen, and it may be difficult to win back the prospect's mind to an attitude that makes a sale possible.

Even when a prospect likes many of the features of a property, his good judgment warns him to proceed slowly lest there be something about the property that is undesirable. His tendency to inject trivial or insincere objections into your sales routine is merely a means of self-defense, its purpose being to delay making a final decision.

The objections that are most difficult to overcome are the

unspoken ones. Often the prospect merely wants to think things over—to test his own judgment by talking things over with a friend, relative, or acquaintance. Except in the sub-division business, real estate sales are seldom consummated at the first interview. Remember that the buying of a home or a business property is usually considered too serious a mat-ter to rush into on the first contact. The prospect must not be badgered into making an immediate decision. To try to do so is likely to make him rebel and refuse to consider the matter further. One must sense to just what degree a prospect may be pressed into taking action.

Always pave the way for a second interview if the prospect appears to be favorably impressed with a property. Leave some opening so that you can call back to resume the negotia-tions. Tell the prospect you will return later with further information after he or she has had time to consider the mat-ter fully. Leave a favorable impression and not an antagonis-tic one as the result of discussions that may have arisen during the sales presentation.

Were it not for objections that arise during the progress of a sale, a salesman would not have an opportunity to pre-sent his best arguments. Instead of letting the prospect load you down with objections, try to turn his objections into rea-sons why a property will meet his needs. The very fact that a prospect offers objections shows that he is genuinely inter-ested; otherwise he would not take the trouble to utter objec-tions.

Don't try to close a sale until you have gotten all foreseeable objections fully answered and out of the way. Serious objec-tions bobbing up during the closing session throw things en-tirely off balance. The prospect may continue to fence with a salesman right up to the last, but his objections may be so patently of a trivial nature that he does not even believe in them himself. Accept such objections but brush them aside and go on with the sale.

Many stock objections have to do with intimate matters concerning the prospect and not the property itself. Convince the prospect that the objectionable features of the property are allowed for in the price asked or are inconsquential. Then tackle the other types of objections, such as the following:

"I can't make up my mind now." [1]

"The man of decision is the man who wins! There is never a better time to act than now. You know of many a man who has regrets passing up an opportunity to buy a piece of real estate before the time to do so was passed. Failure to grasp an opportunity will never make one rich. The advice to 'Do it now' holds as true as ever so far as this property is concerned."

"It's something I can't afford."

"If this property is properly priced—as it is—and if it will serve your purpose, and if you can make the down payment, it is something you can't afford to pass up. If you really want this piece of real estate, you can find means to acquire it. It will give you a good return through its use or the income you will get from it. You are buying a live investment that can't fail to prove profitable in the years to come."

"The price is too high."

"This property is in line with other offerings on the market." [Proceed to quote prices of similar properties in the neighborhood and to appraise in detail the place you are trying to sell. In this way you will establish elements of value in your offering that show the price to be proper and not an inflated one.]

"Not enough money to handle a deal like this."

"Well, Mr. Prospect, you are aware of the fact that it takes only a $5,000 down payment to handle this property, and you confessed to me that you could afford that much. You know

---

[1] Typical objections as shown in *Selling Real Estate,* by Stanley L. Mc-Michael (Englewood Cliffs, N. J.: Prentice-Hall, Inc.)

this is a very fine neighborhood and your wife and children will be happy living here. The transportation, too, is exceptionally good and . . ."

"There's another place on Lake Street I can buy cheaper."

"Yes, that is true. You refer to 1567 Lake Street, which we have listed in our office. It is a nice place but it has one bedroom and one bath less than this property. Also, the lot is only 80 feet wide, while this one is 100 feet. Also, it is farther from shopping and transportation facilities. This house, on the other hand, has exceptional advantages, such as. . . ."

"Give me a chance to talk this over with my banker (lawyer, friend, wife), and then I'll give you an answer."

"That's fair enough, Mr. Prospect, but remember that it is you who are buying the property and not your banker. Our offering will bear the most minute inspection, and, from what you have seen of it, can't you make up your own mind much more readily than your banker can? This property has been accepted for sale by our office, one of the best qualified to pass on offerings of this kind, and we feel that it is properly priced and offers many advantages. Now, don't you admire the sweeping view from that front window? . . ."

"Not ready to buy yet."

"That may be, Mr. Prospect, but let me show you the fine advantages of this neighborhood, the reasonable price, the excellent neighbors you will have about you. . . ."

"Sorry, but I have no time to talk it over further."

"Mr. Prospect, if someone walked up to you at this moment and offered to give you $1,000, would you say to that person that you didn't have time to talk the proposition over? And yet that is just what I am doing in this case. This lot, priced at $10,000, is almost certain to increase in value in the not far distant future. Where, Mr. Prospect, in this entire city, can you find a residential site that has the advantages this one offers that can be bought at such a reasonable price, that. . . ."

"Just bought an automobile. I'll get more fun out of that than out of real estate."

"Yes, that's probably true—for about three or four years. Then the depreciation consumes the principal, and your automobile instead of increasing in value is soon practically valueless, if it is not a constant source of expense. This property, on the other hand, will be right here in three years, or fifty years, worth as much more then as your automobile is worth less. Owning land is the safest, the surest, and the best way to acquire a competence. . . ."

"Can't spare the money from my business."

"This is not a case, Mr. Prospect, where a large amount of money must be withdrawn from your business or other investments, to acquire this property. The terms, as I have pointed out, require only a small down payment, so that the necessity for a substantial withdrawal of cash from other sources is not present. This property, Mr. Prospect, is almost certain to grow in value, and the making of an initial payment, and the meeting of subsequent ones, will prove one of the best investments you could possibly enter into. . . ."

"This is a nice property, but it's too far from the bus line."

"Yes, it is several blocks from the bus, but really, Mrs. Prospect, that is an advantage, for you avoid the noise that would be present if you were on a main thoroughfare. Moreover, all the merchants in the new shopping center offer free delivery, so you won't have to take a bus to shop. Then again, you may be wanting your own car soon. . . ."

"Well, you just give me the location of that place, and I will look at it some day when we are out for a ride."

"Now, Mr. Prospect, this is entirely too important a thing to be taken lightly. I want to give all my clients the very best service I possibly can. Our company has spent months analyzing this property and its surroundings, and you could not possibly know the advantages and disadvantages of this location without having me with you to explain the different things necessary for you to know to make a wise selection, and that is surely what we want you to do. Mr. Prospect, let me drive you out to see this property tonight after dinner! There are two hours of daylight, and I can show you clearly just what the proposition is, and you will know immediately if you want it. There is absolutely no obligation, and I certainly will make every effort to give you a very thorough understanding of everything connected with this property, because I realize the importance to you in making this selection."

"This house is all right, but I don't like the vinyl wall covering in the living room, and my husband doesn't like the sunken tub in the bathroom."

"Yes, both might be improved. Both could be changed at very small expense. Consider the low price on this property, however, and all of the advantages it offers, and you will agree that this is one of the best buys that has ever been offered you. This building is substantially constructed; it is modern and well laid out for utility, convenience, and family use. Isn't that a charming effect, Mrs. Prospect, the architect has obtained in that entrance way? . . ."

"Oh, I guess I have enough real estate now."

"I would be the last man in the world to advise you to own more real estate than you can conveniently carry. But, Mr. Prospect, from what you have told me about your investments,

I feel certain that this would be a distinct addition to your holdings. Do you realize what the income from this property, reinforced by the increment which will doubtless come to it, will mean in a matter of five or ten years? Let me show you. . . ."

"I believe I can buy cheaper later on. Prices may come down."

"Yes, doubtless we all feel that prices ought to come down, but do they? There is no place for real estate to go but up! Buy on a rising market and make profits later on. You will never find prices lower than they are and I sincerely believe they are headed for a steady and consistent rise which will spell profits for the man who buys real estate now and holds it. Remember, people thought prices would go down after World War II, then again after Korea. After Viet-Nam they are bound to drop, so they have said. But they haven't dropped yet, have they?"

"Oh, I'm satisfied with my old place. Guess I'll wait."

"Yes, doubtless your present accommodations are quite comfortable, but have you tried to visualize just what you can do with this property, how it can be made to. . . ."

"Will my money be safe?"

"Your money in properly selected and rightly bought real estate is always safe. No sounder investment for surplus funds can be found than seasoned real estate. No matter what the conditions of the times, it has always been found that real estate is in a relatively better position than any other investment."

**"If your proposition is so good, why
don't you sell it to someone else?"**

"Now, that's a perfectly natural observation to make, my friend. I'm presenting it to you because I believe you need an investment of this kind. I could just as well show it to a thousand other prospects and I could do that with fully as much grace and with the probability that any one of them would seize upon this offering as one of the best propositions ever submitted to him. Now, as I was saying . . ." (Go on with canvass about your property).

"Nothing doing until after New Years!"

"Yes, I know it is only sixty days until Christmas, and that you want to get that out of the way. But, you know, it takes quite a bit of time to select a house and buy it, so why not start early and get possession when you can arrange to move into it." (This is usually an insincere objection. Answer it, dismiss the idea, go on with your canvass, and the prospect will soon forget it.)

"I believe it's cheaper to build than to buy a house."

"That is a general impression, due, perhaps, to the publicity which goes with Federal Housing Administration campaigns. But let me analyze the situation for you, madam. In the first place most of the new building is being done in the outlying areas where location advantages are not nearly so favorable as in the built-up districts where transportation is good and every facility for comfortable living is to be found. Take a soundly built house like this one; adapt it to your needs, and you will find yourself much farther along the way towards having a profitable real estate investment which you can probably sell any time you may want to part with it. Building costs today are higher than ever, largely because of unionization of labor and the increase in costs of materials, which have advanced owing to the very same thing. You can probably buy a house already up for from two-thirds to three-fourths of what it will cost to build it and usually have much better land location factors in connection with it."

"Conditions are uncertain. I might lose my job."

"Life is ever uncertain, Mr. Prospect, but you have to go right on living! If you pay rent, you can't escape that obligation even if you do get into a stretch of hard times or even get out of work. While you are employed you should insure yourself against any such eventuality. Now is the time to go ahead and secure a home and get it paid for as rapidly as possible."

"Won't you call again? I'll see you later."

"Important events have happened, Mr. Prospect, because of delay. Men have been passed by opportunity because they could not reach a decision. Now, this property has all the advantages I have enumerated, namely. . . ."

"I don't believe in vacant property!"

"America's national wealth has its cornerstone set on vacant property, Mr. Prospect. All property was vacant at one time. Improved property is simply land with buildings which earn rent or which are used for homes. Some of the greatest fortunes in this country, those of Marshall Field, Potter Palmer, the Astors, and many others, were based on the purchase of vacant property which they later improved or sold at large profits. Vast increment comes to vacant property if properly chosen and purchased at the right price and on the right terms. Many, many fortunes were started with the purchase of a small piece of vacant real estate which later was sold or improved and which earned good returns for its owner."

"I buy only stocks and bonds. I think the aerospace stocks are the best."

"Most bonds are good and many stocks earn fair returns. But stocks are highly speculative, and under governmental control of the stock market as now exercised the opportunities to make quick or speculative returns are very limited. If speculation will ever pay a profit, it will do so in connection with real estate, in which men have been investing and speculating since the world began. Furthermore, when you buy stocks or bonds you get only a small part interest in an enterprise that is managed by somebody else. When you buy real estate you own it yourself, can go around and look at it and see it grow in value. Vastly more money was lost in the shrinkage of stocks and bonds in the great depression of the thirties than in the shrinkage of real estate. Invest at least a portion of your funds in real estate, the safest and the surest road to financial success."

"Yes, I've been out around there and know all about it!"

"If you know all about it you *must* know that this is a safe and sound proposition. Let me refresh your memory about some of the advantages of this area. . . ." (Always be affirmative in answering this objection.)

CHAPTER 15

Closing the Sale

THERE IS NOTHING MYSTERIOUS ABOUT the part of a real estate transaction known as *closing the sale*. It is not a separate process but an integral part of the sales process that has been in progress from the very time the property was first presented to the prospect. It is that phase of the selling effort that usually ends with a buyer signing a sales contract or definitely rejecting the offering.

The final barrier set up by the prospect—fear—must be gently pressed aside, and the spirit of confidence exhibited by the salesman must be transmitted to the purchaser so that he will take pen in hand and say, as he so often actually does when signing: "Well, I guess I'll take a chance!"

Many salesmen approach the final part of a sales interview in fear and trembling. Many ask for support from more experienced salesmen at this time. Indeed, some offices have men who are technically known as "closers," men who have been through the experience many times. They are confident of their ability to secure a buyer's signature to a contract and are nimble-witted enough to overcome the objections that the buyer will continue, in some cases, to press forward until the very end.

Never forget that some time before final consent has been given by the buyer, he has made up his mind to accept the proposition. He needs just a little more urging to capitulate.

Sometimes he does it very suddenly, but more often with great reluctance, no matter how attractive the offering may be.

Many salesmen have the impression that closing a sale is a high-pressure procedure. This is far from the case. High-pressuring a prospect is more likely to alienate him than to win his consent, particularly so if the prospect is a person of intelligence. He will resent such tactics, and indeed may withdraw at almost the last moment because he does not like the treatment accorded him. Gentle, good-natured persistence, backed with intelligent sales arguments, will do more to win the day than any amount of high-pressure salesmanship. A prospect likes to think he is buying of his own free will, backed by his own good judgment, and resents the idea of someone forcing him to make a decision.

In the earlier part of a sales canvass, the salesman is usually busy answering questions that the buyer asks about a property. Then come objections offered by the prospect, who feels that he should avoid committing himself in favor of the deal until his mind fully is made up and he is satisfied that everything is all right. Once the objections are out of the way, the salesman can proceed to work up to his final task—getting the prospect to sign a contract. The business of signing a contract is an additional handicap in the realty business that usually does not happen in the sale of other commodities. A man will look over a number of suits of clothes, wardrobe trunks, or lawnmowers, and readily answers the salesman when he asks, "Where do you want it delivered?" The salesman of real estate, however, must get the buyer's consent in the form of a signature on a legal document, and it is when the contract is presented that the buyer rears back and exhibits fear, for he probably has never before been submitted to such a formality when buying something.

One way to meet the situation is to get the prospect gradually accustomed to the contract. Fairly early in the final interview, display a copy of the contract and, if possible, get the prospect to look it over. If the terms of the sale are simple and can be anticipated, by all means have the contract prepared in advance. Then, at an appropriate moment, say:

"Let me read you this contract, Mr. Reed, so that you can see that every contingency is being taken care of."

Or, "This contract provides that the deal will be handled through escrow, so that every feature will be taken care of by an expert escrow officer of The Estates Title Company."

Or, "You will notice, Mr. Reed, that the escrow officer acts as a referee in this matter and holds your money in hand until the seller submits a satisfactory title to the property, and it is recorded in your name."

Tell the prospect things that will soothe his fears, if he appears fearful. Answer every sincere objection he may offer, whether it seems important or not, for at this final critical period the buyer may resent having some information withheld.

Selling, after all, is largely a matter of supplying the information a buyer needs to be convinced that he should commit himself affirmatively. Closing the sale is merely applying the finishing touches to the sales interview and is a natural climax of any successful sales canvass.

Don't betray suppressed excitement when you are closing a sale, or appear too eager to force the issue if the prospect is not quite ready to sign. It is simply evidence of the fact that *he isn't sold yet!* Laboring too hard sometimes communicates excitement to the buyer's mind and alarms him, a mental attitude that is not conducive to closing.

Failure to close a sale is usually traceable to poor craftsmanship on the part of the salesman in presenting his offering. Somewhere along the line something has been left unsaid that should be said or something has been said that should have been left out

Frame your questions carefully. Always ask questions that can be answered most easily in the affirmative! Never suggest anything that the prospect can answer negatively.

Good real estate closers are simply men who are aware of the mental processes that are going on in the minds of their customers and who take advantage of that knowledge.

Good clean-cut physical courage is an asset that can be useful in closing a sale. New salesmen, fearing that closing is a complicated matter, often hesitate to forge ahead and persuade customers to take action. They are sometimes *actually afraid of their prospects!* Avoid such a state of mind for if it prevails you will never close a sale. The customer will become conscious of it just as certainly as a highly bred dog can detect fear in a human being. At once the customer will begin to wonder why the salesman hesitates and he may himself become fearful. A scared salesman and a suspicious customer just naturally cannot do business.

Justify action on the part of the prospect at every turn. Give him plenty of opportunities to buy! Ask him:

"When do you want to take posession of this property, Mr. Reed?"

"Do you want to take this in the names of both yourself and your wife?"

"Have you an architect in mind to design a house for this lot?"

If a contract has not been made out before the interview, now may be just the right time to get out a copy and start filling if in, assuming quite casually that the customer has made up his mind to buy. If he is not ready, leave the contract exposed on the table and go right on selling the prospect, giving him more factual information about the property.

Always have a properly functioning pen handy. Lay it down beside the contract. If you think the time has arrived, hand the pen to the prospect and say:

"Now, if you will sign here, Mr. Reed, you will be the owner of a fine piece of property."

Don't hesitate to *pass the pen* if the time seems appropriate. The prospect can't do anything worse than to lay it down again. It may be just the act that will galvanize him into action. If this device fails, take a piece of paper and show him the advantages he will gain by owning the property as against paying rent as a tenant. Emphasize the fact that many a renter who has lived in a house ten, twelve, or fifteen years pays the full price for which he might have bought the place at the outset. Don't act hurriedly or appear flustered. Speak calmly, always with an evenly controlled voice. Don't seem argumentative or give the prospect a chance to resent what you are telling him. Be friendly but firm, indicating that you know what you are talking about and that you are earnestly seeking to help him better his position in life. It is your business to *stimulate his will to act!*

Buyers differ in the amount of time they require to be sold —or rather, to *sell themselves*. You must be patient and must understand human nature quite thoroughly. The personality of the salesman comes into play especially during the closing period. If you have that element of charm and conviction that all successful salesmen possess, you may find it easy to persuade buyers to act. If not, you may have to try again. Unless the propect definitely turns a proposition down, don't fail to go back and try to renew the negotiations. One noted exponent of sales technique says: "Never leave a man's presence without trying four times for an order." That man didn't sell real estate as a business, but the idea is as applicable to the real estate salesman as it is to all others who follow selling as a calling.

If a customer announces that he is not ready to buy, don't become impatient or show resentment. Thank him for the time he has given you and don't fail, if at all possible, to *leave an opening for a return call.* To do so is important, for often, after you have left him, the prospective buyer will begin to think and perhaps overcome some element of fear, so that when he is again approached he may be ready to proceed. Never accept a complete turn-down or dismissal. Leave some opening so that you can still keep your foot in the door! Maneuver things so that you will have a genuine excuse for another call.

Although the customer may say "No," he may not mean it. He may be stalling for time if he says he wants to look into some feature of the property or the terms of purchase. Most often he stalls because he wants more information than the salesman has given him. Some weakness in the sales presentation may become apparent, and to supply the desired information may be the very thing the prospect needs to become receptive to closing.

Closing takes place naturally when the rest of the sales presentation has been conducted properly. Failure to close may be due to one or more of the following:

1. The needs of the buyer were not properly estimated.
2. The prospect has not been properly qualified as to his ability to buy.
3. The salesman, through failure to know fully the conditions and advantages of the property he is trying to sell, has not adequately presented the property.
4. The salesman has failed properly to answer valid objections offered by the buyer.
5. The salesman has failed properly to coördinate his arguments and to present them convincingly to the prospect.
6. The salesman has been fearful of pressing too hard for a close.

Somewhere in the process a gap has been left that has allowed the prospect to escape the salesman's pressure to sign a contract to purchase.

One way to find out whether the prospect is following the salesman in his presentation is to try to commit the prospect as the sales interview proceeds. Ask plenty of questions as you go along that demand an affirmative answer. If the prospect follows along, answering affirmatively, he usually can be led to a decision without much trouble. If he begins to answer negatively, he is off the track and trouble ensues. So see to it that you discover the very moment when the prospect's interest begins to waver.

Getting a prospect to sign a contract brings a thrill to the mind and heart of a salesman. Whether he has sold a lot or a mansion, he has accomplished something worth while. After securing the prospect's signature, be sure to continue to show interest in the customer. Never rush away from a client who has agreed to purchase property. Congratulate him on what appears to be a well-conceived purchase. Continue to discuss the attractiveness of the property and the way it will meet his needs. Follow the deal through the steps it takes to place the buyer in final possession and see that confidence is maintained to the very last, for a satisfied customer may well help you in making other deals with friends of his later on.

Here are the things to remember and to do automatically when closing deals:

1. Dominate the interview throughout—not in a belligerent way but in a calm, positive manner, indicating that you know your business and the property you are submitting.

2. Keep the interest of the buyer centered upon the property. Don't let his mind wander and don't let him side-track your sales presentation with trivial objections.

3. Exhaust *all* of the customer's objections, if at all possible, before you begin to close. Answer the sincere objections; brush away the insincere ones. If objections are offered in the closing period, it is because the prospect has not been sold. Continue to answer them and then press for a close.

4. If at all possible, have your contract written out before attempting to close. Have a pen ready, too, and don't hesitate to pass the pen if the customer will accept it. If he won't sign, go right on selling until his resistance is broken down.

5. Be resourceful and try to understand the motives that influence the prospect's mind. Study his sales reactions. Carry him along with a smooth and interesting sales presentation.

6. Failing to capture a signature on your contract at the first attempt, patiently and skillfully maneuver for a comeback call. Establish some opening for returning. The prospect in the meantime may change his mind and sell himself on the arguments you have presented.

7. Having secured a signed contract, leave the buyer in a happy mood. Congratulate him and continue to give him service. Don't dash away to put the deal in escrow, collect the commission, and forget the prospect. Salesmen who have

treated customers graciously will find that many tips will come later which often develop into more sales.

Remember, too, that to close a sale is not a superhuman achievement that follows a sales presentation; it is a part of the entire sales process and should begin at the opening of the interview and be carried through it until it becomes a natural reward for the salesman's efforts.

CHAPTER 16

What Is

Real Estate Worth?

TO SELL A PARCEL OF REAL ESTATE IT IS necessary to have a wide and accurate knowledge of real estate values. You cannot sell today's real estate on the basis of yesterday's values.

Some buyers refuse to pay the asking price because their investigations reveal that the property under consideration sold for only so many dollars ten years ago. As a speculator and as an alert salesman, you should know that the value of property ten years ago is hardly a factor in what it might be worth today. It is likely to be worth a lot more, but it could be worth less.

Appraising is more involved, more difficult, and more complex than ever before. Still, you are going to have to learn appraising if you are to guide the seller toward fixing a fair price and the buyer toward accepting it.

Modern scientific appraising of real estate is only a few decades old. Until about 1920 the summation method was used almost exclusively by both tax appraisers and those called upon to fix values on which loans were made. By the summation process, the land is valued separately; the reproduction cost of the building is then estimated and a depreciation factor applied to ascertain the value of the structure. The two sums are added and the total is considered the value of the property. The earn-

131

ing power, which in most instances is the real indicator of value, is completely disregarded. The summation method is still used by most taxation appraisers, largely because it can be applied uniformly.

Misconceptions under which appraisers have labored for many years are:

1. That the initial cost of a building, plus the value of the land it rests on, constitutes a warranted value for the property.
2. That cost necessarily equals value.
3. That market value and market price are the same.
4. That every building is worth its cost at the time of its erection, despite the fact that it may be misplaced or an over-improvement.

What is value? As defined by the American Institute of Real Estate Appraisers, value represents *the present worth of future benefits arising out of ownership to typical users and investors.*

There are many different kinds of value, and various kinds of value may exist in a given property at a stated time. Following is a list of terms applied to value, some of which are important and others meaning very little other than a shade of difference between kinds of value: [1]

Absolute value.	Certified value.	Forced sale value.
Absorption value.	Commercial value.	Future value.
Actual value.	Condemnation value.	Going concern value.
Appraised value.	Cost value.	Hold-up value.
Assay office value.	Created value.	Hypothetical value.
Assemblage value.	Depreciated value.	Improved value.
Assessed value.	Economic value.	Income value.
Attached business value.	Established use value.	Imputed value.
Book value.	Exchange value.	Increment value.
Capital value.	Expert value.	Insurance value.
Caprice value.	Face value.	Intangible value.
Cash value.	Fair market value.	Intrinsic value.
	Fair value.	Investment value.

[1] For a comprehensive and scientific discussion of the entire subject of appraising real estate, consult *McMichael's Appraising Manual* (Englewood Cliffs, N. J.: Prentice-Hall, Inc.)

Junk or scrap value.	Productivity value.	Service value.
Justified value.	Prudent value.	Sound value.
Liquidation value.	Real value.	Speculative value.
Loan value.	Realization value.	Stable value.
Market value.	Reasonable value.	Summation value.
Nominal value.	Rental value.	Tangible value.
Normal value.	Replacement value.	Tax value.
Nuisance value.	Reproduction value.	True value.
Physical value.	Sale value.	Use value.
Plottage value.	Salvage value.	Utility value.
Potential value.	Sentimental value.	Warranted value.
Present value.		

Appraisers usually try to establish market value. As defined in the "Appraisal Terminology" of the American Institute of Real Estate Appraisers, market value consists of:

"The price at which a willing seller would sell and a willing buyer would buy, neither being under abnormal pressure.

"The price expectable if a reasonable time is allowed to find a purchaser and if both seller and prospective buyer are fully informed."

One court has defined it as "the highest price . . . a property will bring . . . in the open market, allowing a reasonable time to find a purchaser who buys with knowledge of all the uses to which it is adapted and for which it is capable of being used."

Real estate that is utilized for its highest and best use attains a maximum value. Highest and best use is defined as "that use of, or program of utilization of, a site which will produce the maximum net land returns over a total period which comprises the future; the optimum use of a site." This definition usually applies to land in cities, particularly in highly developed retail sections in business centers.

Under- or over-improvement of a site may detract from its highest and best use. A valuable corner in a downtown section of a busy community may be improved with a small, inadequate building that cannot earn a maximum return. On the other hand, a corner in an outlying business section may have been improved with a large, costly structure for which there was no real need, in which event it cannot be made to pay a reasonable return upon its cost.

Management is an important factor in establishing and maintaining value. Efficient management of a supermarket, for instance, may result in its earning a return far in excess of several small stores adjoining it, which may have an equal land and building area but do not attract the buying power necessary to create as great a net return on the investment. Of course, a goodly measure of the success of the market may be due to skillful and expert management and not to the site or the building occupying it. In that case the element of management must be discounted in making a fair appraisal of the physical property. Also, competition will soon develop in the neighborhood. It is axiomatic that *exorbitant profits breed ruinous competition.* Another supermarket will spring up to share the fancy profits of the original promotor.

The highest and best use of a property may often be found in its existing use. On the other hand, a little investigating may show that another type of business would earn a higher rate of return. Determining the highest and best use demands good judgment and this, indeed, may be the only way by which it may be determined.

The degree to which an appraiser knows his city and the locality in which he is establishing a value are demonstrated by the data he is able to collect and use in any given assignment. An efficient appraiser collects and maintains a volume of facts and figures, which data serve as a reservoir from which he can constantly draw when making valuations of any kind.

Here is a chart of typical data gathered for appraisal purposes:

Concerning the City

1. Location, type, age, history, and outstanding characteristics.
2. Economic status and business, industrial, and social activities.
3. General layout and arterial plan showing the comparative relation of the city to other competitive cities or towns.
4. Availability of transportation facilities, including railroads, boats, interurban bus and air lines, and so forth.
5. Types of inhabitants—a comparison of native and foreign-born residents—and the character of their economic backgrounds. How are they housed?

6. Analysis of educational, religious, recreational, and cultural activities.

7. Geographical, topographical, and climatic data.

8. History as a market center, purchasing power of residents and so forth.

9. Type and efficiency of governmental activities.

10. Taxation benefits and burdens, debt condition, and the history thereof.

11. Review of public service facilities furnishing water, power, light, heat, and so forth, with data concerning reasonableness of rates, costs, and so forth. Availability of cheap power and other benefits from large governmental entreprises, canals, dams, and so forth.

12. Is the city growing? Outline of past history of growth.

13. At what pace and in what manner and direction will it expand? May this affect the property under appraisement?

District Influences

1. Character of buildings in the immediate neighborhood.

2. Transportation facilities afforded the neighborhood.

3. Street plan of the area indicating main arteries which may attract trade or new residents.

4. Topography and building foundation conditions encountered.

5. Available public institutions, such as schools, libraries, churches, theaters, parks, playgrounds, stations, beaches, golf courses, and so forth.

6. Accessibility to central and distant points via the street plan.

7. Hazards, such as possibility of floods or landslides; presence of noisy concerns; nuisances such as dairy barns, smoke, odors, stockyards, chemical factories, oil wells, or airports.

8. Normal rental levels of the neighborhood and probability of their continuance.

From an analysis of neighborhood influences, the appraiser finally estimates the remaining expectant life of the improvements under appraisement.

Economic Trends of the Community

1. Is economic condition improving or retrograding?

2. Past history of business activities and outlook for future.

3. Market conditions in general over a long trend. Active? Medium? Slow? Improving?

4. Average economic status of residents. Well-to-do? Average? Poor? Consider relief activities in area during depression.

5. Analyze demand for real estate and review possible supply thereof. Scan data about number of transfers, type, cost, and so forth.

Data from Public Sources about Property under Appraisement

1. Legal description of property to be appraised.
2. Character of title, whether abstract, insured title, and so forth. Have any defects ever been noted? Does ownership exist in fee simple, or is it an estate interest, a life interest or leasehold, and so forth?
3. Tax information from tax collector's records.
4. Assessed value of land and improvements from assessor's office.
5. Land and building restrictions, easements, rights of way, and so forth.
6. Identity of architect and contractor of improvements, and former owners of the property.
7. Adjoining property owners, tenants, and so on.
8. Encumbrances on property, including mortgages, liens if any, life interests, leases, and so forth.
9. Building department records, including date and amount of building permit for improvements, type of construction, square feet of area, later additions, and so forth.
10. Copies of plans and specifications which may be on file in building inspector's office.
11. Public restrictions applicable to neighborhood, including zoning laws, health, plumbing and sanitary regulations, codes, and so forth.

Data on Which Current Replacement Costs May Be Estimated

1. Size of structure, including square foot and cubical areas, general arrangements of rooms or suites, differences, if any, in types of construction used, number of baths, kitchens, heating and mechanical equipment, and so forth.
2. Age and condition of improvements. Interior finish and character and quality of construction.
3. Cost factors. Assessor's original estimates of cost of improvements.

From these data the appraiser can establish a present-day replacement cost new, including contractor's profits and architect's fees.

Data Concerning the Site

1. Analyze site, topography, soil condition, and location of improvements in relation to position in the block and proximity to corners, alleys, and so forth.
2. Note plantings, trees, and presence of stairways, terraces, walls, or special construction apart from main building.
3. Consider availability of other sites with similar characteristics and elements of usefulness, and determine whether the site under appraisal possesses monopolistic advantages which may add to its value.

4. Consider the availability of the site for a variety of uses.

5. Is the site being used for its highest and best use?

6. Ascertain, if possible, the cost of the site to present owner and whether justified.

From these data, finally, the appraiser can estimate the current market value of the land.

Operating Schedules

Income data:

1. Detailed list of rentals by individual tenants. Check to see whether too high or too low.

2. Special income from telephone service, laundry, resale of water, electricity, or heat, and disposal of waste paper, outmoded equipment, and so forth.

3. Comprehensive data concerning leases, terms, allowances on rent or deposits on same, and so forth.

4. Secure copies of operating statements for several years and average for comparison.

Expense data:

1. Detailed maintenance and repair costs.

2. Taxes and assessments.

3. Wages to janitors, maids, house boys, garage attendants, and so on.

4. Supplies for janitor, office, apartments, and so forth.

5. Insurance premiums for fire, boiler, compensation, elevator, liability, earthquake, plate glass, and so forth.

6. Water, gas, electricity, and power.

7. Coal, other fuel, steam.

8. Rubbish removal, hauling, and so forth.

9. Replacements of furniture and equipment (when carried as expense).

10. Telephone expense.

11. Fees for licenses, inspections, and the like.

12. Gardener and house cleaners.

13. Accounting, legal, and advertising expense.

14. Noncollectible losses and vacancies.

Data Concerning Costs Encountered During Construction

1. Extent and expense of surveys.

2. Extent of financing costs involved in promotion of project.

3. Carrying costs during construction, including taxes, bonds, overhead, insurance, interest on mortgages, legal fees, and so on.

4. Sidewalks, grading, retaining walls, landscaping, and so forth, not in building contract.

5. Rental commissions and advertising.

Maps, Photos and Charts

In making a comprehensive appraisal report on a worthwhile property, the appraiser will make a collection of the following, copies of which should be attached to, and become a part of, the report:

1. A map of the city, or that portion of it that indicates where the property under appraisement is situated.

2, Exterior photographs of the various improvements from different positions.

3. Blueprints showing floor plans of the improvement.

4. A detailed sketch of the property and its immediate environs.

5. Charts or graphs showing rental and occupancy histories of the property, of the district, and of the city itself.

Contingent Assumptions Regarding Data

An appraisal is made on the following general assumptions:

1. The legal description of the premises, furnished the appraiser, is accurate.

2. The title to the property is sound and merchantable.

3. The property is clear of liens.

4. Under any plan of operation outlined, management will be efficient and the property will be adequately maintained.

CHAPTER 17

Elements of

Appraisal Procedure

THE THREE AVENUES OF APPROACH USED
in establishing value are:

1. The reproduction-cost approach.
2. The comparative method.
3. Capitalization of income.

The reproduction-cost approach usually involves the summation method of appraising. A definite value is assigned to the land after it has been compared with other sites of a similar character in the same or a similar neighborhood. If the building is new, its cost is added to the value of the land, and the two represent the appraised value of the property. If the building is not new, a suitable rate of depreciation is applied to the reproduction cost new. Age, physical wear, and obsolescence are thus recognized and allowed for.

The comparative method of approach is a commonly used one. Improved properties of a like character, as well as vacant lots, are carefully considered, and a value is established that bears a relation to other properties of similar character. It is simply a comparison of location, utility, price, and value.

The capitalization approach considers primarily the property's capacity to earn a gross income, from which expenses are deducted and a net income arrived at. A suitable rate of earning is applied, based on that of other properties of a similar character, and a value is arrived at. For a first-class seasoned property, the capitalization rate may be low—6, 7 or 8 per cent, possibly even 10 per cent. Where some hazard is present, such as a location in an outlying business section that has not proved itself, the rate applied may be 12 to 15 per cent. Where expert management is encountered, the capitalization rate may be even higher.

A sound appraisal can be obtained by the application of all three of these methods to a property. The three totals are added and averaged, and the result represents the appraiser's opinion of the market value of the property.

In developing a capitalization rate, the appraiser must gather and analyze all the data about the property itself, such as:

1. Its condition.
2. Its construction. (Will it deteriorate rapidly?)
3. What kind of tenants does it have? For what kinds is it suitable?
4. What kind of leases exist? Are they insured?
5. Can it be converted to other uses? If so, could it be better utilized?
6. Is the management burden excessive?
7. What's the neighborhood like? Is the location improving or worsening?
8. Is the property readily marketable?
9. Is there a prospect for profit in a resale?

But, in addition to studying the property itself, the appraiser must take into account outside factors such as the following that will affect the income from the property during its economic life:

1. Current conditions in the real estate market.
2. Condition of the money market.
3. Competition for, and availability of, investment funds.
4. Interest rates on other forms of investment.
5. Cost of mortgage financing, and basis for obtaining mortgage money.
6. Rate of yield from similar properties in the area.

Depreciation

Elements of depreciation are varied and are due chiefly to three causes:

1. Physical deterioration.
2. Functional obsolescence.
3. Economic obsolescence.

Physical deterioration may be created by such things as:

Dry rot.
Wear and tear.
Corrosion of metals.
Action of the elements.
Settling of foundations.
Decay or disintegration.
Any loss of physical soundness.
Insects, such as termites, and so forth.
Undermining by water, slippage, or earthquakes.

Functional obsolescence may be due to:

Antique elevators.
Ancient plumbing.
Cheap pine flooring.
Too much hall space.
Outmoded architecture.
Excessively thick walls.
Unnecessarily high ceilings.
Out-of-date lighting fixtures.
Lack of wiring for television.
Lack of storage and closet space.
Excessively large rooms in layout.
Lack of sufficient electrical outlets.
Freak or ancient hardware and fittings.
Worn-out furnaces and heating equipment.
Wooden wainscoting, interior walls, ceilings.
Lack of modern air-conditioning installations.
Any element indicating functional deficiency.
Inadequate number of baths, toilets, and so forth.
Excessive gingerbread decorations, inside and out.
Lack of modern kitchen equipment (dishwashers, disposals, built-ins, etc.)

Elements of economic obsolescence may be due to:

Population decreases.
Illegal uses of property.
Incongruous uses of property.
Variations in supply and demand.
Presence of undesirable types of residents.
Legislative action—city, state, and national.
Lack of utilization and desertion of industries.
Unreasonable tax rates, rising debts, and so on.
Invasion of any extraneous conditions which lower values.
Changes in type of buildings, uses, and so forth in a neighborhood.
Shifting economic conditions, changes in value of money, and so forth.

Everyone recognizes the fact that depreciation goes on constantly with the use and maintenance of all structures. Every owner of an automobile knows that when his car is four, five, or six years old it is well on its way to the scrap pile. Many auto users buy a new car every second year to avoid depreciation. This cannot be done where buildings are involved, but judicious repairs, repainting, and maintenance will do much to retain fading value. Periodically buildings must be remodeled or they will degenerate to such a condition of out-of-dateness (obsolescence) that they lose much of their inherent value.

Depreciation may be defined as: Loss, shrinkage, or decline in value, from whatever cause.

Physical deterioration differs among various kinds of property. A building entirely of wood depreciates faster than one of wood coated with stucco, or whose walls are of concrete and brick. Wood must be protected by being painted regularly. Stucco and brick walls must be pointed up where cracks appear, and stucco must also be protected with paint. Trim around wooden windows and doors must be carefully looked after from year to year. Roofs must be renewed. Where termites and dry rot abound, care must be taken to prevent infestation, and they must be eradicated where they appear. Physical deterioration will be apparent to the broker or appraiser at a glance. During periods when depressions and wars prevail there is always the temptation to let repairs and painting get behind, thus lessening the value of properties.

Functional obsolescence is not so easily detected. It is indicated, primarily, by out-of-dateness as evidenced by old-style lighting fixtures, cheap tiling and fixtures at kitchen sinks, ancient fixtures in bathrooms, and often an entire absence of tile in bathrooms. Every year new kinds of materials are introduced into construction of dwellings, and the extent to which they are absent is what spells functional obsolescence.

Functional obsolescence is definitely apparent in aging American cities. In many of those cities are hosts of sound, well-constructed buildings, situated in fine neighborhoods but steadily deteriorating because no one takes steps to remodel or rebuild them. It is likely that the coming years will see an acceleration of remodeling operations in such sections that will tend to recapture values that are definitely fading away through neglect.

Economic obsolescence is represented by the infiltration into a neighborhood of elements that create a discordant note. Persons having a low standard of living soon imprint their mark on a neighborhood. Those who use properties for questionable or immoral purposes soon see their districts slip down in the social and economic scale. "Twilight zones" on the edge of old and worn-out business districts represent economic obsolescence on a large scale. Only total obliteration may cure them. Areas degenerating into slums are hard to regenerate. Only by sweeping them away and replacing them with civic centers or new multiple-dwelling districts can such blots be removed. Federal programs of urban renewal are helping in this respect.

Business depressions leave their imprint on certain sections of cities. Where numbers of persons who are tenants are out of work, landlords are unable to collect rentals with which to maintain their properties. Accumulated repairs mount into the millions during such periods.

The shifting of business districts in large cities is the cause of vast amounts of obsolescence at the same time that new values are created in newly developing business districts. It has been noted that business districts in cities definitely shift every twenty to thirty years. The shifting is due in part to buildings becoming older and not being remodeled to keep abreast of the times. Values are never static in an active business district, for influences are constantly at work that shift trade to new centers. Broadway, in New York, saw business shift five or six times in its march from the Battery and Wall Street up toward Central Park. Chicago's downtown business district has shifted less than in most other large cities, but has moved, nevertheless. Cleveland has seen four or five shifts from the time it was on the river's bank until business marched out Euclid Avenue beyond East 9th Street. Los Angeles likewise has seen half a dozen shifts of its main business center. The shifts left in their wake more or less run down districts that later degenerated to low-grade shopping areas.

The branch of appraising technique with which the broker or salesman will come in contact most often will be that used for residential properties. Most brokerage deals involve the selling of homes, and the salesman should know definitely what a property is really worth before he tries to sell it. While it is the commonest type of appraisal, nevertheless it is one of the hardest to make. The appraisal is usually based on the reproduction cost less depreciation for the house, and on the comparative method for the land. If the dwelling is rented, or can readily be rented, the capitalization approach may be used as a check.

Dwellings are sometimes found to be worth less than their reproduction value at the time of their completion. They may be over-improvements or under-improvements, or freakish in design, either inside or out. On the other hand, a clever builder may erect an especially artistic building worth considerably more than it cost to assemble the materials of which it is built. In such cases the element of *caprice* may enter largely. Women buy most of the houses, and they may have their attention drawn to fancy little touches used in finishing a dwelling, such as mirrors, bits of tilework, fancy grills of iron, planter boxes or what not. The appeal of these things is sometimes so strong that it overcomes whatever objections a woman may have to the house or its cost, and a deal is soon concluded.

Here are elements to consider in making an appraisal of a dwelling house, or in listing it for sale:

General Environment

Current trade.
Living standards.
Population trends.
Governmental trends.
Current credit structure.
Purchasing power.
Costs of living.
Building costs.

Competition.
Zoning and city planning.
Transportation.
National income.
Real estate demand.
Facility for financing.
Workers' incomes.

The Neighborhood

Type of tenancy.
Presence of nuisances.
Suitability of improvements.
Trend of rents, costs, and values.
Directional growth.
Termites, dry rot, and mosquitoes.
Distance to center of town.
District topography.
Soil and foundation factors.
Restrictions, easements, and zoning.
Drainage of area.
Age and condition of section.
Neighborhood changing.
The city plan.
Street layout.
Police and fire protection.
Churches, libraries, and schools.
Markets and shopping centers.
Parks, theaters, and beaches.
Electricity, gas, and water.
Transportation.
Need for more homes.
Type of buildings.
Hazards, floods, etc.
Building costs.
Proximity of buildings.

The Property Itself

Size and shape of lot.
Restrictions and zoning.
Best and highest use.
Soil fertility.
Drainage.
Elevation and topography.
Suitability of building.
Design of building.
Suitable materials.
Adequate heating plant.
Subject to obsolescence.
Fire hazard.
Age.
Cost to reproduce.
Cost justified.
Present condition.
Termites or dry rot.
Maintenance costs.
Taxes and assessments.
Exposure, light, and air.
Enough bathrooms.
Over- or under-improvement.
Plumbing and electrical equipment.
Interior finish.
Room layout.
Utilities all present.
History of owner.

While residential land is usually valued by comparison with similarly located sites, buildings are appraised on a basis of cost.

While some general reproduction cost factors can be assembled as between cities, it is difficult indeed to set up specific cost factors for any given community. That is something the appraiser must find out for himself through study of building records and consultation with contractors and through other means of personal contact and experience.

Two methods are used in calculating costs, one being based on square-foot area and the other on cubic-foot volume. The latter method is used much less often than the former, and then usually for buildings with unusually high ceilings or those of a special-purpose nature such as theaters, halls, churches, and public structures. Labor costs vary from time to time in different localities. They must be considered just as much as the changing prices of standard materials and the introduction of new ones.

CHAPTER 18

Imagination in Selling

BROKERS WHO BECOME THE SUPER-salesmen of the real estate business are the ones who use their imagination in creating deals. Creative selling is one of the highest branches of the calling and is open to anyone who desires to exercise his mental capacity and to train himself in originating ways to sell and improve land.

American cities abound with examples of such work. Large promotional enterprises are to be found on every side that would never have come into existence were it not for little thought germs that originated in the minds of real estate men, who had faith in them and earnestly followed them through until they developed into completed projects. Theaters, office buildings, sports centers, radio headquarters, shopping centers with air-conditioned malls, warehouse developments, resorts of various kinds, store arcades, as well as a wide range of residential developments, stand as monuments to the creative genius of realty men. They have had the promotional urge in their blood and found ways to express it in land and buildings, to the benefit of all concerned.

In many cases the work of such men proves so successful and lucrative that they soon give up their ordinary brokerage activities and become what are known as real estate operators or developers. These are the men who really make big money in real estate, for themselves as well as for their clients. They look about, get ideas for improvements that seem necessary,

147

seek out ways to provide what the public wants, and then go doggedly to work. Sometimes they work for months or even years on such projects before finally accomplishing their purpose. But when they are through they really have something fine to show for their time and effort.

The first thing a realty operator does is to study his city and become thoroughly familiar with its trends of growth. He buys just at the edge of developments and lets the location ripen until it is engulfed by the onward trend of growth. Then the site is ready for development and probably can be sold at a profit. The operator is the city's keenest student of its expansion; he can detect where increases in values may be expected in three, five, or ten years.

A young man once went into the office of a large New York real estate concern and said that he had been studying the possible use of vacant properties in Westchester County, just north of the big metropolis, and that he knew of some that seemed to have great possibilities. Harry Hall, a veteran broker, talked with him; but since the company did not operate outside of New York City, he suggested to the young man that he see certain investors. Several weeks later one of the investors bought a property from the young broker, who got an $8,000 commission, and later several very large deals were also consummated. Only the vision of a young broker was needed to do this, but he got his reward.

In Cleveland, Joseph Laronge, one of the city's leading brokers, came to the conclusion that a new theater district was needed. There were a few theaters in the congested part of lower Euclid Avenue, but they were old and out of date. He solicited capital and developed several important theater projects in the upper Euclid Avenue district. These were among the first theaters in the county in which ample foyers were provided for taking care of crowds in cold and inclement weather.

The promotional genius of J. C. Nichols in Kansas City resulted in some of the highest residential and business developments to be found anywhere in the world. Mr. Nichols started subdividing in a small way. He then began to deal in better types of property, finally going into large projects with separate business districts. Half a dozen outlying business communities stand as monuments to Mr. Nichols' genius.

A broker in New York City, who conducted just an ordinary real estate business, had a hunch one day that a certain property which was ready for a new building should be developed into a headquarters for the knit-goods trade. Without putting a penny into the project, Charles G. Edwards, one-time president of the National Association of Real Estate Boards, accomplished the following:

1. He went to a few engaged in the knit-goods business, and found that his idea was right and that they could be interested.

2. He approached the owner of the land and got a 30-day open option, which he later had to renew for two more such periods. Nothing was paid for the option.

3. Edwards had an architect, without charge, make sketches of the exterior of a building and some typical floor plans, promising the architect nothing but saying that if the building went ahead he would try to get the architect the job.

4. Edwards took the plans to a builder and got an estimate of cost of construction, also without charge. The builder hoped that if the structure went ahead he would get the job (and he later did).

5. Edwards then prepared a "set up," in connection with which it was necessary to get estimates of cost of servicing the building with electricity, gas, water, and telephones. An insurance broker estimated the cost of insurance, and, after a lot of hard work, Edwards had a reasonably accurate idea of the cost of maintaining the building.

6. Then came the matter of getting the money to go ahead, but before doing so Edwards went to one of the large title companies to get a report. He learned that the title to the property was clear and merchantable. With this, and upon representation that a buyer for the property would be provided, the broker interviewed banks and loan companies until he got a satisfactory commitment for a mortgage.

7. Then came the job of getting commitments on the floor space of the large 18-story building. The knit-goods men got together, formed a committee, and agreed to take most of the space, so that problem was solved.

8. With the preliminary work out of the way, the site under option, the cost of the building definitely set, and the cost of operation known, it was a comparatively easy matter to find a buyer for the land, who was also ready to assume the necessary mortgage and provide the additional capital required.

The building was erected. Before the roof went on it was 100 per cent rented. In four years' time the property paid off every dollar the buyer put into it. Mr. Edwards got his commission on the sale of the land, a commission for obtaining the first mortgage, and a part of the insurance commission, and in addition was given a *ten-year contract* for the management of the property—and he had not put a cent of his own into the proposition! *That is creative selling!* Mr. Edwards put through similar deals over and over again in New York City, and it can be done anywhere by anyone who will take the time and trouble.

The phrase "plus value" was invented by an Eastern operator who made it his business to search out sites that needed improving to a higher and better use. He would perceive, for example, that a new theater was needed in a district that was fast going over into that type of occupancy. Options on the land were secured, a building projected, and the entire enterprise pressed through to a successful conclusion. The site occupied by old ramshackle buildings had one value. The beautiful new theater was able to earn a vastly greater return. It gave to the land what the promoter called "plus value," and he was right. "Plus value" can be added to many sites by the application of some mental effort, followed by constructive promotional work.

Many a property, well situated in a mid-town section, becomes a "white elephant" until some shrewd and enterprising broker comes along and envisions a new structure for the site. It is cleared and an appropriate improvement placed upon it, whereupon it becomes a profitable investment if not a virtual gold mine.

In many cities throughout the country, far-seeing brokers realize the need for centering related types of businesses in certain restricted areas. Groups of produce-commission men are housed in large market warehouses. Jewelry manufacturers are grouped in a large single structure. An entire block of stores is set aside for railroad, steamship, and airline ticket offices. Whole blocks of buildings are rented to firms engaged in the household furniture business. In one city a whole district is given over to auction houses dealing entirely in second-hand goods. In Los Angeles, a section of Washington Boulevard became known as "Death Valley" because a score or more of morticians settled down together in a space of two or three blocks.

Chicago has its Merchandise Mart, one of the largest buildings in the country, where hundreds of wholesalers display their goods. This is the outgrowth of an idea born in the brain of a real estate man. Many other cities have similar enterprises.

Almost every city has its medical buildings where doctors, dentists, and X-ray specialists congregate. Indeed, most cities have many small buildings owned by groups of doctors who find it convenient to be in close proximity to each other. Such districts are promotional ventures and for the most part were conceived by realty brokers who had sites listed and saw opportunities for selling and improving them.

Behind many new hotel promotions have been real estate brokers who saw the need and proceeded to do something about filling it. Markets of all kinds, including supermarkets with eight or ten different tenants, are conceptions, in many cases, of realty men.

Perhaps the commonest type of real estate promotion has been the laying out of subdivisions, of which there are many in every city throughout the land. In earlier days the operator of such an enterprise just ploughed parallel ditches and called the space between them streets, sold lots, and promptly, and sometimes hastily, went away from there. That has all changed now. The modern developer installs every improvement and

pays for it, plans and builds a number of houses to establish·
the character of the neighborhood, and then sells the completed homesites to newcomers. This type of development has
been found to be best for the community and also the
most profitable to the operator.

Resort developments seldom come into existence except for
the creative genius of a real estate man. Large beautiful
wooded tracts on the shores of lakes, in the mountains, or along
the ocean are taken over, improved, subdivided, and sold to
eager patrons who would never have had the opportunity of
participating in such an enterprise had not the bright idea been
hatched in the mind of some realtor. New amusement parks
are in the same category, as are marinas, skating rinks, and
bowling alleys.

Even the cemeteries of the country are for the most part the
brain children of promoters who got groups of persons together
to sponsor them. One such enterprise, Forest Lawn Memorial
Park, in Los Angeles, is said to have a total investment in land,
splendid mausoleums, art glass windows, statuary, and other
improvements in excess of $20,000,000. And it all came from
the vision of a man who thought graveyards were gloomy places
to visit and that a resting place for departed loved ones could
be made beautiful and a pleasant place to visit.

Perhaps the greatest promotional enterprise ever sponsored
by a real estate man was that of the great industrial empire,
including a number of huge railroad systems, assembled by
O. P. Van Sweringen of Cleveland. As a boy he sold newspapers
on the streets of Cleveland, with his brother M. J. Van Sweringen. As young men the brothers went into the real estate
business, doing indifferently well until they secured a selling
contract on a large tract of vacant land that later became
known as Shaker Heights. After selling some 2,000 acres of this
original holding of the religious sect known as the Shakers, the
Van Sweringens took on great additional areas to market. O. P.
Van Sweringen conceived the notion of a rapid transit line to
Shaker Heights. The Nickel Plate Railroad was on the market
in those days, kicking around looking for a buyer. He entered

into negotations to get a right of way into the center of Cleveland for his trolley line over the Nickel Plate's tracks. Finding it impossible to negotiate a right of way, Van Sweringen bought the entire railroad and started a series of building developments in Cleveland that ran into many millions, including a 1,000-room hotel, a large department store, a post-office building, and several large and imposing office buildings besides a Union Terminal for half a dozen railroad systems which he later added to his industrial empire. Few, if any, other real estate promoters have ever pyramided their gains to such a large sum as did O. P. Van Sweringen, who, as a warm personal friend of this author, once remarked: "Get a sound idea—stick to it tenaciously, *and you'll win!*"

Every broker and salesman at some time has the chance to develop a good idea through promotional means. Every one of them sees opportunities at times that he *simply just knows* can be made to pan out if they are handled right. The inclination is to let someone else do it, that it is too much work, or too risky, or is not in the regular line of activity that has been engaged in. This is where the initial mistake is made. If it is a good idea, talk about it with someone you can trust and see if you cannot work out a set-up that can be submitted to someone who would be able to handle the transaction. That is the way big promotional enterprises get under way. After handling one of them, the next one comes easier. Eventually the time may come when working on the larger promotional deals may prove much more attractive and profitable than engaging in regular brokerage activities.

Never get the idea that the opportunity for creating new enterprises is not always present. Buildings are constantly wearing out. Old theaters need to be replaced by new ones, as various improvements in three-dimensional photography and projection evolve. The entire country seems likely to work on shorter shifts in the days to come, as much of the heavy and tedious work is done by machinery. Vast opportunities for new forms of entertainment and use of leisure time will become apparent as the years roll by. More playgrounds, more airports, more beach and mountain resorts will be needed. The opportunities seem boundless.

On the ground, in the air, and on the waters of rivers, bays, and oceans—new fast forms of transportation will come into being, and with them the necessity for servicing them.

New ideas will be created for changing the present types of buildings used as dwellings and for business and commercial uses. Here may lie endless opportunities for stimulating the promotional mind.

Harry Hall, of New York, in urging that imagination be let loose to consider creative real estate deals, paraphrased the familiar words of St. Paul:

Though I am as industrious as a bee and wear out a pair of shoes every week pounding the sidewalks and have not imagination, I shall never be more than an average broker. And though I satisfy Diogenes, and have not imagination, I shall never lead my customers to romantic and highly profitable investments.

Imagination discovers things unseen to other eyes, suggests new uses for run-down properties, and anticipates coming expansion.

Imagination rejoices not in the ordinary but in the unusual.

Imagination never faileth but maketh activity in the dullest market.

For some see in part, as through a glass darkly, but imagination makes all things clear.

And so abide industry, integrity, and imagination, these three; *but the greatest of these is imagination!*

CHAPTER 19

Sales Kits, Property

Set-Ups, and Briefs

A WELL-ORGANIZED REAL ESTATE OF-
fice provides its salesmen with adequate sales kits. A broker or
salesman working alone will see to it that he has his own equipment, ready to display to customers when the occasion demands.

A sales kit is really a wide assortment of information about a
real estate man's business, carefully selected, properly organized, and occasionally displayed for the benefit of clients he is
trying to interest in the purchase of listed properties. It may
be in any of several different forms. It may be a small loose-
leaf book in which are crammed typewritten pages containing
a vast amount of detailed information, or a larger loose-leaf
book in which pictures and maps are also included, or an
attaché case in which elaborate photographs, building designs,
maps, and statistical data are presented. A sales kit should
should never be static—that is, the owner of it must be able
at any time to remove some things and insert others that seem
of greater importance and of more interest to prospective
customers.

A sales kit is prepared and maintained for the following
purposes:

1. To maintain in an orderly way the information a salesman

collects about properties, about his neighborhood, about his town.

2. To display maps of a town, of the particular neighborhoods in which a salesman works, and of individual properties or subdivisions he is seeking to sell.

3. To make possible for instant use and ready presentation all kinds of sales information given to the salesman by his office, or which he has assembled, about a wide range of subjects.

4. To back up the personal statements of a salesman. All kinds of authoritative statements and information may be used.

6. Finally, to help a prospective customer visualize the merits of a property so that he will be induced to take favorable action.

In every sale a broker or a salesman attempts to make, he will find that a different line of argument will be needed to influence a prospect. The facts that might apply in one case are useless in another. Seldom is the sales kit used in the same way twice. Properly utilized, it can become a fine-edged tool that will carve out commissions for its user.

Only authentic and authorized information should appear in a sales kit, and a salesman should be able promptly to confirm it if it is in any way questioned. He should be so familiar with his sales kit and use it often enough so that he can almost quote it from memory, and always be able to find any item he wishes without trouble.

Here are some of the kinds of exhibits and information a well-organized sales kit will contain:

1. Maps of the county, the city, and neighborhood.

2. Zoning maps of the city showing all classes of use to which property may be put; also a copy of the zoning ordinance itself.

3. Detailed maps of a subdivision, if that is what a salesman is selling.

4. Maps showing contemplated improvements of important areas, particularly such things as airfields, beach developments, and playgrounds.

5. Detailed schedules of population growth by years and decades.

6. Information about assessed values, tax rates, and ratio of assessments to full market value.

7. Sample contract forms used in different types of sales.

8. Blank offers to purchase which a salesman can use on the spot when necessary.

9. Commission rates and schedules of the local realty board.

10 Records showing the volume of business done by the office with which the salesman has been connected for the past several years, indicating the scope of accomplishments.

11. Tables showing the number of monthly payments necessary to pay for a home, at different interest rates.

12. Information concerning current costs of different types of new buildings, by square foot and cubic foot methods.

13. Costs of adding such improvements as new heating plants, water heaters, new bathroom fixtures, fallout shelters, air-conditioning, and other improvements appearing in house remodeling programs.

14. Information about painting and decorating costs, which can be readily supplied to home buyers.

15. Counts showing percentage of vacancies in a town or district, if such are available and actually exist.

16. Depreciation tables for various kinds of buildings.

17. A table of rentals stated in percentages of gross sales which various retail businesses are able to pay, for use in renting business properties.

18. Model statements indicating the method for arriving at the sales price of a house and of an apartment.

19. Surveys of business and industrial areas which may be available from chambers of commerce and other organizations.

20. For industrial and business brokers, detailed maps showing different railroads, with their connections and principal plants, and strip maps of business "hot spots."

21. Data and statements concerning available power supplies, cost per kilowatt, gas, electricity, and water rates, and so forth.

22. A list of suggestions on how to find prospects, for the salesman to use in refreshing his memory.

23. A brief statement of the best methods followed by experts in making property appraisals.

24. Real estate axioms and quotations by famous men on what they think of real estate as an investment and for home ownership.

25. Codes of ethics of local boards and their national association.

26. Newspaper clippings about contemplated public improvements, estimated growth, and so on.

27. A brief but complete historical sketch of the city or town.

28. Data about number of schools, churches, miles of streets, sewer mains, and information about transportation services.

29. A brief outline of the salesman's real estate organization, how it started, what it has accomplished, who its head is, and so forth.

30. Rules pointing the way for successful selling.

31. A data sheet showing current costs of furniture, carpets, draperies, colored television, refrigerators, and other household equipment for informing prospects who expect to furnish the house they buy. Check with stores every three months for accuracy.

32. The number of different sized lots that an acre can be cut into after allowing land for street uses.

33. Pictures, including actual photographs and clippings from papers and magazines, showing typical and interesting house plans, kitchen and bathroom arrangements, and so on.

34. Detailed information about prevailing tax rates in different districts of a city and its suburbs.

35. Lease expirations, noted well in advance so tenants can be contacted in time to ascertain if new locations are required.

36. A printed or multigraphed schedule entitled "Planning My Day," set up hour by hour so a salesman can sit down at night and plan his next day's work.

37. Data about Veterans Administration and Federal Housing Administration methods and rules for financing property.

38. Reasons for owning your own home.

39. A statement of what a man can afford to pay for a home out of a definitely known income.

40. A schedule showing office rules for dividing commissions on various kinds of deals.

41. Photographs showing houses and business blocks before and after remodeling, and schedules of costs of doing such work.

42. Occupancy maps of business districts showing types of tenants, their businesses, and the rents they pay.

Not every sales kit may contain all of the foregoing, but the list is suggestive of things that may be included and that will be useful in proving to the prospect, from time to time, that the salesman is well versed in his business and knows what he is talking about.

In addition to the kit itself, a broker or salesman should always carry in his car a tape measure and rules, a hammer, nails, and screws, to use when signs are being erected, and a Polaroid camera for taking pictures of interesting houses or vacant lots and their surroundings.

Property set-ups are used in every live real estate office. A broker or salesman may know everything there is to know about a property, but a prospect promptly forgets most of it after hearing it. The wise salesman will leave with the prospective buyer an interesting and well constructed set-up, containing the information in written form so it can be studied by the prospect in the seclusion of his own office or home. Set-ups, which are usually typewritten statements on the letterheads of the brokerage office, include, among other things, subheads dealing with the following:

1. Location of the property and its advantages—proximity to transportation and business districts, churches, parks, and so on.

2. Size of the lot, indicating if it is a corner or if there is an alley in the rear.

3. Description, in detail, of building improvements, including the number of floors, square-foot areas, uses to which various parts are put, and so forth.

4. Statement of income from the property, in detail, with gross income totaled at the right.

5. Statement of actual or estimated expenses, in detail, with a total at the right that can be deducted from the gross income shown under item 4, thus giving a proven net return for the property.

6. Encumbrances on the property—total amount, rate of interest, and date of expiration.

7. Price and terms of sale.

8. Comments of interest concerning the property.

9. Name and address of the broker submitting the set-up.

10. Mention of the source of information outlined above.

Statements may contain one, two, three, or more pages, according to the importance of a property and the broker's desire to elaborate on it. It may go into minute detail or may simply cover the broad essentials the broker wishes to convey to the prospect. Every broker will develop his own technique in building his statements.

A property brief is actually an elaborate, detailed statement or set-up. Most property briefs have attractive covers of special cardboard or paper, frequently in colors. They are usually typewritten. It is not customary to make very many copies. The broker wno assembles and uses them does not broadcast them but lends them out, one at a time, to some qualified prospect who he thinks is genuinely interested in perusing them. He intimates that he is doing the prospect a favor by letting him see the brief at all, and sets a definite time for its return, calling for it at that time. This gives the broker an opportunity to meet the prospect again and to make a final effort to close his deal.

In addition to all of the information contained in set-ups, often greatly elaborated as to descriptive features, property briefs usually include carefully detailed maps of the premises and surroundings, showing the floor areas and the layout of surrounding grounds. Most fine property briefs are got up for the purpose of selling large houses and estates, although they sometimes assume the same kind of selling job in connection with large industrial and business plants.

In addition to floor diagrams, photographs are extensively used in property briefs. These are enlarged so they may form pages by themselves. They show various views of the property —always to the best advantage. The picture may be taken by the broker himself, or they may be the work of a professional photographer if the property warrants it. Large suburban estates lend themselves to elaborate descriptions and fine photographic work.

Set-ups and property briefs are seldom solely responsible for making sales. They are merely tools the broker or salesman uses to arouse attention and interest and to encourage the prospect to make up his mind. No interview about an important property should be completed without some kind of set-up or property brief being left for the client to digest. If it does nothing else, it gives the broker a chance to make a return call on the customer.

Some offices engage in a form of institutional advertising that is often profitable. They create and distribute circulars or booklets dealing with the persons who are affiliated with the organization, showing the scope of its activities and detailing the records and experiences of many of the principal members of the firm. Pictures of the office, its various departments, and some of its activities in the way of subdivisions or business buildings which have been promoted are often shown. Some brokers use circulars outlining the particular activities they engage in, their experience, and so on, and leave them with clients, who thus get a better idea of the background and importance of the person with whom they are dealing.

Use of sales kits, set-ups, and property briefs as well as kindred types of typewritten and printed matter can become powerful weapons in the battle to sell real estate. It takes time, intelligence, and sustained effort to create them, but the results attained through their constant use often spell distinct success in a real estate office.

CHAPTER 20

Income and

Apartment Properties

RESIDENTIAL RENTAL PROPERTIES ARE becoming big business everywhere. The trend is more and more toward apartment dwelling. As families grow up, the couples whose children are all gone find that they can rent an attractive apartment much more economically than they can continue to maintain a house and lot.

The trend is toward high-rise apartments and the newer entity, the condominium, where people can actually *buy* apartments. Any way you figure it, the volume of business created by the transfer of these housing complexes to new owners is running into billions each year. Every brokerage office is interested in income properties and should maintain a department for selling them, and in some cases for managing them.

Income properties include everything from a two-family house up to the largest apartment houses and hotels. They are purchased almost entirely for the purpose of obtaining a return on the funds invested. This applies even to the two-family house where the owner lives in one unit and rents the other to help him pay expenses and secure a return on the cost of his building and land.

The returns on investment funds demanded by the owners of various kinds of income properties differ. A person owning

162

a small four-family building may be satisfied with seven to eight per cent net after all expenses are figured in and due allowance is made for repairs and depreciation. For larger structures, the returns vary in different parts of the country. Most owners like to receive a minimum of eight to ten per cent, though, for various reasons, it is not always possible to do so. And, of course, the yield from residential investment property changes with conditions. Hotels, at one time paying more than ten per cent, are no longer attractive investments. And the motel is no longer the gold mine it once seemed to be.

Every brokerage office, no matter what its size, will attract some listings of income properties situated in its neighborhood. When a broker establishes his office, he naturally makes a survey of his neighborhood to determine what kinds of properties are available. He tries to list those nearest him, or at least to get sufficient information about them to know whether they are soon to be on the market for sale.

If you expect to specialize in this type of brokerage work, you will have to go into matters quite thoroughly. Make a complete survey of a given territory, selected by yourself, and list every building on a card. When information is not forthcoming from occupants of the property itself, the official city or county records will reveal the ownership. Get in touch with the owner and find out whether the property is for sale, or whether it will be for sale later.

It is important to use a good listing card on which all the facts can be listed that you and your client will need to know. Besides a complete physical description of a property, be sure to secure information about the gross income and its sources. Then make a complete check of expenses, including taxes and special assessments, to be deducted from the gross income to determine the net income, which, capitalized, will represent a fair valuation for the combined land and improvements. It is also necessary to be explicit about the price, the terms on which the property can be purchased, and the mortgage encumbrance, including who holds it, the rate of interest, and when it expires. *Get as much information on the first call* as possible. It is usually easier to get the owner to talk freely then than later when you may be involved in a deal.

Having assembled all possible information about a property, it is the duty of the listing broker or salesman to analyze it carefully and prepare a brief or statement, organizing the information and interpreting it for the benefit of a prospective buyer. Some brokers become quite skillful in preparing such statements or set-ups, and thereby assist in the work of convincing the buyer that the property has merit, is correctly priced, and is a good investment. Great care should be taken to present the facts carefully and honestly, as a false statement may bring a suit for misrepresentation should a buyer acquire a property and then find that the facts concerning it were not in keeping with representations to be found in the broker's statement. It is sometimes well to have such a statement approved by the property owner but some brokers feel that if they do this the owner might be so impressed with the advantages of his own property as mirrored in the statement that he may decide not to sell it.

In preparing and submitting statements about properties offered for sale, a broker is dependent almost entirely upon owners for all information. Some owners are very careful to convey correct facts about their properties; others are careless and frequently make misstatements. This may not be intentional, but it may get a broker into considerable difficulty and even leave him open to a suit for misrepresentation if wrong information is conveyed to a client. For this reason many brokers append a paragraph at the end of all statements, reading somewhat as follows:

The above statement is made upon information furnished by the owner, or from sources which we deem to be reliable; for which we assume no responsibility, but which we believe to be correct. This property is offered subject to prior sale, change in price, or withdrawal from the market without notice.

or

Note—This statement has been prepared from information furnished to us by the owner or his representatives, but we assume no liability for errors or omissions therein, and do not guarantee the correctness of any of the information furnished to us by owner or his representatives. It is also given with the understanding that all negotiations relating to the purchase or exchange of the property described shall be conducted through our office.

or

Data and conclusions are memoranda only. No liability for errors or omissions. Subject to sale, withdrawal, or change of price without notice.

Such a notice prompts the client, before finally accepting the statements, either to investigate the statements himself to determine if they are authentic or to require the broker to do so. The following is a typical brief statement on a 25-unit brick apartment building listed at $225,000:

Agena Apartments
1500 Grand Avenue, Middletown

Location. Property is situated on the easterly side of Grand Avenue, which is three streets east of Main Street, and a little over two blocks north of Cordova Boulevard. It is about 300 feet north of Adams Avenue, being the fourth apartment building. Very close to shops, theaters, radio broadcasting stations, studios, restaurants, etc.

This is one of the best renting districts in Middletown, the area being built up with high-grade apartments. A bus comes to the nearest corner and one can walk to the nearest shopping center in five minutes.

Land. The lot has a frontage of 100 feet and is 180 feet deep to a concrete paved alley, 20 feet wide. This lot was recently appraised at $75,000. It is level.

Improvements. The apartment is two stories high, of solid brick construction, covered with stucco, and painted throughout. Unusually attractive in its architectural design, the structure is much better built than the average and is certain to maintain its value for many years with but slight upkeep. The panel section about the front entrance is of marble and the foyer has a marble floor. This latter is quite spacious and has a small telephone room extending from it. The foyer is carpeted, as are also all halls and stairways. Carpets are new and in excellent condition. The property has been owned by a retired contractor, who has taken pride in maintaining it in a first-class condition.

The building contains four large units, one having four rooms and bath and the other three being what are known as doubles. There are also twenty single apartments and a small bachelor room. On the back of the lot, with access from the alley, are ten modern heated garages.

The building is furnished throughout in an excellent manner, with A-1 refrigeration and built-in incinerator. Each apartment is finely furnished and is completely air-conditioned. The building is set well back from the street and there is a spacious platform or balcony at the street entrance level where guests may rest in gaily colored chairs. There is steam heat throughout the entire building, with ample radiation in every suite.

This structure is well above the average in design and construction and is one that will appeal to the owner who may want to reside in his own property. The four-room suite designed for the owner, contains living room, dining room, kitchen, and one bedroom as well as bath. It will be available at the close of escrow.

Income. There are four units at $165, twelve at $120, three at $112.50, and six at $105 each.

Present total monthly income is $4,120, or annually $37,080

Estimated Expenses

Manager (couple)	$270.00	
Laundry	69.00	
Gas, light, water	270.00	
Insurance	22.50	
Taxes ($1860 yearly)	156.00	
	$787.50 monthly, or annually ..	9,450
	Net Return	$27,630

Price. This shows a net return of over 12% on a purchase price of $225,000.

Encumbrances. This property is now held subject to a first trust deed with an unpaid balance of approximately $85,500, repayable $712.50 monthly at 5% annually. There is a second trust deed of record with an unpaid balance of approximately $22,200, repayable $240 monthly at 6% interest. This loan can be paid off at any time without penalty. Present encumbrances total $107,700.

Recapitulation

Net return on rentals annually		$27,630
Monthly payoff on first trust deed	$712.50	
Monthly payoff on second trust deed	240.00	
	$952.50, or annually	11,430
Net cash return is $450 monthly, or annually		$16,200

This is 13.8% on $117,300 required as a down payment.

It may be noted in the foregoing statement that no allowance has been made for repairs or depreciation. Such an allowance is not always included in apartment house set-ups by brokers, as it varies widely and may be figured separately. A property statement seldom contains every item which a buyer of a property must take into consideration.

If a property is owner-managed, it is not necessary to consider the item of management cost; it must be considered, however, if someone must be hired to look after the property.

The most successful apartment house brokers are those who know how to analyze their properties and to prepare and interpret statements of income and outgo, for this is the vital information the buyer wants to know and to have proved to him. There follows a very complete form in which full information is provided for qualified buyers.

Kintups Apartments

24 Apts. Furnished——11 Singles—12 Doubles—1 Bachelor

Location. 2325 Glen Grove Avenue. Ideal, close-in location. Near to park, buses, shops, etc.

Lot. 59 X 153, approximately.

Improvements. Three-story exceptionally well built brick apartment building. Building contains approximately 18,000 sq. ft. Completely furnished throughout. Automatic elevator. Tile floors in baths, showers over tubs. Colored tile sinks. Rooms are all good size. 12 of the 24 apts. are corner ones. Inner-spring mattresses, large dressing closets. Built-in vanities. Built-in dressers. Twin beds in some doubles. Bachelor has twin beds and elec. refrig. Good size dinettes. Ivory woodwork and painted walls throughout. Entire property, including furnishings, in very good condition.

No maid, laundry or phone services furnished. Owner pays for all utilities.

First *Trust Deed.*	$126,000	Payable $963.90 per mo., including 4½% int. Loan runs until paid, which is approx. 15 yrs. $963.90 a month is $11,566.80 per year, which is as of this date $5,670 a yr. int. and $5,895 prin. payments. Loan contains additional prepayment privileges. This is a new loan just placed on the property by the Presidential Insurance Co. of Washington, D.C.
Second *Trust Deed.*	$ 21,000	Payable $210 per month, or more, including 6% int. and running until paid, which is approx. 15 yrs. This is an exceptionally choice second trust deed. $210 a month is $2,520 a year, which is as of this date $1,260 a yr. int. and $1,260 a yr. prin. payments.
Cash Equity.	$ 75,000	
Price.	$222,000	*No Less—No Offers—No Trades*

Income

Total monthly income is $3,066 per mo. Eleven singl. rent from $166.50 per mo. to $114 per mo. Twelve doubles rent from $126 per mo. to $162.20 per mo. One bach. rents for $114.75 per mo. Total yearly income 24 apts. is $36,792.

A SAFE RENTAL BRACKET FOR THE INVESTOR

ANALYSIS

Per Year

1. Income schedule $3,066 per mo., or per yr. $36,792
2. Less manager's apartment at $105 per month, or per yr.   1,260
3. Balance $35,532

ESTIMATED EXPENSES
PER MONTH & PER YEAR

4. Light, water, power, gas, average $264 per mo. $3,168
   Insurance premiums 900
   Manager's salary $75 per month 900
   Taxes, real estate 3,216
   Reserve for allowance for repairs 1,500
5. Total expenses per year .... $ 9,684

6. Balance left if building were clear and before loan requirements $25,848

7. Less 4½% interest on 1st Trust Deed of
   $126,000 per year $5,670
   Less 6% interest on 2nd Trust Deed of $21,000
   per year 1,260
   Total interest charges on trust deeds per year .... $ 6,930

8. Balance left before principal payments on loans per
   year $18,918

9. Less principal payment on 1st Trust Deed per
   year $5,895
   Less principal payment on 2nd Trust Deed per
   year 1,260

   Total principal payments on Trust Deeds per year .... $ 7,155

10. Net Cash Spendable Dollars Left Per Year $11,763

SUMMARY

11. Cash return per
    year .... $11,763 or approx. 16% on $75,000 equity
12. Payoff on loans
    per year 7,155
13. Total return per
    year .... $18,918 or approx. 25½% on $75,000 equity
14. Reserve for possible
    vacancies 10% of
    rent schedule per
    year, or .... $ 3,553
15. *Annual Return*
    after 10% allow-
    ance for vacancies $15,365 or approx. 20½% on $75,000 equity
16. Depreciation on
    building and
    equipment .... $ 4,200
17. *Total net yearly re-*
    turn after all ex-
    penses, principal
    and interest
    charges on loans,
    allowance for va-
    cancies & depre-
    ciation .... $11,165 or approx. 15% on $75,000 equity
18. The four percentage figures above total approximately 77%

19. 77% divided by the 4 percentages shows an over-all average per cent per year return of approx. 19% on $75,000 equity
FOR FURTHER INFORMATION CONSULT . . . . & Co., Exclusive Agents.

Sales methods used in disposing of an apartment in no way differ from those governing other types of real estate.[2] Having advertised the property in the newspapers or by means of circulars and personal contacts with prospective buyers, the salesman finally finds someone who, he is convinced, should own the property. He centers his selling technique on the prospect, presents his statements, shows the property, hammers away at the advantages the prospect will enjoy through ownership, and finally gets a purchase offer signed, accompanied by a check.

In a city where many apartments are constantly passing from owners to buyers, it is well to build up a prospect list and to use circulars, which can carry the message more fully and convincingly than a mere newspaper advertisement. Contrast the following advertisement used for a different property but by the same company that issued the foregoing complete statement and analysis. You can see how much more convincing the statement is.

Pays

$13,200 a Year

NET ON $45,000 CASH EQUITY. Splendid close-in location. On South Madison near 6th. Well built, 2 story, large lot, 27 singles, 1 bachelor, furnished. All apartments large and light. LOW RENTS, average $84. Monthly income $2340 or $28,080 a year. Taxes only $1536. No laundry or services. Very economical to operate. BRAND NEW 16-YEAR 5% insurance company loan. Price is right. No offers, no trades. Principals only.
    . . . . . & CO.

[2] See Chapter XVI, "Selling Mupltiple Dwellings," in *Selling Real Estate,* 3rd Ed., by Stanley L. McMichael (Englewood Cliffs, N. J.: Prentice-Hall, Inc.)

The ad interests prospects who desire to acquire an apartment property, but the foregoing statement becomes a sharp-edged tool in the hands of the salesman to drive home his sales arguments.

Who is a prospect? Anyone who has funds to invest is a partial answer to the query. Add to this owners who have sold properties and are again in the market to buy. Their names can be gleaned from newspaper articles, from county transfer records, and from remarks made by friends and acquaintances. Many prospects telephone in response to ads or visit real estate offices. If their names are not recorded on prospect cards, they are soon lost sight of until *some other broker* contacts and sells them!

There are two distinct types of apartment projects. One is the property with suites that are unfurnished. A tenant must have his own furniture to move into a building of this type. The other is the furnished apartment house, usually comprising many small units of two or three rooms with baths, which are practically a type of glorified hotel suite except that they include kitchens. Some owners prefer unfurnished suites because their tenants do not move so often. On the other hand, such suites do not rent for as high prices as do the furnished ones. The broker must be able to weigh and analyze the type of property he is selling and advance the necessary arguments to make it an attractive investment.

Rental properties at resorts, beaches, and mountain retreats often prove profitable investment ventures and are sold regularly through brokers' offices. In normal times such properties have high income returns for several months and then close for the remainder of the year. There are certain hazards in connection with their ownership that should be carefully considered.

Dealing in income properties is an important branch of work in any brokerage office, and it should be constantly fostered and developed by examining the way in which other brokers operate and through experience gained by the actual handling of such deals.

CHAPTER 21

Business Property

SEVERAL IMPORTANT FACTORS MUST BE considered in the purchase of business property. Among them are the *type* of real estate, the *location*, the *terms*, and the *use* to which the property is to be put; that is, whether it is to be used for the investor's own business or leased to tenants who will pay rents and thus provide an adequate return on the money invested, allowing for maintenance and amortization over a term of years.

There are many types and sub-types of business properties, including skyscraper office buildings as well as groups of three or four one-story fifteen-foot stores in a neighborhood business center. Most of the larger cities went on a skyscraping spree in boom days, and scores of huge buildings were erected. There was only a promotional urge behind many of them and little actual profit was realized on the invested capital after they were completed and partially occupied. Many of those structures went through real estate liquidation, fell into the hands of mortgage holders, and were resold for fractions of their original production costs. To the average investor who desired to secure a satisfactory return on his money, or to the promoter who was willing to take a chance, many such properties offered opportunities of profit when resold.

Many large downtown buildings in most cities have been erected as the direct result of promotional activities by an organization or an individual who desired to erect a building as a civic or personal monument. Probably fewer of this type will be built in future years. Exceptions are large department stores, theaters, and hotels. The average investor might well keep away from large promotional enterprises.

Small downtown business properties may occasionally be acquired at reasonable prices. That is, they may be a good investment to a buyer if he has a use for them in connection with his own business. Booms in many cities have caused retail business districts to stretch and burst their economic boundaries. For blocks beyond the point where the pedestrian traffic provided natural retail buying power, business buildings were erected and in most cases temporarily occupied. When a depression came, scores of small commercial enterprises went out of business or consolidated. Chain-store growth aggravated this condition. Decentralization of business to outlying areas helped a bit, too. A result was that there came into existence during a depression a black border of vacant store and business properties around the fringe of active downtown business areas. Some such buildings have scarcely ever earned their taxes and property maintenance charges. They would scarcely be bargains at any price unless one had a definite profitable use to which to put them. This, then, is the answer to the problem of downtown business property: Don't buy such property unless there is a definite use for it, or unless, upon careful analysis, the property shows concrete evidence of honestly earning sufficient income to pay for its carry, and a reasonable return on the investment placed in it. Then it can be recommended to clients.

Brokers are warned against the selling and buying of business property in so-called blighted districts or twilight zones to be found in every large city about the outer edge of its downtown business areas, extending out, in some cases, into residential districts beyond. Only if there is a proven, profitable use for such property should it be considered.

Actually, the downtown situation is continuously depreciating in a major proportion of our cities. Even those downtown properties which are in good business districts may not be able to hold up over the long haul. Both brokers and speculators should survey the local trends. Fortunately, some cities are solving their downtown deterioration problems by creating shopping malls, constructing small parks, providing adequate parking, etc. So, in some situations, and depending upon the trend, downtown property may be expected to grow in value. But the watchword is "caution."

Broadly speaking, there are three general districts where business property can be bought and made to pay its way. With good business conditions, some such properties may be made to return handsomely on their investment cost. The first is to be found in outlying business neighborhoods of cities, including any existing or potential neighborhood business center where there is a density of population growing up around a natural trading spot, which does not too closely adjoin another such center to offer too great competition.

Many existing subdivisions, established in earlier years in many cities, will continue to grow and build up their purchasing power, which will naturally be translated into business activity in the shopping centers in such localities. The chief difficulty is that the owners of vacant business properties in such centers often want to skim all the cream, and their asking prices are usually out of line with what such properties can be made to earn. It requires keen study and analysis to select the right spot and establish the right price for live business properties in such areas.

The second place in which there are often chances to buy good business properties is in the satellite towns around a big city. Indeed, there is nearly always a chance in any live outlying town to convert a choice centrally located site into a real revenue producer by changing tenancy from old-line stores into new, snappy chain stores with tenants who go out after business aggressively and are willing to share profits with landlords through percentage leases on gross sales. In many satellite towns near large cities, radical changes in tenancy can be brought about that will result in substantial increases in the earning capacity of properties which have good futures and will steadily improve in value as the communities in which they are situated grow in population and buying power.

The third place where potential business properties may sometimes be acquired is at natural suburban cross-currents of vehicular travel—which today may be occupied by gas stations but which ten, twenty, or twenty-five years from now may be important business centers.

Every observer of realty growth knows of important outlying business intersections which twenty or thirty years ago were hay or grain fields. The population growth of large cities may not proceed at the same rate as in the past. Nevertheless there will be important gains and shifting in population, much of which will have a tendency to settle in new outlying neighborhoods, supporting new business centers, which will spring into being from small beginnings or, as in the past, develop from vacant cross-roads into busy marts of retail trade.

The investor interested in retail business property naturally is attracted by the probable net yield of such property, after all charges have been taken care of. A seasoned downtown business property that definitely yields 8 to 10 per cent and that seems stabilized, with a good future assured for a number of years, should be a satisfactory one in which to invest money. The risk always sets the investment rate of return. Outlying "hot-spots," where chain stores prevail, may be purchased on a 10 to 12 per cent net return; less important locations, in less favored neighborhoods, pay more.

Business property is probably the most liquid type of real estate there is; that is, it can be sold most readily and the investor's money realized on the shortest notice, provided it is really a sound investment and is priced in keeping with its earning capacity. At all times it has a strong element of safety, for even in depressions, prime business properties hold up better than any other investment and are more readily merchandised. At almost any time of the realty cycle, carefully selected business property in strategic locations offers good investment possibilities. Reasonably acquired, it can usually be depended upon to maintain its value.

Almost any kind of real estate, carefully chosen, is a good investment. Every family should own its own home, first of all. There are excellent possibilities of profit in the ownership and operation of various kinds of multiple dwellings, furnished apartments, and hotels. Many kinds of industrial and commercial properties can be operated profitably. Every manufacturer should own his own factory. When it comes to selecting the best and most profitable type of property for investment purposes, however, the wise and cautious investor usually turns to retail business property, if he is able to finance his purchase.

Buying and selling business properties are involved and complex operations, for there must be careful study of every locality and, particularly, a critical analysis of every property to determine its risks, its advantages, and its earning capacities. A broker or a salesman interested in the soundest realty investment in the world today should explore this most attractive field.

CHAPTER 22

Industrial and

Commercial Properties

IN AN AGE SUCH AS OURS, WITH ITS RAPIDLY expanding population, active economy, and technological breakthroughs, the need for new factories, commercial properties, and business enterprises is snowballing beyond all expectations. Now that atomic power for the wheels of industry, exploration of space, and numerous innovations for the home and for recreation are inescapable elements of the modern scene, there must be an enlargement of industrial facilities. This means that lands for factories must be made ready and sold, that new buildings must be erected, and that money must be spent for every conceivable item that human beings may come to need or desire. All of this is very good for the real estate business.

Property used by manufacturing concerns is usually considered *industrial*, while that employed for warehouses and similar purposes is known as *commercial*, as distinguished from *business* property, where retail stores, banks, hotels, and office buildings predominate. Industrial and commercial properties are usually segregated in areas by themselves, and in larger cities are rigidly zoned, some being devoted to what are known as "light" manufacturing and others to the "heavy" type, which include machine shops, foundries, steel mills, and so on.

Industrial properties are for the most part found along the borders of railroad tracks and adjacent to rivers and harbors where piers and wharves can be built to service vessels. Commercial properties are generally located at the edge of town in what becomes known as "the wholesale district." They do not necessarily have railroad trackage, as auto trucks now handle many types of shipments. Trackage, however, is desirable and necessary for larger enterprises.

Industrial property in almost every city has several characteristics:

1. There is almost always an excess of vacant land, near railroads, which owners desire to sell for factory use.

2. Buyers of this type of land seldom purchase until just before they plan to build.

3. The result is often a lack of price standardization, because locations are all different and offer varying advantages and disadvantages.

4. Owing to an excess of supply in normal times, the buyer can dictate prices, to some extent, thus playing off one owner against another.

5. Frontage on certain railroads can be sold at a premium over that on other and less favored lines.

6. Area, as represented by square footage of land, is often considered more important than highway frontage.

7. High-grade commercial property may have a chance, at a later time, to graduate into business property of a minor type, because of its proximity to a growing business district. This sometimes occurs quite speedily.

Factory property is, for the most part, appraised and sold on a square-foot or acreage value as against the front-foot value usually applied to commercial and business property. Just enough space for an office building is about all the frontage required by most concerns, which would rather pay less money per square foot for interior land that can be utilized for factory buildings and storage uses.

In buying industrial property, it is extremely important that an adequate allowance be made for the amount of land needed for the parking of employees' cars. (Experience shows that many companies underestimate the number of workers who will come and go in their own cars.) Some large plants even operate garages where employees' cars may be repaired while they are at work, regular standard charges being made for such work. This often eliminates absenteeism and lateness in getting to work.

Large plants that process ores or chemicals, where heavy amounts of waste materials pile up, may be interested in land where fills may be made. Some such plants may fill many acres with waste material to depths of 50 to 100 feet or more. Land bordering on swales or swamps can be so utilized to advantage.

Recent years have seen a reshuffling of the industrial map of the United States. With government money, many great and small plants were brought into being in sections of the country where comparatively little industrial activity had existed. New industries blossomed overnight. The germ of industrial activities was widely spread and many of the plants were later reconverted to other uses. Common labor, at the outset, was converted into more or less skilled labor, anxious to continue in industrial life. There were the plants, there was the labor supply, and there soon came the insistent demand for more consumers' goods of all kinds. This finally spelled the building up of new industrial empires in many parts of the country, to grow and furnish business for real estate brokers.

To engage in the sale of industrial property, a realty broker must learn a few fundamental facts about the needs of his clients. He must put himself in the position of a concern that is about to go into business and desires to get the best available site at the most reasonable price. Among the factors concerning plant location are:

1. Availability of materials used in the business.
2. Location of the markets to be served.

3. Transportation facilities offered: railroad, truck, ship—together with rates, schedules, and so on.

4. Labor supply—suitability, attitude, number, and probable efficiency. Are union demands unreasonable or is labor coöperative?

5. Climatic conditions as related to plant operations.

6. Water supply, sewage facilities, electric current, mail service.

7. Living conditions for employees. Is housing available for a growing work force? Room for expansion?

8. Are there oppressive laws and ordinances, or are factories welcome?

9. Are taxes high and will they increase?

10. Do local financial institutions coöperate with business?

11. Is there a sound economic need for the industry?

12. Will it be welcomed by its neighbors, or be considered undesirable and harassed?

13. Is the site under consideration one that will carry heavy buildings?

14. Is the location of such a size and topography that a layout of tracks and buildings can be arranged that will permit of good railroad service and economical handling of freight?

15. Are railroad, trucking and cargo rates such as to enable the industry to compete with rival concerns throughout the country?

16. Is this the best location for an industry to settle on or would one in another part of the same city, or some other city or state be better suited?

17. If improved, is the property general or special in construction?

18. Does the local zoning law permit the kind of industry under consideration?

19. Will the property resell readily if later vacated?

20. Is the price asked a fair one in relation to comparative sites?

These are only a few of the many things which an industrial realtor must know about. The average broker, only occasionally selling such a property, will be called on for the answers, too. His ability to furnish them may be the controlling factor in closing a deal.

One of the greatest problems in connection with selling industrial lands is their financing. Except in the case of large and strong industrial units, the average concern is loath to use its capital for the purchase or erection of a plant, preferring to keep its money working within its own sphere of action. Purchase of land and the erection of buildings makes it necessary to secure additional funds. Investors in that type of improvement are not readily found, except in large cities where the call for industrial sites is frequent.

Banks and mortgage companies, in most cases, do not look with favor on the financing of new industrial enterprises, considering that the hazards outweigh the benefits. Live local chambers of commerce can sometimes influence financial institutions to give support to industrial expansion, but only if a newcomer puts some money into the enterprise. Where financial aid is provided it is usually stipulated that standard factory or warehouse buildings be erected, so that if a buyer later fails to make good or to carry out terms of his lease, little difficulty is found in selling or leasing again. In good times factories fill up with owners or tenants and everything looks rosy in an industrial district, but in periods of depression many idle plants lie for months or years without producing a penny of income for their owners, some of whom were former mortgage holders.

During recent years efforts have been made to standardize factory buildings so that they may be used for a wide range of operations. Large construction companies, working on mass production principles, with prefabrication of much of a factory building done at a company mill or foundry, turn out acres upon acres of factory buildings at reasonable prices. These buildings can be used for a wide variety of purposes, and it is this type of construction that is favored by those who are responsible for housing and financing new enterprises. Mass production of buildings is thus encouraged.

A development of recent years has been the creation of well-financed enterprises which erect large, fully equipped industrial districts, with adequate railroad and other necessary facilities, and then lease space to tenants on reasonable terms sufficient to provide for management, upkeep, and a profit on the invested capital. These are to be found in large industrial cities such as New York, Chicago, and Los Angeles. The idea is adaptable, however, to smaller communities and may be used on an extensive scale when necessity demands.

An industrial realtor must acquire a wide knowledge of the various railroads catering to the city in which he is located. He must be familiar with rail rates, sources of materials, and markets reached. Each road has its own advantages as well as its drawbacks. If the city has a "belt line," the broker must know all about that, also. A belt line is a road that circles a city like a huge belt, tapping all the existing railroad lines and tying them together for shipping and trans-shipping purposes. Belt lines are strictly freight carriers and for the most part serve intermediate properties not reached by trunk lines. A factory on a belt line has access to all other lines operating in or out of the city. By establishing universal freight stations at different points, a belt line can accumulate shipments of less than car lots which, after sorting and routing, can be placed in cars for their destinations. This saves time and money for the shipper and adds to the value and usefulness of his location.

Waterfront industrial locations are of great importance in cities where there are large shipments of bulk goods such as grain, iron ore, and oil. Waterborne freight can be carried much cheaper than by rail. It is much cheaper to send a cargo of goods by a long water route from New York to Los Angeles or San Francisco, via the Panama Canal, than it is to ship it on a direct rail route overland.

Most important American cities have grown up on river banks or on lake and ocean harbors, and most of them have waterfront shipping facilities. The amount of waterfront property is less and consequently is higher-priced. Once proper wharves and piers are installed, however, the saving in rates is so great that eventually the waterfront site may become cheaper than a rail site, particularly if the location has both rail and wharf facilities. Care should be taken by a broker in listing a waterfront site to ascertain definitely whether the ground is of such a type that heavy building foundations may be placed upon it. He must also find out the condition of the channel, whether there is sufficient depth of water for a ship to tie up at a dock that may be constructed on the property, or whether it will require expensive dredging operations to make the site usable. Two types of materials are usually used in docks; concrete and wood piling or wood sheath. A concrete dock costs about twice as much as a wood one but lasts much longer.

With large earth- and sand-moving machinery now available, well-located river, lake, or ocean frontage can be increased in size by reclaiming large areas, by installing piling and pumping in vast quantities of sand. Such made land is useful for storage of many materials, such as lumber, or as sites for light warehouses, small factories, or shipyards.

How are industrial sites disposed of by the broker? They certainly do not sell themselves. What is the best way to go about finding a buyer? There are a number of ways. Signs are very useful on both vacant or improved property. The sign should be dignified and should bear some relation to the size and value of the property offered. Most newspapers in the larger cities have advertising columns devoted to the sale of industrial sites and buildings, and these can be used profitably. The broker can use direct-mail letters to selected lists of companies and individuals he believes might be considered as prospects. With such a letter might go a circular, attractively illustrated, showing the size and layout of a plant offered for sale and stating its possibilities in detail. It is assumed, of course, that before going to any great expense in advertising a property the broker will have secured for himself an exclusive contract to sell it. In the presentation of all of his advertising the clever broker will hold back one thing—the price! To do so requires an interested party to make an inquiry in such a way that his identity can be established, and the broker is thus able to get in touch with someone genuinely seeking information about an offering.

Some industrial realtors periodically issue catalogues of their listings, sending out 10,000 or 15,000 to a select list of manufacturing concerns which might be interested, throughout the country. This catalogue shows locations and gives data about both improved and vacant offerings, and reveals enough to whet the interest of a prospect so that he will seek more information. The same catalogue often results in new listings of both improved and vacant properties which owners are seeking to dispose of. With such a catalogue a return card can be sent so that the person or firm receiving it can easily acknowledge its reception or ask for further information. Four-page attractively illustrated circulars are most often used when a full catalogue of listings is not mailed.

A broker, in securing a request from a concern to advise it upon securing a new or large plant, should by all means make an inspection of his prospect's premises so that he will be better able to understand what is needed in a new location. This also gives the broker an opportunity to establish a personal contact with a new client.

American industrial activities, originally centered in New England, have spread throughout the entire country. First they marched across the middle western states through Ohio, Pennsylvania, and Illinois. Then came a shifting of the textile and shoe factories from New England to Southern states. After World War I, industrial activity began to spring up on the Pacific coast, and with World War II came a huge growth in the manufacture of airplanes and ships all along the Pacific slope. The space age has stimulated new industries everywhere, particularly in the Deep South. Those new manufacturing centers all seem destined to grow and provide business for industrial realtors.

Dealing extensively in industrial property eventually results in a broker becoming a specialist in that line and devoting his entire time to it. Only in cities of some size is that field profitable. In a smaller city or town a broker or salesman may sell an occasional industrial property along with his other activities. He will find problems in connection with them that he does not encounter elsewhere, and for this, if for no other reason, he should have some general knowledge of the procedure followed in that branch of the real estate business.

New industrial plants mean so much to the economies of communities that the acquisition of new plants has become a major interest of chambers of commerce. Many chambers have organized industrial districts, acquired properties, and are actively engaged in selling to desirable industrial interests.

This trend places real estate men dealing in industrial properties in a type of competition with the chambers of commerce. But the wise real estate agency will cooperate with these interests, because the gaining of new industry is a boon to every member of the community. On the other hand, if an agency is able to acquire listings for highly desirable properties, then a liaison may be entered into with the local chamber of commerce and its industrial committee. Such committees can help you sell the properties you have on exclusive listing, while at the same time they seek properties for their own listing to attract new industries which may consider locating in the community.

CHAPTER 23

Short- and
Long-Term Leaseholds

LEASING LAND FOR SHORT OR LONG terms, either separately or combined with structural improvements, has become such a general practice in American cities that a thorough knowledge of the fundamentals is essential to salesmen. This is particularly true of long-term leases for fifty or ninety-nine years. Short-term leasing of stores and buildings for business purposes also has become one of the most important branches of the realty business.

Leasing is distinctly a brokerage activity and something which a broker can learn not in a month or even a year but only by actually engaging for a long time in the business.

What is a lease? Here is a definition:

A lease for years is a contract between an owner, called the lessor, and a recipient or tenant, called the lessee, for a recompense by rent or other compensation on the one side, and the possession and use of lands and improvements on the other. A lease is the written document and the leasehold represents the rights conveyed.

Long-term leasing, dating back to the early Roman Empire, is shrouded in antiquity. Rulers of the early empire controlled all the land and apportioned it among a favored few who became the overlords. Having large areas of land and not being able to cultivate or realize a return from them, they

186

devised a rental or leasing system which has its counterpart in our long-term leases today.

About the fifteenth century, during the baronial period, the practice came into existence in England. All land was held in the name of the king and huge tracts of acreage were granted to favored lords and barons, who paid land rentals to their king and in turn sub-leased their holdings. Leases in England were made for 99 years and some for as long as 999 years. Why the term is 99 years and not 100 is a mystery, but there seems to have been an early custom or law prohibiting the making of leases for 100 or 1,000 years. In early English literature on this subject, too, reference is continually made to "three generations," and 33 years may have been considered the life of a generation.

Strange and peculiar leases exist in England and European countries, but many made in the United States are quite as unusual. A lease was made several centuries ago in Boston for 1,000 years on a business frontage on Milk street. Payments of rent were to be made in a specified amount of Russian sable iron, a fine grade of iron used in the arts and crafts. Time came when it could not be procured, so the lessor sued to dispossess the tenant. The court held that the tenant's action in tendering an amount of money equal to the last market price of Russian sable iron was sufficient and decreed that, therefore, the lessee would remain in possession of the premises. Then there are several so called "sky leases." In such a case the site is already improved with a building sufficiently strong to carry additional stories. The owner of the ground and basic building sublets the air space above the existing structure. The lessee or tenant builds above and pays rent for the privilege of erecting additional stories with access to the street below. In Pennsylvania a site for a church was leased to a congregation, the only rental being a red rose from each parishioner each year, placed on the church altar on a certain date.

In 50- or 99-year leases the rental usually is what is said to be "net," that is, the tenant pays a stipulated sum for the use of the land and in addition agrees to improve it adequately with a building, and pay all taxes and carrying charges for proper maintenance of the property.

If long-term leases are sane and equitable and are not made vehicles for the attempted collection of speculative profits, they have definite advantages to both the tenant and the owner of land. Most of the long-term leaseholds that have caused trouble have done so for two very definite reasons: (1) The owner demands and receives an unusually large and unwarranted rental for land from a tenant who was gambling on a speculative future, which does not materialize. (2) In a leasehold taken for speculative reasons, adequate building improvements may not have been placed on leased land sufficient to insure the landlord that the tenant was going to carry out the covenants of the lease. At the first sign of trouble, therefore, the tenant walks out and the leasehold collapses.

Great skill and care must be exercised in making long-term leases if they are to be used as instruments of occupancy of lands in American cities. Owners must curb selfish desires to demand the last possible dollar in rent and must establish rental on a basis of current warranted value. In return, the tenant must have a very definite stake in the deal by contributing adequate improvements. Thus, when hard times come, the tenant may carry on and at the same time the land owner will receive his rent.

Long-term leases, at least the kind which have been adapted for use in the United States, originated largely in Great Britain, where land values were comparatively static and where violent realty booms were seldom or never encountered. To take such an instrument and transplant it to America, a rapidly growing country, entailed considerable risk. Particularly has this risk been apparent because periodically this country has gone through real estate booms and ensuing depressions, in which latter period many leaseholders have gotten into serious trouble and lost their equities.

Definite changes are being made in the way leases are drawn and operated. One manifestation of change is the introduction during recent years of percentage leases, particularly for short-term use. By this method a minimum rental is fixed which usually covers the current expenses of the property and a minimum investment return to the owner. Then a rental rate is established, according to the type of business involved, by which the tenant agrees to pay the landlord a certain percentage of his gross sales. If the tenant prospers, the landlord does likewise. If the tenant finds it impossible to make money, the lease usually contains an owner's recapture or "escape" clause which permits its termination.

A novel suggestion for the operation of both short- and long-term leases has been made to assure the owner an equitable return in rental on his property. This contemplates a provision permitting rental adjustments to be made from time to time, such changes to be fixed by the changing value of the dollar. Based on an index which denotes the current purchasing power of the dollar, rental would fluctuate up or down, according to the capacity of a dollar to purchase goods. It is maintained that this would afford the land owner a steady stream of buying power to which he might apply it. Rental would fluctuate, it is true, but it would seem to be a fair arrangement for both landlord and tenant.

There have been three commonly accepted types of long-term leases in recent years. First is the flat, straight, or ungraded lease. The second type is the graded lease by which rental is stepped up over future terms of years. The third is the so called reappraisal or revaluation lease whereby appraisers representing each party determine a rental value every ten years—unless lessor and lessee can agree between themselves as to the rental to be charged, which is seldom the case. The flat lease is the fairest. Rental should be fixed on a property's current warranted value. Never under any circumstances is a reappraisal lease recommended, and very seldom a graded lease. Improvements cannot be financed under a reappraisal lease and the tenant is inclined to want to walk out at the end of ten years, as he finds himself deprived of any increment which has come to the property.

Negotiating a lease, whether short or long term, is a complicated procedure requiring technical skill, knowledge, and experience. It should not be attempted by a salesman or broker till he has had some experience in the field. The compilation of the lease document itself is usually left to lawyers skilled in this work. The number of attorneys able to compile leases has diminished because of the comparatively few long-term leases negotiated in recent years. Lawyers can be found in most communities, however, who are capable of preparing these documents. Short-term leases may be taken care of through forms issued by companies that print legal documents of various kinds, or developed from sample forms.

In larger cities, many large and active real estate offices maintain departments that specialize in leasing. Salesmen in that branch of the business familiarize themselves with certain "hot spot" locations where business districts are springing into existence, or with their "100 per cent leasing district," which is usually in the heart of the downtown business sections. In both types of districts chain-store concerns of different kinds vie with each other for locations and pay unusually high rentals for favored spots.[1]

There are about 200,000 multi-unit retail trade establishments in the U.S., and the list continues to grow each year as concerns branch out with new outlets. National chains grow from smaller chains in states, which in turn have expanded from live businesses which have established numbers of local branches.

One of the most puzzling things in connection with chain-store leasing on a percentage basis is the selection of the exact percentage rate to be used in a lease. A list of such percentage rates may be found below. These must be applied cautiously and only when local conditions are known. Manifestly it is impossible to compile such a table that will apply equally throughout the entire country. A thorough knowledge of local

---

[1] The entire subject of leases, including chain-store percentage leases, is completely covered in *Leases-Percentage, Short and Long Term*, by McMichael and O'Keefe, 5th ed. (Englewood Cliffs, N. J.: Prentice-Hall, Inc.)

conditions and the rates generally in effect is necessary if a broker is going to get his parties to agree.

Rental Percentages for Retail Stores
Based on Gross Sales

Type of Business	Per Cent	Type of Business	Per Cent
Appliances	3-4	Furniture	4-6
Auto:		Fur stores	5-6
Accessories	2-4	Hardware	4-5
Agencies, new cars	1½-3	Hosiery	7-10
Bakeries	4-6	Jewelry	8-10
Barbers	7-10	Liquor	4-5
Beauty parlors	7-10	Millinery	7-10
Book stores	5-10	Office supplies	5-6
Candy and confectionery	8-10	Paint and wallpaper	4-6
Cigar stores (tobacco shops)	6-8	Pharmacies	6-10
Clothing stores:		Photographic supplies	8-10
Children's	6-8	Shoe stores	5-7
Family	4-7	Sporting goods	5-7
Men's	5-7	Stationery	5-10
Women's	4-6	Supermarkets	1
Drug stores	4-6	Variety stores	5-6
Florists	8-10		

CHAPTER 24

Vacant Property

LISTING AND SELLING VACANT PROPERTY
is always an important activity in any real estate office. There
are many kinds of vacant tracts of land, most of which are in
demand constantly. The brokerage commissions to be earned
on such sales are not so large as those coming from the disposition of more expensively improved property; nevertheless
this branch of the business is important and requires constant
study and attention.

First of all, the broker should become familiar with and list
all vacant property within the radius of his operating activities. There are always dwelling sites that remain unimproved
and that can readily be sold to persons desiring to build new
homes. Locations for business buildings may be found along
partially improved business thoroughfares. There are sites for
manufacturing plants and for commercial firms requiring warehouses. Farther out, on the edge of a town or city, are many
tracts of vacant land in demand for small rural homes, chicken
farms, and other enterprises requiring larger spaces than ordinarily found in city lots. Finally, there are the farms spreading
out mile upon mile from a city's borders, the sale of which in
itself constitutes a more or less specialized business.

A real estate office should have suitable listing cards for
vacant properties, including city lots, industrial acreage, rural
sites, and farms. Complete information should be secured at

the time a listing is first made, so that the card will present a fairly accurate picture of what is offered for sale, the encumbrances against it, if any, and the price and terms at which the property can be acquired.

Since no one resides on vacant land, a search of county records may be necessary to discover its ownership. Accurate dimensions of the property should be inscribed on the listing card; also the assessed value and the taxes, together with any information that may be available concerning easements, restrictions, and so on.

Having obtained the owner's name and address, the next step is to get in touch with the owner, either personally, by telephone, or by mail. A personal call is usually the best way to get a listing. You get acquainted with the owner and perhaps make a contact that will serve you well later on. Your main purpose in talking with the owner, of course, is to get some idea of his notion of value. Here you, as a broker or salesman, must use tact and diplomacy, especially since the owner often has very little idea of the market value of his holding. If you ask him right away for a price, he will naturally play safe and quote it at as high a figure as he thinks the market will stand, which is usually beyond the price an average buyer would be willing to pay for it.

Right here is where a knowledge of values and a means of establishing them comes in handy. The inexperienced broker, lacking detailed knowledge of values as established by sales that have taken place in the neighborhood, is at a distinct disadvantage and usually winds up with a listing at a price higher than he can get a buyer to pay. The canny broker, who knows how to establish an appraised value for property, should be able to convince the owner that the figure suggested by the broker is more nearly the market value than that announced by the owner. The broker, at the outset, should be in a position promptly to name a value and price for the property that will permit him to sell it and still obtain for the owner the highest return current market conditions will afford.

The broker or salesman should try at all times to be fair,

but at no time should he let himself be imposed upon by an owner who seeks to list a property at a higher figure than the broker can reasonably expect to sell it for. In such a case a listing should be accepted with the reservation that as good an offer will be secured for it as possible, or it should be politely refused. Overpriced listings are never good merchandise in any office. They clutter up the files and serve no useful purpose. If a broker knows his business and has a knowledge of comparative values, he can, in most instances, persuade the property owner to consider a price within the realm of reason. If he cannot, it is probably because the owner doesn't want to sell the property anyway. So, why waste effort on it?

Vacant residential lot values can usually be checked with sales recently made in a neighborhood. It is significant that home sites, in most instances, are priced at the time they are first placed on the market at about their peak value. After a few houses have been built, the prices may be upped a little, but then they sag back to about a uniform level. Lots that have remained unimproved for long periods of time seldom gain much in value, and then never in proportion to the loss sustained through carrying charges, such as interest on the investment and taxes and assessments.

Vacant lots in neighborhoods zoned for multiple dwellings start off at fairly uniform prices and may advance owing to speculative influences. Then they halt their advance until some new and attractive buildings are erected. If there is a scarcity of such lots, their price may advance again. There is always a limit to which the prices for vacant lots can go, however, and that is set by the amount of income that can be derived from improvements erected on them. In large cities some brokers specialize in so called "income lots," dealing with speculative builders and individuals seeking to erect apartment houses.

An interesting and profitable branch of the realty business is the sale of lots having business frontage on thoroughfares zoned for retail business, usually on the fringe of built-up areas. These lots are in the pathway of retail and commercial development. Over the course of the years they sometimes advance in value to an extent little dreamed of by the early inhabitants of the district. Such property may increase in value because of the steady advance of commercial growth, evidenced by the erection of new store buildings. It may be definitely influenced by an important development such as a large department store coming to the new neighborhood, which is certain to attract a heavy pedestrian traffic. The new improvement must be something which will attract people, who in turn become purchasers of the wares of local shops. The local businessmen, in turn, stand ready and willing to pay the prices asked if they can do a volume of business that will leave them a profit after rent, taxes, and other expenses are paid.

Erection of churches, theaters, community fallout shelters, boat piers, and similar enterprises does not necessarily stimulate real estate prices, except momentarily. It may be true that large numbers of persons patronize such places, but they are not of the buying type that merchants seek.

Unless vacant land is being bought for a purely speculative purpose and with the hope that a considerable profit can be wrung from the property at a later date, it should be improved within a reasonable time, for carrying charges eat away anticipated profits speedily. Considering interest on the investment and the usual taxes and assessments, a property must double in value every eight or nine years just to allow the owner to break even. In other words, a vacant property can be said to "eat itself up" every eight or nine years!

Most vacant property is, or at least should be, acquired just prior to improvement. Every year vast sums are lost to owners who carry dead horses in the shape of unimproved real estate, and this is an argument that sometimes moves an owner to sell after he has carried a tract of unimproved land for a long time. One of the curses of the average American city is that altogether too much land is subdivided and furnished with public service improvements for years before it comes into actual use. Both the land and the public service facilities, such as sewers, water mains, and pavements, fail to earn their keep until put into actual use. Cities sprawl out over vast areas long before their populations come to build them up and use them.

It is significant that real estate activity can usually be found at the center and at the circumference of a community. There is activity downtown, where high-pressure demand exists for 100 per cent business sites. Then there is a long gap between the edge of the active downtown business section and the newer residential sections which are building up. This gap consists of old subdivisions, improved, for the most part, but static in growth. Shopping centers spring up in outlying sections of the larger cities, and vacant land in such areas is often in active demand. And on the rim of a city can usually be found an active demand for homes.

The automobile has done much to stimulate the demand for vacant land. Hundreds of small rural homes, clustered about cities, would scarcely ever have come into being were it not for the ease with which automobiles have solved the transportation problem.

The increasing amount of leisure time available to the average worker is another important factor in the gradual disappearance of vacant land near cities. Large numbers of families have moved from comparatively small and modest quarters in cities to outlying areas where they are able to have the kind of gardens they want, together with space for a tennis court and a swimming pool. Brokers on the edge of large cities are constantly catering to such clients—who are likely to increase in numbers as years go by and work weeks are shortened, making more leisure available for many workers.

Even so-called "gentleman farming" may offer an opportunity for the sale of vacant land. Many businessmen have set up stock farms, horse farms, and the like that may often be operated as much for a hobby as a business.

A broker should be careful not to establish his office in a worn-out district that is slipping rapidly because buildings are becoming older and more run-down each year, where all vacant property has been built up and there is little room for new expansion without wrecking existing buildings. Settle in an area where there is still a sprinkling of vacant lots, or where new devolpment in the form of subdivisions and shopping centers is in progress. This applies, of course, to larger cities. In a smaller community a broker can locate downtown and cover his entire territory from there.

Don't waste time trying to sell vacant property in blighted districts. You may find lots that have stood for fifty years — from the time the area was first subdivided—and are still vacant. There is seldom any justifiable use for such property, and it is effort wasted to try to sell it.

A profitable type of business may be found in the selling of vacant acreage for new factory sites and warehouses. Such land is found along railroads and on water frontages. Here again the land is bought usually just before it is improved. An abundance of such sites is offered, usually, since everyone who has land bordering a railroad considers his parcel to be the best factory location in the neighborhood. It was once good farm land on which crops were raised, but in all probability it has long remained idle awaiting a buyer. It requires a good deal of knowledge of comparative values for a broker to list and sell such property. Study and close attention are needed. Land on one railroad will be worth more than on another line. A buyer usually seeks to locate his plant on the line with the most direct outlet to his customers. Industrial lands are usually valued on a square-foot basis. Square-foot area is more important than a long street frontage. Some concerns prefer rough terrain because it gives them facilities for dumping refuse that would otherwise have to be carted away.

Vacant lands bordering on river fronts and lake or ocean harbors are in demand by large manufacturing concerns. Many problems are again encountered in the listing, pricing, and selling of such properties. Depth of water in the channel beside which the land is located must be sufficient for boats to tie to docks, which must be constructed. Marshy ground sometimes makes it impossible to build wharves and piers. Railroad connections are extremely useful, particularly for large enterprises.

How may values and reasonable selling prices of vacant lands be learned by the new broker or salesman? Principally through deals in which transfers have been actually made. These represent market value to quite an extent. The local assessor sets certain ratios of values on vacant land, but these may actually represent from 25 to 125 per cent of actual market value, according to the condition of the real estate market, the demand for vacant property, and the time assessed values are computed. Tax valuations are seldom of much use to the broker in ascertaining genuine value. Studies of actual sales of vacant properties will always be the best means of establishing values for new listings.

Vacant properties can usually be most easily sold by means of signs placed upon them. It is not difficult for a prospective buyer to look at a lot on which a sign is placed and decide whether he would like to own it. He can see the neighborhood stretching away on all sides. He probably knows much about the district itself. A sign may spur his interest into active consideration of the property, and it will often be found that more prospects will be contacted through signs than by any other means.

Selling vacant property is not the most important activity in any realty office, but it is always an interesting and lucrative one and well worth paying close attention to.

CHAPTER 25

Subdividing Land

A SUBDIVIDER IS JUST WHAT THE WORD implies—one who takes a large tract of land and divides it into smaller units or lots. The character of a subdivider is indicated by the improvements he installs on the property and the extent to which he goes to promote a low-, medium-, or high-grade project. Frequently—in recent years—he builds up his entire property with finished homes, ready for occupancy and financed to suit the needs of the tenants.

A subdivision is just a little part of the great mosaic that makes up a town or city. For identification and control, all vacant land is platted and registered with a county official, usually known as a recorder. Each plat, or tract, or subdivision has a name or number. Maps are filed indicating the manner in which it has been cut up or subdivided into individual lots. The sizes of the numbered lots are shown, with frontages on streets of stated widths. The subdivider usually files a set of regulations, known as restrictions, which govern the types of buildings that may be erected, how far they must be set back from property lines, in some cases the amount they must cost, and whether plans must be submitted to the subdivider or his representative for approval before work may proceed.

Since the beginning of recorded time mankind has been taking possession of land and subdividing it. It is one of the oldest businesses on record and is the first way in which the real estate business itself became identified with human activities. Adam was the first tenant, with Eve as co-tenant, in the Garden of Eden. Unfortunately he voided his life lease on the premises by breaking restrictions and was evicted. One of the first recorded transfers of land may be found in Genesis 23, wherein Abraham purchased, from the children of Heth, a burying ground for the interment of his wife Sarah. It was the cave of Machpelah, for which Abraham paid 400 shekels in silver, about $256 in American money. The owner did not want to sell but Abraham insisted and the deal was finally consummated and "made sure."

According to the Bible, the first real estate salesman of record was Hanameel, nephew of Jeremiah, who said to the prophet (Jeremiah 32–7): "Buy thee my field, for the right of inheritance is thine, and the redemption is thine; buy it for thyself." And it is recorded that Jeremiah bought the field and weighed out 17 shekels of silver in payment therefore. He also "subscribed the evidence and sealed it and took witnesses." So present-day formalities had their counterpart in that earliest transaction. The chapter is replete with the formalities which surrounded the acquisition of land, in ancient times as now regarded as a solemn proceeding by mankind.

The first president of the United States, George Washington, was one of America's first great subdividers. He was a civil engineer by profession and, as an associate of Lord Halifax, who owned over 5,000,000 acres of land in the Shenandoah Valley and Northern Virginia, he subdivided and sold vast quantities of it to newcomers from Europe. Washington planned and subdivided the city of Alexandria, Va., opposite Washington, D.C., where today a bronze tablet marks the site of his real estate office on Cameron Street just east of St. Aspath Street. A shrewd trader and at times a speculator, he was well-grounded in the fundamentals of realty development.

Subdividing is intimately associated with city growth. City planners control, coördinate, and improve the efforts of subdividers, who create cities piecemeal, tract upon tract, until a vast expanse of buildings houses sometimes millions of inhabitants. Most cities, like Topsy, "just grew." The earlier efforts at city planning resulted in a hodge-podge of subdivision street systems that were quite uncoördinated. The result is, in many old cities, that streets start nowhere and end nowhere. Only since city planning commissions have been established and at work has an orderly system of street design resulted.

There are two distinct types of subdivisions, considered from the standpoint of design. One has a rectangular block layout; the other has curving streets, with long blocks and fewer cross-streets than where the rectangular system is used. Design, to an extent, must always follow the topography of the parcel of land that is being subdivided. It is desirable to secure an artistic layout while continuing to secure the most serviceable number of useful lots.

Until the latter part of the last century, subdividing as a business was a haphazard occupation. An owner would find himself encumbered with a piece of land, hire a surveyor to cut it into lots, put up a sign, and offer the lots for sale. Purchases were made entirely upon a cash basis. Installment buying of real estate was unheard of. This was the kind of realty development that went on until the 1880's.

William E. Harmon was America's first professional sub-divider and he is credited with evolving a system of lot sales that was later copied by hundreds of subdividers. Harmon was educated as a doctor but never practiced, becoming instead a salesman for a tree nursery. He lived in Cincinnati. One day, while passing a large field near town, he saw a beautiful oak tree and became inspired with the idea that it might be a fine thing if the average man could own a home site with big trees on or near it. He thought it might even be possible to sell a lot for a few dollars down and regular payments as low as $1 a week. His friends scoffed at the plan. Finally he convinced Charles E. Wood and his own brother, Clifford B. Harmon, that the plan would work. Together they assembled $3,000 in cash and bought a 30-acre tract of land near Cincinnati, operating under the firm name of Wood, Harmon & Co., which later developed into one of the largest concerns of its kind in America.

The first subdivision was called Branch Hill. The thirty acres were cut into 303 lots, which were priced at $25 each. The new subdivision was seven and a half miles from what were then the city limits of Cincinnati. The sale was slated for December

14, 1887, almost the middle of the winter season. Advertisements went up and the new developers waited in fear and trembling. The first day a few lots were sold, more the next, and by the end of four days the entire subdivision was completely sold out. Down payments were $2 in cash, with weekly payments of twenty-five cents.

Thus was founded the business of selling lots in subdivisions on a purchase contract basis. Tract after tract was placed on the market and soon disposed of. Like wildfire the idea spread to other cities, and during the ensuing years hundreds of thousands of lots were sold to eager purchasers. Some of those early subdivisions were indeed sorry affairs. Groups of streets were indicated by ploughed furrows; wooden stakes marked the location and sizes of lots. No improvements were installed when the properties were sold. These came later and had to be paid for by the lot owners.

As years went by the demand for better types of subdivisions became insistent. The subdivider added more and more street improvements and merged the cost into the selling price of his lots. City planning commissions began to enforce regulations under which subdividers might operate in many cities, and the character of the newer allotments improved. Today streets in all new subdivisions must articulate with those tracts previously sold in the neighborhood. This does away with blind streets and sudden jogs in others. All public service facilities such as gas, water, sewers, and electricity must be installed before lots are sold, in most cities. Pavements must be laid and must pass inspection of public works departments. This makes for an infinitely better type of development and is a distinct advantage to the buyer as well as being more profitable to the promoter.

Subdivisions are not confined to the accommodation of persons who want to build homes. There are numerous subdivisions of business property, particularly where crossroads of traffic indicate a developing town site. In some large subdivisions many acres are set aside as business centers; these are subdivided further and sold separately. Industrial subdivisions in large cities function as a part of large warehouse and terminal developments. In recent years near large cities there have been many large rural subdivisions, with lots an acre or more in size, zoned to permit the raising of horses, chickens, rabbits, ducks, frogs, and even fish.

Naturally, the selection of land suitable for home sites is not a simple problem. Many factors must be considered. There must be adequate transportation for home owners—paved highways and freeways, busses, or trains. Retail stores must be within reasonable travel or walking distance. There must be schools, libraries, and playgrounds. Public services such as water, sewers, electricity, gas, and mail service must be available at reasonable cost.

Land to be platted must be reasonably priced. It must be purchased at what might be considered a wholesale figure, because it must be improved with utilities and disposed of in small units at retail. In earlier days, when few improvements were installed by the operator, he could afford to work on a 1 to 3 basis; that is, he could pay $500 an acre, expecting to resell it for at least $1,500 an acre or more in parcels of any size. Today, with the high cost of public improvements, many subdividers believe the ratio should be one to five, or more; that is, if $1,000 an acre is paid for land, it must be sold for at least $5,000 per acre at retail. Remember that an operator must set aside some of the land for street purposes—with small lots, this would be about 25 per cent; with larger lots, less. But land may also be set aside for other purposes, such as schools or playgrounds, or even community swimming pools.

The following table shows the number of typical lots obtainable per acre. Allowance is made for the lots to front on a fifty-foot street, with cross-streets every 800 feet for the smaller lots and increasing proportionately up to 2,000 feet for the largest.

Size of Lots	Number of Lots per Acre	Size of Lots	Number of Lots per Acre
50 X 150	4.74	80 X 200	2.35
50 X 175	4.14	80 X 240	1.99
60 X 175	3.48	100 X 250	1.54
60 X 200	3.10	120 X 200	1.61
70 X 175	3.00	120 X 250	1.30
70 X 200	2.67	200 X 200	1.00

Subdivisions are all different; every design is different; topography varies; curving streets allow wide frontages with lots narrowing as they recede. Any table like the one above is approximate only, but reasonably accurate for most purposes.

Pricing lots in a subdivision must be done skillfully and by experienced persons; otherwise it may not prove a profitable venture. Indeed, the subdivider must be able to take a tract of land, briefly lay out a design, estimate the number of lots available, and ascertain what his return will be before he even contracts to buy the land! To do this he must have a fairly complete knowledge of appraising technique.

Negotiations for the purchase of land for subdivision may be conducted directly with an owner or, preferably, through a broker. If an owner believes some prominent developer wants his land, he will promptly overprice it and defeat the purposes of all concerned. A capable broker can quietly approach such an owner, discuss the listing of such property, preferably concluding his negotiations by obtaining an exclusive contract to sell it. Many owners of "raw" land do not realize that to produce salable, improved lots costs as much as the land, sometimes more. They quickly estimate the retail price of lots in their neighborhood, then ask the prevailing price for their land. That is the reason why some greedy land owners go along for years still owning vacant acreage that should be improved with homes.

Financing subdivisions, in many cases, is almost as difficult as financing industrial enterprises. Banks and mortgage companies are seldom interested, since they do not make a practice of lending on vacant land of *any* kind. The following methods are used:

1. The developer may arrange with a property owner to buy his land, making a substantial down payment, the owner taking back a mortgage for the rest but agreeing to release lots, pro rata under the mortgage, as they are sold. In lieu of making a cash payment the subdivider may only agree to install expensive improvements throughout the property. This is to the advantage

of the property owner, provided he is dealing with a substantial developer who can provide sufficient money to pay for all of the improvements as the disposition of the property takes place, and it is ripe for marketing.

2. Syndicates are sometimes formed, embracing three, five, or even more persons who are given a "split" on the profits as they are earned.

3. A subdivider may get an individual to buy the land for him, replacing the former owner, allowing the new owner a substantial profit on the operation. Or a partnership may be formed with one or more persons to float the transaction.

4. A corporation may be formed and stock sold. Such an enterprise might run into difficulties with corporation laws in some states, and this matter should be looked into at the start.

Numerous legal matters must be provided for in the subdivision business. At the outset, restrictions must be imposed on the property. Usually the more complete the restrictions the higher grade the property will be. Easy restrictions permit cheap development, and the property is then not selective enough to attract good prices. Restrictions include such things as set-back of dwellings from front lot lines; whether the garage may be separate or must be attached to the house; whether fences may be built instead of hedges; whether buildings must have a certain minimum cost; whether plans must be submitted for architectural approval. Sometimes provision must also be made in the subdivision for easements, such as those for underground power lines.

In addition to restrictions and easements there must be forms of contracts of sale, deeds, preliminary deposit receipt agreements, deeds of trust, and of course titles to be provided by a responsible abstract or title company.

Selling lots in a subdivision is relatively simple as compared to general brokerage activities.[1] The main advantage the tract

[1] For further data in regard to selling subdivision homesites see Chapter XIV of *Selling Real Estite*, 3rd Ed., by Stanley L. McMichael (Englewood Cliffs, N. J.: Prentice-Hall, Inc.)

salesman has is the knowledge that he *can deliver the property at the price asked.* He can be coached by a sales manager and in a few days know all about the advantages and selling points of the property he is handling. His sales canvass can be learned so thoroughly that it seems to bubble out spontaneously and convincingly. His competitors are limited to other subdivisions some distance away which may not attract the attention of his prospects. Many successful real estate brokers and operators got their initial training selling lots in subdivisions, graduating later to more complex deals.

Selling subdivision lots is unlike other types of real estate selling in that fixed prices prevail. No offers are taken or considered, as lots cost just so much and must be bought at that price without haggling.

A potent sales argument for selling lots is the enforced savings that it requires on the part of the buyer. Many a person began his investment career by buying a homesite. A buyer may be urged to invest in a lot simply to establish a thrifty practice which may mean much to him later on.

In addition to being given a thorough grounding on the advantages of the property he is selling, and being coached in selling techniques by means of lectures, demonstrations, and mock sales, a subdivision salesman is usually given a sales kit, attractively bound and containing good-sized pictures of houses, a map of the property, and attractive layouts of kitchens, bathrooms, and so on. The sales kit is arranged so that its contents follow the normal progress of a sale. It is in many cases actually a silent salesman. It first seeks to emphasize the psychological order of securing attention, arousing interest, stimulating desire, establishing belief, and securing action. Then it makes an effort, through its pages, to breathe life and warmth into the subject being discussed, through the use of colored illustrations of attractive houses for which plans are shown. The presentation and use of a sales kit must not be tedious, and the salesman must be encouraged to change his timing and material now and then; improving it with the introduction of new ideas gleaned from newspapers and magazines and from personal contacts with new customers, who often have excellent suggestions to offer. Without a sales kit, many agents would fail to present the property in the way the owner desires.

Compensation for selling subdivision property differs throughout the country, ranging from 7½ to 15 per cent. To men remaining throughout the year some companies give a bonus of 3 or 4 per cent in addition to the regular commissions earned. This is to reduce turnover of the sales force.

One of the evils of the subdivision business is the over-production of lots in a market not able to absorb them. In good times some men try to subdivide and sell property in a market not able to absorb more than a limited number of home sites. Every city has subdivisions that have "gone dead" and have been passed over for others farther out. If the realty board or the city planning commission had made a survey and ascertained approximately how many home sites were needed to meet a normal demand, much of this over-development of property might have been avoided and much loss prevented.

A plan followed by many wise subdividers is to improve and sell only a part of a large acreage at one time. A comprehensive master plan is evolved for the entire property but, if the tract contains 100 acres, only 20 acres are improved with streets and public service facilities for the initial offering. A sale is announced and within a reasonable time the lots are disposed of. As it becomes apparent that more lots are needed, another street or two may be installed on ten, fifteen, or twenty acres, and that new section, in turn, is offered for sale. In this way the operator saves overhead cost on expensive public improvements, which do not deteriorate and are new and ready when needed.

Most successful subdividers in recent years have been those who have built new houses on their own properties. They sell completed projects and control the manner in which building takes place as well as establishing the character and class of their developments. They make a profit on the land they sell and on the improvements placed on it. A new, modern house, attractively and soundly built and properly financed, offers much more interest to a prospect than a vacant lot which he may have to take a great deal of trouble to improve with a dwelling about the construction of which he knows very little.

New subdivision developments should be reasonably geared to other developments near by. It is foolish to attempt to install a high-grade development in a neighborhood already built up with cheap or even medium-priced ones. Such an effort will in all probability fail, and the tract will soon deteriorate to the level of the developments nearby. When and where such a mistake has been made, it is wise to admit it speedily and sell out the remainder of whatever lots are left at prices the market will absorb.

In earlier days, when cities grew in a star-shaped pattern, it was necessary for subdivisions to be near street-car lines. That they were star-shaped was due, in most instances, to the influence of street cars operating on roads radiating fanwise from the center. Today, with motor travel having taken the place of street cars, a subdivision may be located almost anywhere.

Zoning laws in cities have done much for the protection of subdivision property and its owners and the orderly growth of communities. Zoning laws frequently set up the minimum acreage for lots (for example, half an acre or a full acre) to prevent land exploitation and the cutting up of valuable areas into small building lots long before the time needed for them. Master plans adopted by governments will also affect the development of subdivisions by setting aside land for parks, by laying out road networks, and the like.

Subdividers are the city builders! Great oaks from little acorns grow, and many an important subdivider got his start by buying a ten-acre tract and cutting it up, astonishing himself at the profit he made; for, if rightly done, subdividing is a profitable business!

CHAPTER 26

Selling Farms

SELLING FARMS IS A SPECIALIZED BRANCH of the real estate business extensively engaged in by certain brokers who devote most of their time to it. Occasional farm deals come up in every realty office, however.[1]

At the outset the farm broker must be careful to conserve his time by "qualifying" his prospect; otherwise he will be shuttling about all over the country with "buyers" who are simply going along for the ride.

"I'm just looking around to see what I can find in a good buy," announces the prospect as he drops into a chair in the farm broker's office. He suggests that someone take him around in an automobile and show him places. He *may* really be a potential buyer, but more likely he is just a sightseer. Tactful handling of the situation may soon reveal the purpose of the man's call. Let him remain seated. Suggest that, as a real estate man, you might help him find the kind of property he wants, but to do so you would need more information about what he wants in the way of the "good buy" he has mentioned. Ask him for what he

---

[1] This chapter is devoted largely to methods followed in the farm brokerage offices of Strout Realty, whose headquarters are now in Los Angeles, and which in the past sixty-six years has sold over 100,000 farms through its associated offices. The Strout organization is the largest rural land-selling concern in the world, has survived several boom and depression periods, and has thoroughly tested its sale methods. Several times a year it issues a 175-page illustrated catalogue listing hundreds of farms situated from coast to coast, which is mailed to hundreds of farm prospects.

209

intends to use the property, whether for farming, for investment, for a home, for speculation, or for commercial use. Ask him how large a down-payment he expects to make and what size and price range he is interested in. If the visitor is sincere, he will answer these and other reasonable questions. If he evades your questions, you may be sure that you are entertaining a man who wants a buggy ride but not a farm.

If the prospect has responded to a specific ad, and if he requests information about the property and asks to see it, invite him to be seated and offer to give him additional information about the property before showing it.

Give the visitor some general information about the property. Tell him that when the listing was taken the owner was advised to set his price as low as possible, and that the down-payment agreed to is as low as is consistent with the conditions of the sale. This is done to forestall any future attempt on the part of the newcomer to chisel or beat down the price and terms when he knows all about the listing offered.

In presenting a farm property to a prospect, be careful to make no statements that may later get you into trouble. Don't say, "This grove is frost-free." Say, "It is reported by the owner that this grove is frost-free." Don't say, "Sales from this orchard last year aggregated $10,000," but again quote the owner as making the statement. Don't promise glowing profits to be obtained by re-selling a farm property. Just tell the truth and guard your statements, and there will be no unpleasant "kickbacks."

Because of the amount of traveling and running about a farm broker is called upon to do, he must conserve his time and efforts and not make needless trips. Try to find out exactly the kind of property the prospect wants and whether he is able to make a reasonable down-payment. Then match him up with two or three properties that most nearly approach his needs and that have in general the qualifications he demands. Don't drag out listing books and batches of photographs, unless you want the prospect to announce that he would like to see all of them. It would mean taking him around for a week at least. It is wise to take him to one farm and try to sell him the place. If that farm doesn't suit him, pass on to a second one that may meet his requirements. This is where the process of qualifying the prospect eases the salesman's task.

Ask the prospect plenty of questions and give him plenty of chances to volunteer information, because thereby he will divulge the very information about his needs and his mental processes that a salesman should know. Some prospects are uncommunicative and try to hide their thoughts from the salesman, especially if some high-pressure salesmen have tried to sell them properties that did not meet their needs. You must establish a friendly relationship with the prospect, so that he will thaw out and will frankly indicate whether he likes a place and is willing to buy it.

Don't be deceived about the price a farmer will pay for a property. Though he says he has only $10,000 to invest and that he does not want to assume a heavy mortgage, if he sees a $40,000 property that requires a $15,000 down-payment, he may very well buy the place *if it is what he wants!* Prospects for houses and other types of property will do likewise. If a prospect really becomes sold on a place and wants to own it, it is surprising how he will manage to get the necessary cash.

It is possible to talk a prospect into buying a farm and then, by continuing, to talk him out of buying it. Answer every question honestly and frankly, even if it means revealing some unfavorable features about a property. If the prospect asks a question which a salesman is not able to answer, the latter should frankly confess it and then, or later, get the information. Never fail to furnish all the facts.

It is well to impress the prospect with the fact that comparatively few desirable properties are on the market, that most owners are satisfied and do not want to sell. That is usually the truth, except in times of deep depression, for the percentage of sale listings to all properties is always relatively small. Create the impression that the district you are visiting is full of contented farmers who are prosperous, thereby stimulating desire in the prospect's mind to live in that community. If you can show him something desirable and rightly priced, a sale is almost certain to result.

A farm salesman must have a wide range of knowledge about many things. He must know local geography, soils, markets, shipping rates, taxes, availability of all kinds of farm supplies, and the prices paid for different farm commodities and machinery; distances to different towns and cities; the location of schools, churches, libraries, and fair grounds; the prices paid for fuel and groceries and livestock, and a mass of miscellaneous knowledge that the buyer is bound to want from time to time. The salesman must read, besides the local papers and magazines, the farm and stock papers and state and government reports dealing with farms, farmers, and their interests.

Find the best approach to a farm that is about to be shown to a prospective buyer. The best approach is over the shortest distance and over the best-paved road. Every piece of real estate has some good points which should be emphasized. However, do not try to gloss over any poor qualities by misrepresentation. Satisfied customers are the best advertisements a real estate broker can have.

Never discuss commissions with a prospect or reveal what commission you might make if you sold him a property. Don't give him the impression that you are merely trying to make money out of his patronage.

Be careful how you bring a prospect into contact with a farm. When the property is listed, the owner should be coached a little on how to act and how to talk when prospects come to see the property. Urge the owner to assume a positive rather than a negative attitude. Though he wants to get rid of his farm, advise him to speak favorably about it, to point out its good points and never to say anything that might startle, scare, or antagonize a buyer. Once a farmer's wife remarked, as she showed a prospect and a broker through her house: "I haven't had a chance to clean this room since my sister died."

"Oh, have you recently lost your sister?" asked the buyer's wife, who was along.

"Yes, she just died of cancer in this very room!"

That sale collapsed right then and there and could never again be revived—with that customer at least.

The Strout Company issues a booklet telling owners how to act and talk, suggesting conversational methods which are cheerfully constructive rather than sadly destructive and discouraging.

Owners are always asked in the booklet to coöperate with the salesman by observing the following suggestions:

You can help sell your property, when writing or talking to prospective purchasers, by avoiding mentioning any sad, unfortunate or repulsive ideas connected with you, your property, your town or anything else.

Success or failure in advertising and selling is determined by the right or wrong appeal.

Folks' main ambition is to attain more success, more beauty, more cheer, more happiness.

Therefore, in selling, never refer to disasters, accidents, sickness, deaths, or hard luck of any kind.

Never refer to another property for sale when speaking to a prospect. It gives him an idea that the whole neighborhood is for sale and if he does not decide at once to go elsewhere, he will not decide on yours until he has seen the other places.

Never refer to unfavorable marketing conditions, poor roads, poor schools, poor neighbors, droughts, blights, windstorm, hailstorm, extremes of weather, mosquitoes, greenhead flies, lack of labor, poor shipping facilities or any other general condition that would create an undesirable impression on his mind.

When the prospect has looked over several farms and has finally whittled down his choice to one in which he seems greatly interested, the time now comes for the salesman to close his sale and get a deposit. He must, at this point, evidence complete confidence that he is going to make the sale, and might, as a means of securing action, ask "When would you want to take possession?" or, "What kind of down payment would you like to make?" Something—anything—to secure action! As in selling every other kind of real estate, *give the prospect plenty of opportunities to buy!*"

Now is the time to pass the pen! Have a contract form all ready and calmly begin filling it in, asking the prospect whether he wants to take title in the names of both himself and his wife.

At this point some prospects begin to make offers—"verbal" offers. The bargaining instinct begins to show itself. The offer may be within reasonable striking distance of the price asked, in which event try to get him to raise it to the price at which the place is listed. If it is impossible to do so, suggest that he give you a written offer with a substantial deposit as good faith. Tell the prospect that if the owner does not accept the offer, and if you fail to get the owner and the buyer together on some kind of contract arrangement, the buyer's deposit money will be promptly returned without any further obligation. Sometimes an offer lower than the price asked is accepted and, in any event, the buyer has committed himself as wanting that particular property. If his low offer is not accepted, he may be persuaded to raise it to the necesary level to make a deal.

The buyer who wants to make such a verbal offer may say to the broker: "You go to the owner and tell him I'll give him so-and-so for his place."

A "conversational" offer of that kind is worthless, for the buyer may change his mind the next minute and there is nothing to hold him to the deal. *Don't consider verbal offers.* They are evidence that you have not sold the prospect sufficiently.

Every farm broker and salesman should have some kind of contract-to-purchase form on which to inscribe the buyer's offer and (when and if it is accepted) the seller's name. Then you have a contract to purchase real estate—a meeting of the minds that has earned the broker a commission.

After filling out the contract with the terms that have been discussed, call for attention and read the contract to the buyer. Then ask the buyer to make out a check for the deposit. This should never be less than the amount of the commission, and in large deals should approximate from 5 to 10 per cent of the total consideration. You may have to take a smaller deposit, but at least you can ask for enough. If the buyer is really in earnest and means to go through with the deal, he will not object to making a substantial down payment.

See that the check is correct and then casually place it safely in your wallet. Even at the very last minute many prospects have been overcome with fear and reclaimed their checks, thus terminating negotiations. In nearly every deal some degree of fear is indicated by a client about to make a purchase. It is usually expressed by the remark, "Well, I guess I'll take a chance!" as he writes his check and signs the contract.

Now comes the time for presenting the offer to the owner of the property. If it represents the price and terms of a listing and the listing is still good and in effect, little trouble should be had in securing acceptance of the offer. If the property has been listed for some time and it is not an exclusive listing, the owner may have changed his mind, either deciding not to sell or raising his price. The desirability of exclusive listings on farm properties is apparent. It takes a lot of time to list and show a farm, and probably it is as much work again to persuade the buyer to act. In addition, advertising must be prepared, signs erected, and other work done, all of which makes it desirable for the broker to have a listing that he knows will "stay put" until its term has expired.

Assuming the parties have both agreed to the deal, it can then either be put in escrow or completed in the office of the broker or an attorney representing one or both of the parties. The broker should keep all papers and data together on each deal, and place them in a folder or a large manila envelope, properly marked as to date, names of buyer and seller, and terms. Later it is an easy matter to resurrect the folder if information about the transaction is needed. Keep all listing cards and other data, as the property may come up for resale three, five, or ten years later, and exceedingly valuable data will then be readily available. Whether possession is given immediately or not, commissions on real estate deals are due the broker at the close of escrow, when papers are recorded in the name of the new owner. The rate of commission will be charged in conformity with the usual rates for the locality.

When a good-sized deal is completed it is well to write an account of the sale and send it to the local newspapers where the property is located. Publicity of that kind is appreciated by both seller and buyer and is definitely useful to the broker, as it shows that he is actively at work. Such stories are often responsible for worthwhile farm listings being sent in.

There is no sacred place in which a contract should be made out and signed. It does not have to be in a broker's office. You can keep a pad of contract blanks in your car or brief case, and one can be made out on the front seat while chatting with the prospect, or on the front porch after you have wandered around the premises and the prospect gives evidences of having been sold. Don't be afraid to ask the prospect to make his offer, and never hesitate to ask for a deposit to bind the deal.

Many farm deals are not made upon the first visit. The prospect often wants additional information that can be obtained only by means of a soil survey, or a visit to the county agricultural agent, who can tell what crops and livestock can best be raised in that particular section of the country. He may want to talk with other people in the vicinity, and may hang around the locality several days before he can make up his mind. Help him secure comfortable accommodations and assist him in every way to secure the information he needs. It may be the biggest deal he has ever engaged in, and he wants to know he is doing the right thing.

Clever farm brokers become good advertisers, for they learn what people want to know about their commodity. Here are some of the things to include in farm advertisements:

Information about electricity and telephone service.

Does the property front on hard-surfaced state or improved highways?

What livestock, tools, equipment, crops, household furniture, etc., are included?

Large acreage when it is very reasonable, even though it isn't too accessible.

Large hay crops. Tillage workable by tractor.

Bordering or overlooking lake or river.

If owner has made money by taking summer boarders, state the amount in any one season.

Mention the good deer or bird shooting and the fishing if they exist— and state the kinds of fish.

Wood or timber on the farm.

Large and commodious barns and outbuildings.

Buildings in good repair.
Low down payment or easy terms.
If tax rate is low, mention it.
Nearness to thriving towns, where farmers attend Grange meetings and where there is a high school, good churches, movies, fraternities; creamery; milk, egg, and poultry collection, or milk shipping depot, and such other attractions as will help make the life of a farmer profitable and enjoyable.

When a property is listed, all of the information above and more should be obtained so that you will have plenty of ammunition. Avoid careless or misleading statements. Know the facts are exactly as you state them.

If you can use a half-tone engraving of the dwelling and the largest barn on a property in an ad, do so. The Chinese proverb, "A picture is worth 10,000 words," is as true in farm advertising as in anything else. Obtain complete data on the interior of the farm dwelling, and be able to tell a prospective buyer how he can enlarge it with additional rooms if he has a large family.

A farm broker should take plenty of pictures to show to prospects. Many a sale has been made by showing an attractive photograph and enlarging on it so eloquently that the prospect at once becomes interested.

Occasionally a broker lists a property occupied by a tenant who does not want to move. Such a tenant usually "knocks" the property when it is being shown in the hope of killing the sale to avoid moving. Never engage in an argument with a person of that kind. An effective way to handle the situation is to talk about like this: "How long did you say you have lived here, Mr. Tenant?" "Isn't it too bad you have had to live so long in a place that doesn't meet your needs? Tell me just the kind of place you want and if I learn of such a place I'll be glad to tell you about it—and won't charge you anything for helping you find it." Next time you show the property he is likely to refrain from "knocking."

Selling farms is not unlike selling other kinds of real property. It presents the same problems, the same arguments, the same tussles with human nature, the same rewards when a job is well done. Farmers are as well read, as well informed, and just as intelligent as city people. They are nice people to work with, honest and considerate. The broker or salesman who wishes to succeed must study constantly and daily translate his newly gained knowledge into useful practice in following up his deals.

CHAPTER 27

Rentals and

Property Management

EVERY BROKERAGE OFFICE FROM TIME to time engages in the rental of houses and apartments in its own neighborhood, but only the well-established office in an area with many apartments and houses for rent can operate a regular rental department successfully.

A rental business is supposed by some to be a feeder to the sales department where tenants are converted into home owners. There is considerable doubt as to whether this is actually so. If a rental department is to be operated, it should stand on its own feet, earning enough commissions to make it an independent entity in the business.

Rental properties commonly encountered include unfurnished and furnished houses, unfurnished and furnished apartments, flats and units in two- and three-family houses. Rentals of business and industrial properties are not usually included in a regular rental department but are handled through a leasing department set up separately for that purpose.

The most successful rental department is usually included as part of a regular management business that takes complete charge of large apartment buildings, business blocks, and other real estate enterprises that depend for their income on rentals derived from their tenants. Rentals are incidental to the carrying on of management operations, but are only a part of them. Most cities have firms specializing in this type of business. In addition to renting and managing, they take charge of all repairs, decorating, furniture, linens, and general equipment. Such a rental office, provided it has enough properties, can show excellent returns from year to year.

At the outset a rental department must assemble its listing cards for different types of property and application forms to be filled out by prospective tenants. This information is necessary and in many cases must be turned over to landlords before a tenant's application for a rental will be accepted. Anyone contemplating the establishment of a rental department should make a trip to large cities near by and visit rental offices, learn their techniques and obtain copies of their various forms; or should obtain books on the subject that discuss in detail many of the problems the rental manager encounters.[1]

To obtain rental listings, a new office should conduct a survey of all properties in its neighborhood, calling upon apartment-house owners as well as homeowners and getting acquainted with those residential units which are for rent or may become available from time to time. In this way a personal contact is established with managers and owners. When a vacancy does occur, the owner's first thought will be to call the rental office and register a listing. Most active rental offices carry advertisements in daily newspapers soliciting listings. Signs on the front of offices requesting rental listings are also effective. Mailing lists can be made up of the owners of all rental properties contacted, and these can be circularized occasionally. The rental agent must keep himself well and favorably known to the property owners who will occasionally make use of his services.

Diplomacy is necessary in handling rental prospects so that they may be properly placed in accommodations that meet their needs and where their particular type of tenancy is wanted. The prospective tenant is asked to fill out a listing blank, or

[1] See, for example, Part VI, "How to Manage Real Property" in *Real Estate Encyclopedia*, E. J. Friedman, (Englewood Cliffs, N. J.: Prentice-Hall, Inc.)

at least to give the information necessary to do so. The rental agency must use considerable tact in fitting tenants into the right locations. Many landlords are particular about the tenants they will accept, and it is time wasted to try to settle a tenant where he will not be happy or where he is not wanted.

When a prospect stops at a broker's office and requests an accommodation, the agent in charge of such work will at the outset have a conversation with the visitor to find out what type of quarters are wanted, the rent the applicant is prepared to pay, and information about the tenant's business and general responsibility. It is necessary to get this information, since some property owner is going to demand it very shortly and the best time to get it is at the initial interview. While obtaining the information the rental agent carefully sizes up the prospect and decides on the type of place to suggest. The next thing to do is to show the tenant what is available. This will depend largely upon the type and volume of current rental properties. At certain boom times they are scarcely obtainable; in periods of depression there is sometimes a surplus.

Never show a prospect so many properties at one time that confusion results. This warning applies to vacant apartments in a building as it does to houses. Settle on one, or two, or perhaps three places and get the tenant sold on one of them. Some tenants will shop around for hours or days if the agent lets them. To do so is a wonderful way to waste the agent's time and patience. By qualifying a prospect as to his needs and his ability to pay rent, much time and effort can be saved.

An agent should be careful not to promise special concessions which a landlord may later be loath to give. There should be a very definite understanding between the owner and the agent about the exact size and condition of the premises to be rented, the amount to be charged, and any special requirements the owner may insist upon. When the tenant is shown the premises, care should be taken to quote the exact price and any other conditions required by the landlord; little difficulty will then be encountered. Don't promise anything the landlord has not already agreed to give.

Don't argue wth a prospect and don't talk too much. Give the prospect plenty of opportunity to sell himself on what is offered. Tell the truth and don't attempt to hide apparent defects. Give the prospect credit for having a brain. If there are serious defects in a property, better not list it or attempt to provide a tenant until the defect is remedied. Avoid high-pressure salesmanship, and encourage a prospect to return at a later date.

As in selling a property, so in renting it—give the prospect plenty of chances to close. If the prospect seems well satisfied with what you have offered, proceed to close the deal right there by getting a deposit and an agreement to rent the premises. Have this accepted by the landlord, deduct your commission from the deposit, turn the balance over to the property owner, and you have completed a deal!

Quite frankly, unless a brokerage office intends to make it an integral part of its business in an extensive way, it is doubtful whether a rental department is worthwhile in the average small office. It entails a lot of trouble and grief, and the returns seldom are great enough to justify the time and energy expended. If a regular management department is found desirable, one person should be placed in charge of it and trained for the work, if such training has not already been secured through experience with another office of the same kind. The rental manager can expect to be a busy person, for calls will come not only in the daytime but also at night when plumbing fixtures break or get stopped up, or something happens to electric wiring, or tenants keep television too loud.

Besides becoming familiar with leasing arrangements and lease forms themselves, the property manager will have to copy or create forms that will include a tenant's application, lists of furniture and equipment to be found in furnished units, notices to quit when eviction of a tenant seems to be required, various house rules to govern the conduct of tenants in buildings being managed, and other forms found necessary in this branch of the realty business. Most of these forms will have to be supplied in quantities, and many will have to be printed.

A property manager gets to know a good deal about human nature when it comes to handling tenants, and this applies especially to collections of rentals. Some tenants pay on the dot every time the rent is due; others seem intentionally careless and forgetful. Some are deadbeats who move from building to building, or from neighborhood to neighborhood. Care in selecting tenants and securing references or information from former landlords will tend to prevent deadbeats from plying their trade too boldly. Then there is the type who comes along with just a part of the rent due and promises to pay a little more next week and the balance by the middle or the end of the month. These are troublesome and annoying types and should be dealt with sternly if they appear to be taking advantage of the property manager. Another kind of tenant gives a bad check after having overrun his rent-due date. Keeping track of all kinds of tenants and their weaknesses tests the patience of the most even-tempered rental agent.

A typical form which a tenant is asked to sign when making an application usually has a place for at least three references from former landlords, and the last two landlords should be included. Not until the former landlords have been contacted and the record of the tenant made known should an application be finally accepted. Better to turn away a tenant than invite trouble from an unstable one. The tenant's employer and his bank should be asked for references when the tenant moves in, and in the event he gets behind in his rent another check with them is desirable. Some rental agencies turn over the matter of references to professional credit agencies that are in a position to collect and interpret data about those they are asked to investigate. For a fee, a very complete report will be furnished, from which the property manager can make up his mind as to the desirability of the applicant as a tenant.

A rather extensive bookkeeping system is necessary if many properties are being managed through one office. A set of books must be kept for each property, income and expenses noted, and a balance secured at the end of the month to be forwarded to the property owner indicating his return on his investment. A good bookkeeping system will show:

1. The financial condition of a property when first listed.
2. Every transaction recorded as it occurs.
3. An account for every tenant, with income received from each apartment or dwelling.
4. A report, submitted monthly, showing condition of each tenant's account and standing.
5. A report showing amounts spent for each kind of expense.
6. An annual report showing total cash receipts and expenditures.
7. A yearly profit and loss statement for the property owner.

Large offices have enough work for a bookkeeper. In small offices the books may be kept by the rental agent. In brokerage offices where only an occasional rental is made, each one can be considered the same as a deal that is handled by the office bookkeeping system.[2]

The alert executive of a management business will seek constantly to expand so as to include as many important properties as possible. Volume counts here. Where should one seek new business? Among others the following should be contacted:

1. Owners.
2. Estates.
3. Trustees.
4. Attorneys.
5. Receivers.
6. Savings banks.
7. Trust companies.
8. Insurance companies.
9. Chain-store concerns.
10. Syndicates owning real estate.

[2] See Chapter 26, "Apartment House Management," *Real Estate Encyclopedia*, E. J. Friedman, (Englewood Cliffs, N. J.: Prentice-Hall, Inc.)

11. Building and loan associations.

12. Elderly investors who do not want the bother of managing their own properties.

13. Non-resident owners of real estate.

14. Institutions owning real estate that are glad to engage expert service in this field.

Before the creation of any management business on a large scale is contemplated, a survey should be made to ascertain the possibilities of obtaining enough customers to make the venture a profitable one. Sources of business should be carefully investigated, and the volume of income that can be obtained must be estimated. It may be found that not sufficient revenue can be expected to maintain such a department, which requires a good-sized yearly budget to support it. Perhaps there is too much competition in the field already, making it difficult to obtain patronage.

Compensation for managing properties is a matter of contract between owner and agency. It may range from 5 to 10 per cent of total rental collections, or it may be arranged on a stated monthly sum to be paid for the service.

Some real estate brokerage offices have headquarters in large office buildings, which they manage. The problems of the office-building manager are not unlike those encountered in the apartment-house field. He does not always have to be so particular about the personality of his tenants. It is desirable, however, that he make a close scrutiny of his prospective tenants, their past activities, and their credit backgrounds, if only to avoid trouble at a later date.

Real estate brokerage offices that specialize in the selling and leasing of commercial properties keep complete records of lease expirations of merchants and storekeepers. Checked some months in advance, prospects for new locations are often turned up. Stores to be vacated furnish listings for which tenants may be secured.[3]

Rental departments are frequently productive of news

[3] For detailed accounts of store-leasing practices, see *Leases: Percentage, Short and Long Term*, by Stanley L. McMichael and Paul T. O'Keefe (Englewood Cliffs, N. J.: Prentice-Hall, Inc.)

stories that attract business. Occasionally something of interest transpires in an apartment house, or a visitor of note moves in, or the property is sold at a large figure. Information sent in to the city editor or real estate editor of a newspaper will always receive attention if it has news value. On the other hand, it is always desirable to avoid *unfavorable* publicity, as when a fire occurs, a tenant or one in his family commits suicide, a murder takes place, or some other unfortunate event occurs which does not redound to the credit of the property. Not much can be done about it except an appeal to city editors to refrain from mentioning the street number or name of the property where the event occurred. When chain-store leases of considerable magnitude are made through leasing departments, publicity can always be obtained in daily newspapers.

Offices that manage real estate properties on a large scale often maintain departments for the purpose of making repairs, decorating, and so on. An additional revenue can be obtained from this source and prompter service can often be secured through a department's own employees than by securing bids or hiring itinerant workers to do the work. Great care must be taken to maintain such a department on a strictly business basis, asking only a fair trade profit and not making a racket out of it, as has sometimes been done in large cities, thereby giving the agency a bad name among property owners.

It is customary for operators of office buildings to have regular repair and decorating staffs, manned by several employees who care for emergency work and redecorate wherever it seems desirable to have the work done. Those staffs are usually under the direction of a building superintendent, who also supervises elevator operators and janitors. Well-maintained repair and decorating programs are worthwhile and help fight the grim monster of obsolescence, which threatens to shorten the life of every large building, whether it be an apartment house, a hotel, or an office building.

To the newcomer in real estate, consideration of rental departments is largely academic, for he will probably not be concerned with the matter for some time. Later, as he develops his own business or becomes associated with one of considerable size, the question of whether to go into the rental business and operate a management department will come up. At that time the entire matter can be gone into by studying the subject and visiting other cities where ideas may be obtained for promoting such work.

CHAPTER 28

Trading Real Estate

EXCHANGING LAND AND THE IMPROVE-
ments thereon is one of the oldest branches of the real estate
business. Before money was invented and came into general
use, all trade involved bartering one thing for another. It was
difficult, at times, to make deals on a fairly equal basis because
equities in different things varied greatly. Nevertheless it was
the way exchanges of goods and properties had to be made.

In some exchanges of real estate no monetary consideration
is involved, and the most difficult problem is how to pay the
broker for his services. He may have to take notes, payable
over a term of months, or he may even have to accept an
equity in a property as his reward, reselling it later for cash.

Some brokers and salesmen take naturally to trading while
others seldom, if ever, indulge in it. One requires the shrewd
instincts and patience of an old-time horse trader to engage
in "swapping" one piece of property for another. Few men follow it as a calling exclusively, but almost every broker makes
an occasional trade in the course of his business activities.

Trading is encouraged by income tax laws which exempt
many exchanges of real property from taxation. (Gain on a
sale of real property is generally taxable, with a limited exception for homeowners acquiring and using a new residence
within a specified period after the sale of the old.)

The problem with trading is in matching the needs of two

(or more) parties. Experience shows it takes a peculiar type of alert mentality to develop into a successful trader of real estate, and comparatively few succeed in this branch of the realty business.

A brokerage office should always maintain an exchange file and carefully tabulate all listings that can be traded. There should be a cross-file, in one being the listings to be traded and in the other cards indicating what prospects need and what they will trade for.

Typical conditions under which trades can be made are the following:

1. An owner of vacant property, tired of paying taxes and losing interest on unproductive land, will consider a trade for income property.

2. The owner of the income property will make a trade because he is tired of managerial problems, or has quarreled with his tenants, or feels his property is getting old and will require a lot of money for rehabilitation.

3. A farmer will trade for a home in a town or city, having decided to retire.

4. A city man, impressed with the security of the person who owns his own ranch, orchard, or farm, will exchange his city residence for a country place.

5. An owner of property in one community, desiring to remove to another for business, health, or other reasons, will trade his home or business property for a like holding in the city where he plans to go.

6. Occasionally an owner who has a lot of small properties —sometimes known among the real estate fraternity as "cats and dogs"—will trade them for one large property, often assuming a mortgage on the latter in doing so, but getting rid of small unprofitable ones.

7. The man who takes in the properties in the foregoing paragraph may be a trader who will fix them up and sell them at a profit, or trade them again, getting a little cash out of each deal.

8. In an active building market, apartment-house builders

often trade new income buildings for vacant land on which
they can again build, together with a little cash to pay commissions and "sweeten up the deal."

9. Property holders who are about to have mortgages renewed or foreclosed and who are tired of their holdings frequently resort to trading in an effort to improve their positions.

10. An owner may become imbued with the idea that he
wants to own a certain type of property, such as an apartment, hotel, beach cottage, or suburban home, and he will
straightaway be interested in a trade of his home or miscellaneous property, probably adding some cash if necessary.

A broker, to be successful at trading, must have a shrewd
knowledge of realty values. He must be able to analyze every
property offered him for trade and make up his mind as to
the inherent value it possesses. *He must know what it is actually worth!* With this knowledge he can proceed to offer
some other property on the basis of what it is worth, and arrange for one or the other owner to pay the difference in cash,
accepting a mortgage or adding another piece of property to
even up equities.

Knowing what a property is worth, the broker immediately
knows whether its owner is quoting it at an inflationary price,
a fact that must be taken into consideration by the broker in
approaching the man who is to trade something for it. This
man probably offers something in trade which is also inflated.
The owner of the better property boosts his price in the somewhat vain hope that he will have an advantage of the other
party to the deal, while the owner of the poorer property also
elevates his price in self-defense. Both know their prices are
too high and definitely inflated, and it takes the broker to
bring them down to earth and together in a deal. This
takes some plain and fancy maneuvering. The broker must
dominate the deal or the two traders may get to quarreling
or drift apart. He must persuade each one in turn that a
fair price must be set on a property to make it an acceptable
subject for trade. Seldom are the parties to a trade actually
brought together until their minds have met on terms ac-

ceptable to each. Each is shown the other's property. Advantages and defects are pointed out. All bulges and wrinkles in the deal finally having been ironed out, they can then be brought together in escrow after each has signed an exchange agreement in which every detail is carefully explained and accepted. After signing such an agreement, it is the practice of some brokers to take the parties into escrow separately, not risking any chance for further arguments.

In many trade deals, one or both of the properties involved is what is known as a real estate "cripple." There is something the matter with it. It may be simply that it is not readily salable and a trade seems the best way out. It may be in a poor state of repair and require considerable money to be spent on rebuilding operations. An owner may have "gone sour" on a property and simply made up his mind to get rid of it. It may be that taxes are high, the property provides little income, and the owner is tired of carrying a "dead horse." There are many things that may be wrong with properties involved in trades, and the broker must be able to detect the trouble instantly. He must at the very outset ascertain in his own mind the real and actual motive each owner has for wanting to trade his property. If the broker fails to find this out, and the party to whom he presents a property does, the deal may collapse. It is wise in many cases to dwell on the actual defect of a property, sometimes making it appear worse than it really is. Then, when the prospect sees it, he will be prepared and perhaps admit that it is not nearly so bad as the broker painted it.

Each party to a trade is, at the outset, naturally suspicious of the offering of the other fellow. He wonders what is wrong with it, if anything. If investigation develops that something is actually defective with an offering, the broker should not seek to deny it or brush it aside, but should delve into the matter in detail and ascertain if it is important enough to prevent the parties from getting together. Complete frankness and honesty are his best defenses at this time.

Trading properties in different cities occasionally results in the earning of substantial commissions. A man in Buffalo wants to retire and move to Los Angeles and would like to dispose of his Buffalo real estate holdings for something in the Western city. A Buffalo broker communicates with a realtor in the coast city and outlines what he has to offer; the other broker finds that he has a man who found that he made a mistake in retiring and wants to get back in harness again in Buffalo. The two are brought together and after a good deal of inspecting and bargaining they make a trade. Deals of this kind are going on constantly throughout the country. Sometimes offers to trade property may be found in the classified ads of metropolitan papers. A variation may be found where a man from one city goes to another, likes it, and seeks to trade his back-home property for something in the new location. Such deals all necessitate careful appraisals of property, either by the broker or brokers involved or by expert appraisers hired for the job. When an expert appraiser is called in, if the properties are within a reasonable distance of each other, it is wise to have *the same appraiser value both properties.* Members of the American Institute of Real Estate Appraisers (M. A. I.'s) do this work constantly.

The most likely prospect to be willing to trade his property is the distressed or harassed property owner who is in difficulty over his mortgage, which may be about to be foreclosed. For various reasons he may not be able to sell despite the fact that he possesses a sound equity. This man will "trade down," that is, he will take an inferior type of property provided it has no encumbrance against it—vacant land, an old dwelling, building lots, or what not. The party who accepts the distressed property may be able to repair it, or change the type of occupancy, or do something to it that promptly cures its defects, whereupon little difficulty is found in refinancing it.

Trading, in addition to requiring a wide range of appraising technique, also calls for extensive knowledge of financing, leases, earning capacity of property, how to set up statements of income and expenses, how to figure operating profits and the net income of a property, and similar matters. It is not a field for the newcomer to enter until he has had sufficient training and experience to know his way about.

In periods of economic depressions, trading is much more active than in boom times when property can be sold for cash. When an owner faces a long siege of lowered income, he is usually willing to cast off his responsibilities for certain properties he owns and becomes a docile client, willing to make any fair deal that may lighten his burden. The property-exchange market, however, never amounts to more than a small proportion of the total volume of real estate transferred.

The cash value of a property is usually greater than can be obtained in a trade but not much or it would be sold for money and not traded. Many owners boost their prices on trades above the cash prices, but in the end they get less in a trade than they would if they sold for cash. The practice of boosting prices when trades are involved sometimes makes it difficult for the broker to get his parties together, but if he does succeed in making a deal on the high figures, his commission is correspondingly greater.

It takes much determined effort to originate and carry through trade deals to successful conclusions. Unless a broker is willing to stick to his deal until it is consummated, sometimes months later, he is wasting his time, for trade deals seldom slip through as easily as do cash sales. Suspended trades sometimes come to life at a later date, when they can be revised and consummated.

Traders are sometimes, but seldom, accused of sharp practices. Most brokers are honest, are licensed, and are held to strict accountability for their actions. In many instances the broker has to keep constant watch to ascertain if one or the other of his trader principals is acting squarely. The best insurance against anything untoward happening is for the broker to be thoroughly familiar with each property. Then, if he sees one party taking advantage of the other, he can make the necessary revelations, which may keep his record clear if a blow-up occurs later on.

Trades involving transfers of city dwellings for suburban homes are frequent. Nearly everyone at some time in his career gets the "farm bug" and wants to live in the country. It usually comes early in life, while one is ambitious and likes hard work.

It is easy to interest him in a trade of his city property for a suburban home. On the other hand, the owner of the country place has found that there is a lot more work involved than he realized, that his taxes are high, that laborers are arrogant and expensive at times, and that the time spent in traveling to and fro might be better used in some other more profitable way. Here are two persons with definite motives, ready and willing to act, just as soon as the broker can get them together. To do so is sometimes quite a task, but that is what makes up the real estate trader's business.

A realty broker can be of great service by trading property that is in the hands of a misfit or turbulent owner. A turbulent owner is one who is not interested enough in the real estate he owns to look after it the proper way. He may quarrel with tenants, neglect them, fail to keep his property in habitable shape, and generally fail in his duties as a landlord. To trade such a property out of such hands is to perform a genuine service to the neighborhood and to the property involved, which might prove a good investment to someone who knows how to care for it. It takes ingenuity to rescue thin equities in income or business properties and get them transferred into more friendly hands.

In times of depression, when mortgages default, some financial institutions such as banks, mortgage and insurance companies become the possessors of large quantities of property which they are compelled to repossess, rehabilitate, and sell. Frequently it is possible for a broker to take several such properties and trade them in on a larger holding, such as a hotel or apartment house, which, with some remodeling and skillful management, can be liquidated more easily than can the individual properties. In good times banks repossess very little property and are usually able to sell it readily for cash. Some of their "white elephants," however, are traded to persons who are willing to work them over into merchantable realty investments.

The non-resident owner of either vacant or improved real estate can frequently be persuaded to become a party to a trade for a property in his own city, where he can see, watch, and manage it. After a broker has found a choice piece of acreage, for instance, which belongs to an owner in a distant city, St. Louis, for instance, he can run an ad in his local paper and secure the attention and interest of some former resident of St. Louis who still owns property in that city and who might want to trade it for the acreage. A swap results, and each party is happy in that he has secured property near-by that he can plan to use to advantage, or subdivide and improve, or sell. Trades like these are made frequently.

Sometimes estates which are in the hands of individual executors, and which are made up of miscellaneous properties, are consolidated by being traded for a large property that can be placed in the hands of a responsible manager. This is particularly advantageous in the case of distantly located farm properties or vacant tracts, bringing in little income, with taxes being paid regularly every year.

Few successful trades are made except through careful planning. Hit-and-miss listing and sales methods get a broker nowhere. Very seldom indeed does a trade just happen by someone listing a property one day and someone else taking it the next. Real effort, backed with knowledge and experience and an eternal insistence that a fair and equitable deal shall result, are behind practically every worthwhile trade that is consummated. If a broker is not capable of studying, analyzing, and valuing properties, he might well direct his efforts in other directions.

The broker must be more than careful to be fair and honest in executing trade deals, for he may be charged with misrepresentation, if in the negotiations he makes assertions or presents facts that later are found to be untrue. He must be on his toes, mentally and physically, if he is to make a success of trading.

Some traders emphasize the fact that they just exchange equities and are averse to quoting definite cash prices. This, in a way, is good practice, for it is the equities that are being transferred, and if each party can be satisfied that he is getting fair exchange value, a trade is possible. In such deals physical values are not considered and cash prices are not quoted, or if talked about, are in general terms. After the deal is closed, the broker can sit down with each party and arrive at a basis on which a commission is to be paid.

This leads directly to the matter of compensation to be paid for the broker's services. Where a single broker brings two parties together, each with a property to be transferred, and an exchange is made, under rules of real estate boards he is entitled to and can collect a commission from each party, on the well-grounded assumption that he has performed a definite and useful service for each party. It is wise at the outset for a broker to advise his clients of this fact, to avoid difficulty when the matter of commission comes up. In an exchange contract the payment of commission is always provided for. If one broker is involved, he gets commissions from each party to the deal. If a different broker represents each side, then a single commission is due each one.

Only occasionally will the average broker be called upon to negotiate an exchange of properties. He must realize that in trading he is simply engaged in a double-barreled deal in which two owners are seeking to sell to two buyers. He must serve two masters with the consent of each, but he must guard the interests of each just as carefully as he would in an ordinary transaction involving a seller and a buyer. The sales technique may be a little more involved, but the reward for his efforts will be well worth while if he can close his deal.

CHAPTER 29

Financing Real Estate

WITHOUT FINANCIAL ASSISTANCE, RE-latively few real estate or building transactions would be completed. Rare indeed is the buyer who has cash for the entire purchase price—and it is somewhat unusual to find a seller who is willing or able to finance the transaction. Of course, some sellers will take back a purchase money mortgage either because the return they can get is greater than that of other investments, or because of possible tax savings.

Most mortgage financing, then, has to be obtained from outside sources, such as:

1. Commercial banks
2. Savings banks.
3. Savings and loan associations.
4. Insurance companies.
5. Trust companies.
6. Mortgage companies.
7. Individuals.
8. Endowed institutions.
9. Pension funds.
10. Other investors.

Practices observed by those different lenders will be considered in detail below. Conditions vary from state to state and between distantly separated sections of the nation, but for the most part they are found to be fairly uniform in principle. [Generally, the limits or restrictions noted below do not apply in the case of Federal Housing Administration (FHA) and Veterans Administration (VA) guaranteed loans.]

Commercial banks will make loans on both residential and income-producing property, although their most important function is in providing construction financing. Generally, commercial banks chartered by the states will limit their mortgage loans to 66 2/3 per cent of the apraised value of the property even if the state permits a larger percentage. (In some states the limit is only 60 per cent.) National banks can make mortgage loans up to 75 per cent of the appraised value, but the loan must be amortized over its length. Ten-year mortgages for up to 66 2/3 per cent of appraised value can be made if 40 per cent of the loan is amortized during its life. Most commercial banks confine their mortgage activity to a limited area around their office or offices.

Mutual savings banks, although found in only 18 states, are an important factor in real estate financing. Mortgage loans by such banks generally must be made on improved property, and frequently only on property within the state in which they are chartered or within a limited distance from the home office. (But, for example, New York savings banks may make mortgage loans in Connecticut, Massachusetts, New Jersey, Pennsylvania, Rhode Island, and Vermont.)

The loan-to-value ratio of savings bank mortgage loans ranges from 60 per cent to 90 per cent of appraised value, depending on state law. Loans of 80 per cent or more are generally limited to new single-family homes—and these constitute the bulk of savings bank mortgage loans, although, particularly in the larger cities, such banks may concentrate on multifamily, commercial, and industrial properties.

Savings and loan associations (including building and loan associations, coöperative banks, and homestead associations) must invest the bulk of their funds in home mortgages—making them a most important source of funds for such mortgages. These associations may be chartered under state or federal law. In general, they are limited to making loans within a fifty-mile radius of the home office, although, under some conditions, federal associations may make loans outside their regular area. Federal S & L's can lend up to $40,000 on a one-to four-family house; they can also finance (1) small multi-family dwellings and (2) the acquisition and development of land for home building. They may also buy participating interests on mortgage loans on one-to four-family homes anywhere in the country. State chartered associations generally operate under similar restrictions, though their loans are often confined to single-family dwellings.

Loans can be for 80 per cent of appraised value with a twenty-year maturity, or, except for some state associations, 90 per cent in the case of single-family homes.

Life insurance companies invest a large share of their assets in mortgage loans of all kinds, although they are apt to concentrate on income-producing property rather than homes. While such companies are chartered under state laws and are subject to numerous restrictions as to the investments they can make, generally there are no restrictions on the areas within which they may make loans.

As a general rule, life insurance companies can make loans of up to two-thirds of the appraised value. Higher ratios can be used in some states if the company sets up a reserve for the excess, and in others if the loan is self-liquidating or the amortization schedule will insure payment in full within a limited number of years.

Trust companies and banks with trust departments have funds of personal trusts and estates that they must invest, and in some areas this source has become a substantial factor in the mortgage market. While there are cases where they may originate and hold mortgages, much more frequently trust companies or departments purchase outstanding mortgages or shares in savings and loans institutions (thus indirectly investing in mortgages).

Mortgage companies organized under the business corporation laws of the states generally have very broad mortgage lending powers. Not only will they originate mortgage loans, but they will act as loan correspondents for insurance companies and some of the larger mutual savings banks. These companies are a particularly important source of mortgage financing in the South and West. Because they usually have broad lending powers and do not have to account to directors or trustees, they can act very quickly.

Strange as it might seem, it is estimated that individuals hold between 20 and 25 per cent of mortgage loans—and yet they are not an important factor in the normal mortgage market for homes or income-producing property. The answer to this seeming paradox lies in the fact that most such loans are either purchase money mortgages taken back on the sale of a home or other property, or are second mortgages which lending institutions are not permitted to make. Nonetheless, almost every community of any size has at least one individual who will make mortgage loans because he likes the high return —and the alert real estate broker will make certain he knows who this person is, since this can be an important source when money is tight.

Mortgage investments are ideal for the endowed institution where liquidity is a minor consideration. Whereas banks and life insurance companies must be prepared to have substantial amounts of cash withdrawn, endowed institutions rarely need to touch principal—hence their interest is primarily in a safe investment yielding as high a return as possible. Some institutions handle their own investments, others entrust their investments to banks or mortgage companies.

While lending institutions must constantly seek savers to supply them with lendable funds, pension funds do not have that problem. As with the endowed institution, the main problem of a pension fund is to find safe investments yielding the highest possible return. Investment in mortgage loans is one answer to this problem, although only a small percentage of such money is now invested in mortgages, with the bulk being put in stocks and bonds. There is, however, a trend towards diversification of pension portfolios, with more money being put in mortgage loans, principally those that are government-backed. As the funds gain more experience in mortgage investment, a larger share of the funds may go into the conventional loan field.

Other sources from which mortgage money may be available are fraternal and benevolent associations, individuals acting as administrators, executors, and trustees of estates, and investment trusts—possibly even the tax-sheltered Real Estate Investment Trusts.

What are the instruments used in financing real estate? Primarily, they are: (1) the note or bond indicating the obligation of the borrower (mortgagor) to repay the lender (mortgagee), and (2) the mortgage or other security instrument subjecting the real estate to the payment of the indebtedness. The latter instrument takes different forms in different states. However, whether the instruments are called mortgages, installment contracts, deeds of trust, warranty deeds, or vendor's liens, in substance the same situation exists.

The important factors in any of the instruments are the terms of payment and the rights and privileges of the parties. In long term borrowing, the rights and privileges can be especially important. For example, if the borrower does not have the right to pay off all or part of the mortgage in advance (prepayment privilege), the lender may legally demand the payment of all interest that would be due up to the normal maturity date of the debt, or may refuse to accept prepayment regardless of any premium that may be offered. (Prepayment privileges are generally readily available when interest rates are low, but much harder to obtain when interest rates are high. Lenders must include a prepayment privilege in all FHA and VA loans.)

If a note (a simple written promise to pay) is used as one of the primary instruments, the chief advantage is that federal documentary stamps need not be affixed. Rarely do the notes include a waiver of homestead and exemption rights, but they usually do contain a waiver of demand, notice, and protest, as well as a provision that the borrower will pay any attorney's fees in event of default. The note may also include other technical provisions, such as for a grace period.

If a bond is used instead of a note, the purpose is to insure payment of any damages resulting from the seller's failure to pay the mortgage loan according to the contract. The penalty provision in the bond is frequently for twice the indebtedness, but in no case can more be collected than the indebtedness, plus interest and costs, according to the contract.

Either the note or the bond may be "sealed" in order to extend the time for any legal action based on it.

The legal effect of the mortgage, the customary security instrument, depends on state law. In some states, the mortgage conveys legal title to the lender until the indebtedness is paid, at which time title reverts to the mortgagor. But in most states, the mortgage does not transfer title but merely creates a lien on the property under which the lender may liquidate the property in the event of default. In any case, when the debt is paid, the mortgage is extinguished, although evidence of payment of the debt must be recorded.

In many states, a good deal of property is bought under contracts to convey at some future date. These may be called installment contracts, land contracts, contracts for deeds, sales contracts, or other names.

Basically, such a contract provides for the purchaser to make a down payment, followed by a specified number of payments of a stated size to be made on specified dates. When the last payment is received, the purchaser receives a deed for the property. (The contract sometimes provides that, after a specified portion of the total price has been paid, title will pass, subject to a mortgage for the balance.)

Installment contracts are especially useful to builders and developers in the low-priced home field, and in other cases where the down payment is too small to make it possible to obtain a mortgage.

If the financing is to take the form of a deed of trust, the borrower first executes a promissory note (or notes) to the lender. The seller then transfers title to the buyer (usually through an escrow) and simultaneously the buyer executes the deed of trust which conveys the legal title to a third party trustee. The trustee holds the title as security for payment of the note (and of any other obligations contained in the deed of trust). The deed of trust is frequently used in California because, under that instrument, the borrower has no right to redeem after foreclosure, while under a mortgage he can redeem the property any time within a year. Deeds of trust are also commonly used to secure large loans on commercial property when the borrower already has title. The sale procedure in case of default under a deed of trust is generally shorter, less complicated, and less expensive than foreclosure and sale under a mortgage.

Warranty deeds are used in Georgia in place of a mortgage, and may also be used in other states where a mortgage does not provide adequate security under the law. Such deeds usually contain the same provisions as a mortgage.

A vendor's lien is used extensively in Louisiana and sometimes in other states. Again, it is generally resorted to when it is felt a mortgage does not provide adequate security. Under the vendor's lien, the property is conveyed to the lender and then is reconveyed to the borrower with the lien, which contains conditions similar to those found in mortgages.

The following are four commonly accepted types of tenure in the United States:

1. *Fee simple* represents complete and absolute ownership. An owner may sell, encumber, lease, or otherwise dispose of his property in any way he chooses.

2. *Estate for life* represents an interest in land and improvements which may be held and enjoyed by a person for the term of his or her lifetime, whereupon it passes to another in the same form or to be owned in fee simple. An estate of this character is often created by a husband to take care of his widow during her lifetime, the property thereafter going to surviving children.

3. *Leasehold* represents an interest less than fee simple. A lessee may take possession and have full rights to use a property, subject to whatever rental or other obligations must be paid for the privilege.

4. *Land contracts* are used in the purchase of property by partial payments. The title remains in the owner until the

buyer, after making his initial down payment and completing all payments called for thereafter, is entitled to have the property transferred to him in fee simple. Land contracts are most commonly used in the purchase and sale of subdivision property although they may be used for acquiring houses and for many other purposes in the conveying of real estate.

Lesser interests in land are represented by such things as easements, rights of way, and liens.

Attributes of an ideal investment in real estate are:[1]

1. Acceptable duration.
2. Unlimited durability of enjoyment in the investor.
3. Freedom from liability.
4. Ample and constant security for capital invested.
5. Perfect liberty in ownership.
6. Constant and unfluctuating return, sufficient to pay the agreed rate of interest, and, in the case of a terminable estate, to provide the annual contribution to the necessary sinking fund for replacing the capital invested; in other words stability of income.
7. Immunity from anxiety and trouble.
8. Ease and readiness in realization of capital when desired.
9. Potential appreciation in value.

What relationship should price bear to value in a real estate transaction? In an active boom market, prices are usually higher than actual value as established by reliable appraisals from disinterested sources. In times of depression, values come down until sometimes they are less than reproduction cost less adequate depreciation. Definitely tied in very closely with financing real estate is the ability to establish value through modern appraisal procedure. In fact, the roots of all financing practices are sunk in proper appraisal methods as used by honest, well-informed valuators.

[1] Suggested by Robert F. Bingham and Elmore L. Andrews in their book *Financing Real Estate*.

CHAPTER **30**

Developing

Business Centers

A FERTILE FIELD FOR AN ENTERPRISING
real estate broker is the creation and sale of business property in outlying subcenters of trade. These centers may be
already in operation or in process of establishment, or they
may even be in the creative stage in the mind of someone
who is convinced of the success of such a venture.

Every city of any size has witnessed the springing up of
little subcenters of trade at outlying crossroads of travel.
From a few stores initially, these in many instances have
grown into important districts where real estate values have
expanded on a large scale. Surrounded by expanses of residential property on which are being built homes, the new
owners of which readily afford great increase in buying power,
these little satellite business communities present rich opportunities for brokers and salesmen to make sales and leases.

Even more important in recent years has been the growth
and development of the so-called shopping center—whether
it be the neighborhood center of 10 to 15 stores and service
shops, the community shopping center of 15 to 35 stores, or
the regional center with 50 to 100 establishments. For example, in 1949 there were approximately 75 shopping centers in the United States; in 1961 alone, 1,000 *new* shopping

245

centers were opened. It is estimated that in 1962 one-quarter of all retail sales were made in shopping centers.[1]

Today's modern shopping centers had their birth in the mid-1920's, when developers such as Jesse C. Nichols of Kansas City, Missouri, laid out the first community business centers. The experience gained from early mistakes and from the large number of such centers built since World War II makes it possible to put out some very general principles that should be observed (or at least considered) in the planning of any such center.

The first problem in developing any center is the selection of a suitable location. Population questions are the first factor in making this choice. For any particular location, it is possible to work out on a map a reasonably accurate forecast of the area from which the center will draw its patronage, and, subsequently, of the population itself. (The larger shopping center may draw as much as 20 per cent of its business from outside the normal trading area, but in a neighborhood center only rarely would as much as five per cent of the business come from outside the trade area.) This analysis must also take into account population trends in the area. Remember, too, that it is not enough to just have the simple figures about the population from which the center will have to draw its customers. The economic level and purchasing power of the prospective patrons should be studied.

With the car so important in today's world, the location of the shopping center must take into account its accessibility by car—and, of course, make adequate facilities for parking. Distance by itself is not as important in determining the trade area from which the center will draw as is the acceptable travel time. Twenty to twenty-five minutes seems to be about the outer limits of the time people will travel (and this only for a large regional center) regardless of whether the distance covered is fifteen miles or five miles.

Naturally, no study of a possible location would be com-

[1] Figures from "Suburban Shopping Centers," Robert H. Myers, in *Small Business Bibliography No. 27*, Small Business Administration, Washington, D. C.

plete that did not take into account both existing and possible future competitive facilities.

The topography of the land where a shopping center is to be created has much to do with its planning. Do not place stores on hillside locations. Try to select level land, because hillside sites cause increased construction and maintenance costs and are less flexible. Of course, grading of the site is often possible. While this may be expensive, the lower land costs of a topographically undesirable site may offset the grading charges in whole or in part.

Don't forget, too, that the slope of the land may interfere with access to and from the site and with the site's visibility from the adjoining roads, as well as with the use of the property.

Governmental planning and zoning should be taken into account. While rezoning is often possible, this is apt to be time-consuming, and if expensive property has to lie idle awaiting such changes, its cost increases even more.

To obtain a site large enough for the center being planned, it may be necessary to make some compromises. Remember, however, that it is cheaper in most cases to buy extra land than to provide for double-deck, or even triple-deck, parking. Try, also, to obtain a fairly regularly shaped site and one not divided by streets. Pedestrian or vehicle bridges are not only expensive, but they restrict the cohesiveness of a center.

In selecting a site, the developer must, as we have already indicated, take into account the zoning of the property. But he should also pay particular attention to the zoning of the surrounding properties. If the abutting properties are zoned for business use, the possibility is always present of competitors moving in, or of small stores acting as parasites, using the parking lots of the center and feeding on its customers. Whenever this possibility exists, it is generally wise for the developer to buy this additional land. While the price may be high, the land should increase in value—and it can either be sold later with restrictions, or used for future expansion of the center.

When the property around the center is primarily single-family residential property, it may be desirable to set up buffer zones between the center and the homes. When zoning changes are necessary (and this is usually the case with a center of any size), good public relations can be vital in bringing about the desired changes as quickly as possible. The developer should cooperate to the greatest extent possible with the zoning board, remembering that proper zoning protects the neighborhood around the center and thereby helps to insure its economic welfare.

The smallest shopping centers are generally built with a supermarket as the major tenant and drawing card. Larger centers are apt to have a large variety store or limited department store as the center of attraction. Finally, in the large regional center there will be at least one, and often two department stores to serve as a nucleus. Because the major tenant is so important to the shopping center role, efforts should be made to line up such a tenant as early as possible. Experienced department stores and chain stores, for example, will want to make their own population surveys, traffic counts, etc., and will want some control over the planning of much of the operation, such as the other tenants who are to be sought, the type of architecture to be used, how much parking is to be available, and the like.

Too many factors enter into the picture in deciding on the number and type of other tenants for a center to lay down any rules. Consideration should be given to local buying habits and needs, to the reputation of local stores, to competitive aspects, and to the type of shopper expected. If recreational services are to be available, such as a movie house or bowling establishment, space considerations may become important. Each center, really, requires its own tailor-made list of tenants designed to fit its own needs and opportunities.

Once the site has been selected and the choice of tenants pretty well made, an architect will have to be engaged to help plan the buildings, the parking, the pedestrian area, the servicing area, and the like.

For a shopping center to do its job well, it must be designed to generate pedestrian traffic—that is, the shopper must be gotten out of the car and, if possible, guided past other stores as he or she walks to the intended destination. But the shopper is not going to walk if the distance seems too far, or if walking requires being subjected to crowds, noise, dirt, or hazards like automobile traffic and truck deliveries. This is the reason that, even in the smallest center today, the stores are set back from the street, with the parking in front of the stores and deliveries being made from the rear. As the center gets larger, some or all of the following other measures are almost always taken in an effort to increase pedestrian traffic:

1. All delivery trucks and other service traffic (such as repairmen and garbage trucks) are funneled through basement and underground tunnels. In this way the customer is separated from the noise and fumes of the trucks, and from the hustle and bustle of deliveries as well as from the dirt and garbage they create.

2. Pedestrian promenades are made as attractive as possible. Plantings, pools, fountains, and even pieces of art not only make the walking more pleasant but tend to slow the shopper down and thus lead to more window-shopping. Roofs, screens, and walls are built to protect the walker against the elements and even to shield him from more unsightly elements, such as deliveries and parking lots. Indeed, some malls are completely enclosed and even air-conditioned!

3. In some cases, the main windows of the stores face on an interior court with only blank walls or small showcases facing the parking lots.

4. Children's amusement areas and temporary exhibitions (such as antique cars, or paintings) can increase the number of pedestrians.

5. If the center is readily available by public transportation, the location of bus stations, subway entrances, or the like can have an important bearing on the flow of pedestrian traffic.

6. In almost every case, shopping centers set up restric-

tions on the type and size of the signs that may be used, as well as on their location. Signs are not permitted to interfere with the walkways and must be in harmony with the surroundings.

Before any pedestrian traffic can be generated within the center, the shopper must have arrived there. This requires careful study and designing of the access roads and exits to and from the property. A vital part of such a study is taking into account the traffic flow the center will generate in the surrounding areas. It is important to try to keep nearby residential areas as free of new traffic as possible. Failure to do this is apt to result in such areas rapidly running down, and this in turn will lower the chances for the center's success.

How much parking space will be required? No simple formula can be given. Of course, there are rules of thumb, such as three or four times as much parking area as rental area, or 5 to 10 cars per 1,000 square feet of rental area. But these are over-simplifications. Any formula must take into account the size of the shopping center (generally the larger the center, the lower the ratio of parking to rental area), the type of stores in the center, the economic status of the customers the center draws, and the availability of public transportation, among other factors. It will also be necessary to decide, as a policy matter, how much space should be alloted to each car. The tendency today, particularly with ever-larger cars and doors that swing very wide is to allow more and more space per car. Indeed a buffer space is frequently painted between each parking stall.

Efforts have been made to fix a safe ratio to use in arriving at the number of square feet of floor space for stores in relation to the population to be served. Many formulas have been used and in most of them the amount of commercial space needed has been overestimated. It is a good idea to have a complete plan made for as many shops as may be required some years hence, and then start with a relatively small number of them, adding units later as needed.

Practical needs of merchants should not be sacrificed to secure architectural perfection. Architects are apt to design more elaborate buildings than warranted by the rentals to be obtained. A good architect should be employed, but he should understand that he is building a commercial enterprise and not a monument. It is wise to use one type of architecture throughout a development. Merchants can be given individual fronts to their stores if they desire and a blending of styles can thus be obtained.

Store fronts should be as fluid as possible so as to permit future changes. Indeed, the original fronts should not be installed until the wishes and needs of the tenants are known. Store fronts should be open and clear of columns so that any kind of finished front can be installed. Steps or ramps into stores are bad practice. As far as possible, all store entrances should face the main flow of foot traffic. There should be plenty of electrical outlets in windows and throughout all store premises.

The arrangement of the stores within the center is of vital importance. We have already noted that each center generally has one or two stores that serve as the major drawing cards. But the layout of the other stores must also be designed to attract as much pedestrian traffic past them as possible. Generally, there will be a number of secondary traffic attractors among the tenants—for example, banks, post offices, shoe stores, or the like. These will draw much of the traffic from the primary center. Hence, they should be placed so that people going to them from the department store or supermarket will have to pass stores that have little pulling power. This will increase the traffic in the latter stores and thus increase the rent they can afford to pay.

Grouping of merchants is important. Don't put a hardware store, a shoe-repair shop, or a house-equipment merchant next to a women's dress shop. Keep the women's shops by themselves; also service stores and five-and-ten cent stores. Florists, jewelers, apparel shops, camera shops, drug stores, gift shops, and book stores are all good types of tenants. Offices of public utility companies, where home owners come to pay gas, water, and electric bills, are good tenants, but they should not occupy prominent spots. Service shops, not able to pay high rentals but necessary to a well-developed center, can be accommodated in "off-locations," if accessible. They often help to get a small center started.

What are the latest trends in shopping centers? For one thing, the discount store, at one time almost anathema to shopping center merchants, is now often eagerly welcomed as a tenant. And frequently this has led to the upgrading of the merchandise of the more traditional stores to avoid competition at the lower price ranges.

Shopping centers are becoming true community centers in many instances. Meeting rooms, assembly halls, movie houses, and even legitimate theatres, in conjunction with other recreational facilities, often make the center the hub of community life. Flower shows, fashion events, and even symphony concerts are not uncommon occurrences.

Particularly important from the real estate man's view is the increasingly scientific planning and development that is going into the centers. And even after the center is underway, new systems of center expense classification make the collection and analysis of operating data easier, so that results can be compared with other centers and others in the same industry.

The regional center has had the most growth and seems to be becoming larger, while the neighborhood and community centers seem to have had more problems. Perhaps this is due to the fact that, by its very nature, more planning and work went into the establishment of the regional center.

In any case, it seems clear that the day of the "fast buck" for the shopping center developer is over. Profits are still there to be made—but only by developers and merchants who are interested in careful and thorough planning.

CHAPTER 31

Building

AS WE MOVE SWIFTLY TOWARD THE LAST quarter of the twentieth century, many innovations of the real estate business are emerging. For one thing, the real estate business is becoming much more diversified.

Traditionally, real estate men were content to allow speculators and builders to develop properties and to pay them fees for the sale of these properties. And, no doubt many agencies will continue to sell already-developed properties for fees.

But there seem to be two patterns emerging. In the first place, builder-developers have become reluctant to turn their properties over to agencies and to pay what seems to them to be exorbitant fees for the sales. "Why not organize our own sales force?" has been the reaction of many builder-developers. This they have done; and, within the context of such enterprises, the real estate salesman carries on much as before. But the developer has become more of a salesman, while the salesman has necessarily availed himself of understandings of the building game to undergird his selling techniques.

The second pattern is that the real estate broker, seeing that the sales function is being incorporated into the building-developing process, visualizes his future as a combination man, too. He seeks understandings about building and developing, enters into liaisons with building contractors, bankers, surveyors, etc., and comes forth with his development-building-selling firm.

And so the pattern goes. Real estate men are going into developing and building, and builder-developers are organizing selling arms for their enterprises. And with it all, the real estate broker must often diversify or perish.

Some brokers in active real estate markets have made money by forming syndicates for the purpose of acquiring lots zoned for business purposes and erecting thereon rows of stores, which after renting and being allowed to season for a time are sold at good profits. Profits are divided among the syndicate members, of which the broker usually is one. He is also allowed extra compensation for promoting the idea and supervising it until completion and sale.

Many real estate brokers have made money by buying old run-down houses, completely rebuilding them, and then re-selling them. Under FHA's Title One, a borrower is advanced money for rebuilding work, the loan being guaranteed by FHA but supplied by a financial institution. This field provides excellent training for the building of new houses, if the broker cares to venture into that field. Millions of old houses require rebuilding, new bathrooms, kitchens, and heating plants. As of 1960, there were over 58,000,000 housing units in the United States almost half of which (46.5%) were at least 30 years old.

Real estate men frequently are the leaders in rebuilding programs conducted on a large scale, especially those concerned with business properties. Many smaller towns and cities have buildings lining their main business thoroughfares which have been in use thirty, forty, fifty years or longer. A meeting of property owners is called and a vote is taken to ascertain how many are willing to coöperate. An architect is called in and designs are made, each one different for each property but harmonious as a whole. Three story buildings are lowered to two stories in some instances, while a one-story structure may have another added. Bids are asked and contracts awarded. The work can proceed slowly along the entire block until it is rebuilt, in as modern a manner as if the structures were all new. Business goes on in the stores as the work progresses. This is a way in which vanishing real estate values can be recaptured at comparatively small expenses, and it often prevents business from shifting to another neighborhood where new buildings are available. A vast amount of rehabilitation of business areas is in sight, and the next few years offer a good field for the realty man with vision and aggressivenes.

Among the best customers the realty broker has in an active real estate market are the speculative builders who are seeking lots on which to erect houses or apartment buildings. They buy readily, pay current prices, and make quick deals if they are shown something they can use. Some brokers are constantly on a hunt for properties to sell to such buyers. These operators transform vacant lots into complete homes or apartment structures in just a few weeks, often carrying on a number of building jobs at one time. They finance their operations through local banks and building and loan associations, and from their own funds. The broker may sell a lot to a builder and may also secure a listing on the property when it is completed.

One successful method of selling houses has been used by subdividers for many years. The "model" house, though erected for sale, is kept open so that hundreds of visitors can walk through it and see the latest construction features, including the very newest equipment for bathrooms and kitchens. Such homes are artistically decorated inside and out and set in a modern landscape, often of a lavish character. Here is a demonstration which appeals to the home-hungry hearts of hundreds of persons who roam through such a dwelling and get ideas for their own home-to-be. Many sales are made through the medium of model houses and many new prospects are contacted who buy later on.

Building operations require proper planning and usually the hiring of an architect. The owner for whom the building is to be erected can, however, be most useful in helping to sketch out on paper the kind of structure he wants. This

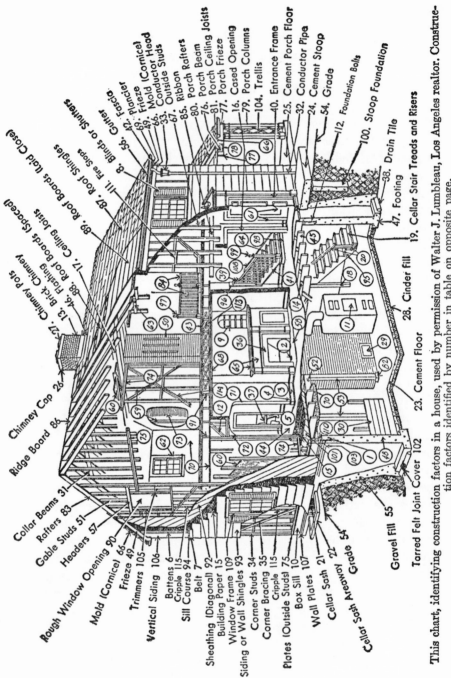

This chart, identifying construction factors in a house, used by permission of Walter J. Lumbleau, Los Angeles realtor. Construction factors identified by number in table on opposite page.

will give the architect something definite to start from. Even a floor plan clipped out of a magazine or newspaper and modified may be helpful in crystallizing the ideas of the prospective owner. It is possible, at times, to purchase what are known as "stock" plans from certain building organizations which specialize in their preparation and sale. Stock plans include complete sets of blueprints which can often be used in the erections of good-sized buildings. Some well-known magazines regularly print pictures of prize-winning houses, plans for which can be acquired and modified in any way the pro-

Index to Drawing on Opposite Page

1. Anchor bolt	61. Interior doors and trim
2. Ash dump	62. Interior window trim
3. Base	63. Lookouts
4. Base mold	64. Main stair treads and risers
5. Base shoe	65. Mantel shelf and trim
9. Book shelves	66. Mold (cornice)
11. Boiler	68. Picture mold
12. Bracing	70. Plaster
14. Bridging	71. Plaster arch
15. Building paper	72. Plaster arch brackets
18. Cellar stair post	73. Plaster base
20. Cellar stairrail and post	74. Plates (inside studs)
29. Cleanout door	75. Plates (outside studs)
30. Coal bin partition	77. Porch frieze
36. Damper control	78. Porch soffit
37. Dining nook	82. Porch base blocks (precast cement)
39. Easing	
41. Face string and face mold	84. Rails and balusters
43. Finish floor—1 × 2″ strips, deadening felt—diagonal sub floor	91. Second floor joists
	95. Stair carriage
	96. Stair partition casing
44. Finish floor	97. Stair landing newel
45. First floor joists	98. Starting tread and riser
48. Foundation wall	99. Starting newel
50. Furring strips	101. Sub floor (diagonal)
52. Girder	103. Termite shield
53. Girder post	108. Wall stringer
58. Hearth	110. Mud sill
59. Inside studs	113. Cross bridging
60. Insulation	114. X bracing

spective builder desires. Every prospective owner of a house will have his or her ideas to be incorported, and the more completely these can be set down on paper the more readily an architect will conceive just what is wanted and prepare finished plans.

It is sometimes advantageous for a realty broker to have associated with him a building contractor, sharing the same offices and coöperating in deals as they develop. The broker is a specialist in land and the builder knows how to improve it. What could be a more natural combination? One can send business to the other as the occasion permits, and each will benefit from the association.

The American Institute of Architects does not publish fee schedules. The development and publication of fee schedules are the prerogative of each individual chapter of the AIA. A uniform national fee schedule or scale would have no meaning, nor would it represent the conditions that cause variance of fees from area to area. Fee schedules that are developed by individual chapters are based upon their own local conditions. Geographical location, labor market, geologic conditions, building types and scope of architectural services are just several items that affect fees.

Generally, if agreed to between the owner and the architect, the architect will perform services up to and and including construction contract administration, which includes periodic visits to the site to check the progress of the construction. This, of course, is wholly dependent upon the particular situation. Generally, the architect's services are complete upon the owner's final payment to the contractor. Of course, many architects are called upon by the owner during the one-year guarantee period or longer should any special guarantee be part of the construction contract. However, most architects, if called upon by the owner during this period, are paid a fee, usually an hourly rate, by the owner. If, however, the case is clearly due to an error or omission on the part of the architect, then the architect, of course, can be held liable.

It is wise for a realty broker, if engaged in building operations, or representing clients who want to build, to have definite written contracts with both an architect and a contractor and with others who may provide special services such as landscaping and construction of a swimming pool.

To keep abreast of building operations, the broker should subscribe to at least one good architectural magazine to keep him posted on new things in the building field and changing styles of architecture as they develop from year to year. He can thus be helpful to clients who intend to build or remodel, even if he does not engage in construction operations himself. If he is an appraiser, he will find it absolutely necessary to know building costs and trends and be able to translate them into appraisal reports.

CHAPTER 32

Advertising, Publicity,

and Promotion

ASSOCIATED CLOSELY with the successful operation of a real estate office is the judicious use of advertising and publicity.

The advertising media generally used are newspapers, magazines, signs, direct mail in which circulars and property briefs are extensively employed, multiple listing bureaus conducted under the auspices of realty boards, and window displays in offices with ground-floor locations. Radio and TV presentations may also be used occasionally.

Advertising is the contact the realty broker or subdivision developer establishes with the general public. The largest and most important business concerns in the country are often the largest advertisers, but unusual splurges on the part of a realty broker seeking to attract buyers may not be necessary. A great deal of money has been made through the use of advertising and also a great deal has been lost by useless expenditures on advertising that has failed to yield any real return.

A broker establishing himself in business should proceed rather slowly until he finds where the expenditure of money brings best results. There is always the temptation to listen to alluring sales talks by advertising men who want new brokers to launch big and expensive campaigns. Quite frequently this is a useless expenditure of money, as results are not forthcoming. Almost every newly established brokerage office goes in heavily for advertising of one kind or another for the first several months, then simmers down to a volume that is found best adapted to the needs of the office. A little cautious consideration of the whole subject and the judicious selection of the right places to spend advertising money might have saved a considerable amount that was spent.

The classified columns of daily newspapers or weekly publications usually draw the best response for the amount of money expended. There is usually one newspaper in a city or town that attracts most of the real estate advertising, and it is well to patronize that paper, even if its rates are higher than those of a competitor. Judicious use of space in such a publication will bring inquiries from many sources. It is not necessary to use large bombastic ads to secure public attention. State the facts fully and in an interesting manner, and readers will respond.

It should be understood that advertising does not actually sell property. It simply puts the broker in touch with persons who are interested. The selling process goes on from there. Once the contact is established, the broker must use his own good judgment on how to proceed.

Newspapers in most cities now limit their real estate classified advertising columns to small (agate) type, arranged under property classifications which readers can easily turn to. Few papers now permit pictures or engravings of any kind in classified columns, and most limit the size of type for headings that can be utilized. This has a tendency to make the classified columns look crowded, rather dull and prosaic, and it becomes necessary for the ad writer to inject genuine interest in his appeal.

There is no quick and ready way to learn to write ads. It is gained through experience and by carefully studying the methods employed by others who are using the same advertising columns. Sometimes a small classified ad cleverly written will bring better returns than a long-winded one that fails to spark appeal because of its dullness. The newly established broker will do well to study and use the classified columns for a time to the exclusion of other types of advertisements.

Display advertising, the kind that appears in other portions of a paper than on classified pages, has its use for certain purposes but is seldom productive of much return when utilized for selling real estate. Well-written display ads in the financial or real estate pages of a Sunday paper often bring good results. This type of advertising is more expensive than classified and should be used sparingly until the advertiser is sure that it will bring returns.

Weekly papers in communities where there is no daily will probably bring equally as good results as those obtained through the classified columns of the town and city dailies. Here again the newcomer should make tests and comparisons to ascertain the best methods to employ in telling the world about his wares.

Here are some simple rules for the preparation of copy for classified advertisements, suggested by a man who has had wide experience in this field:

1. Carefully inspect the property to be advertised.
2. Select the most attractive features of the property.
3. Decide the type buyer that will most likely be attracted by the property to be advertised.
4. Draw a mental picture of the property to be advertised and put that picture into words.
5. Do not go into minute details which are of no real importance or significance.
6. Avoid the use of descriptive adjectives.
7. Do not use stereotyped phrases.
8. Avoid having the advertisement appear sensational.
9. Have the advertisement set up so as to be easily read.
10. Use the individual advertisement in preference to block advertisements.
11. Always give price and terms.

In preparing copy for advertisements, particularly those used in newspapers, care should be taken to employ type that is easy to read.

To prepare copy that will be smooth and effective, observe the following rules:[1]

1. **Attract attention.** Use striking headlines, colorful copy, and good layout.

2. **Arouse interest.** Headlines serve to create attention and interest. Beyond that, the interest is created principally through the manner in which the property is described, the selling points presented, and the price indicated. No general rules can be laid down, but it is best to have the leading sentence short and the words as simple as possible.

3. **Create desire.** Describe the merits of the property. Emphasize the most attractive features. Make the copy complete enough to convey a picture of the offering. Don't give every detail, but arouse the reader's curiosity by leaving something to his imagination.

4. **Convince the reader.** For convincing copy:

   (a) Use simple, direct, and understandable language.

   (b) Make the copy concise.

   (c) Be specific. "Big" or "large" with reference to room size, for example, doesn't convey the same picture as "accomodates a concert grand."

   (d) Eliminate the superlatives. Understatement is preferable to overstatement.

   (e) Choose the vivid word. Use strong nouns and verbs in place of adjectives.

   (f) Give the reader a valid reason why the price is low.

   (g) Admit the faults of the property.

   (h) Repeat the principal appeal (on occasion).

A real estate firm with a reputation for honesty and integrity can be fairly certain that readers who know it will have confidence in its message. However, since many of the readers may not know the reputation of the advertiser, the aids for making copy convincing should be used without exception.

5. **Ask for action.** The suggestion for action can be a direct command or an invitation to investigate. It may come at the beginning or, more often, at the end. Some ideas for closings that suggest action:

   (a) Show the consequences of delay.

   (b) Give the reader an inducement for prompt action, such as a reduced price for prompt sale.

   (c) Invite the reader to inquire further.

[1] Adopted from the Prentice-Hall Real Estate Service. Used by permission.

Caution should be used about advertising in the miscellaneous weekly neighborhood and trade papers that abound everywhere. These media very seldom are worth while for advertising real estate, and money is wasted when they are employed without careful tests being made. Programs used in theaters and for benefits, picnics, sports, and charity events are likewise poor producers for the most part; it is seldom that business can be traced to them. This applies also to annual outings, games, and so on, conducted by police and fire departments and public service bodies of all kinds. Money spent on them should be considered as a gift, usually pried out of a real estate man who hasn't the stamina to say "No!"

Printed and painted signs are indispensable to the realty broker. For their cost and productiveness, they are the cheapest and best way to advertise real estate. A broker should have an attractive design made of his name and business by an artist, usually employed by a sign company which he patronizes. Something distinctive and eye-appealing will attract attention when it is found attached to buildings or standing on stakes on vacant property. A sign costs little but goes on day after day sending out its message to the hundreds and often thousands of persons passing by it. Different sizes of signs should be used according to the importance of the property. Signs should be in colors, the background being one color, with lettering in another color, sometimes in two colors if the design permits.

Never fail to ask permission to put signs on vacant properties. Persons seeking locations in the neighborhood will be attracted by a sign and will immediately telephone or call at the broker's office for information. The same applies to signs tacked on houses that are for sale. A sign often costs no more than what is paid for one day's insertions of an ad in a daily paper, and it goes on for days or weeks making its appeal for attention and action. Signs are usually purchased from professional sign makers in lots of 50 to 1,000 or more. They may be of metal, plain wood, or plywood, properly braced to keep them from warping under exposure to the elements. Keep plenty of signs posted around your neighborhood and they will bring business. This includes large and attractive signs on the broker's own place of business.

Direct-mail advertising is used by many brokers when they have special properties to be disposed of. Attractive circulars are printed, or elaborate property briefs are reproduced and sent out to selected lists of persons whom the brokers believe might be interested. Cheaper types of advertising can be reproduced by multigraph or mimeograph. Postcard messages by the hundred and the thousands can be broadcast when a broker wants to announce to fellow brokers or to the public that he has a property for sale. Some farm and industrial brokers publish catalogs, which they issue from season to season. These are sent to selected lists locally and throughout the state and nation.

Some brokers make a specialty of preparing property briefs, often on an elaborate scale. These are for the use of selected clients who evince interest in the properties shown. Such a property brief contains detailed descriptions of the premises, with all of the neighborhood advantages carefully enumerated. Also included are maps and photographs of the property, showing it from different points of view; a statement of the cost of maintenance; and, if it is an income property, a set-up of the income and expenditures, with a final net figure shown as the return the property produces. For valuable, choice properties, briefs are well worth while and frequently go a long way towards selling them. They are usually got up in loose-leaf form with a binder, with a printed diagram of building plans and photographs to match.

Realty boards in many parts of the country conduct multiple listing divisions to which members contribute listings of properties that they get from owners on exclusive basis, agreeing to list them with other board members. Such listings are distributed in card or circular form to the various members of the bureau, who are then able to present them to their clients. Any commission earned is split with the listing broker, and a small fee goes to the board for its service.

Brokers who maintain ground-floor offices face the problem of offering attractive window displays or simply painting them with signs. Attractively prepared photographs and printed descriptions are read by persons passing by, and buyers frequently are attracted in this manner. There is a temptation to start off with a fine window presentation and to wind up a few months later with the display of a solitary potted plant! If the broker really desires a window display, he should make it worthwhile and appropriate to its setting. The degree of attractiveness of a ground-floor office mirrors the success of the broker maintaining it.

Advertising over the radio has seldom proved profitable for real estate. Some subdividers can attract prospects through a radio program but the average broker gains little from radio presentation unless it be in the form of general publicity of a favorable character. Real estate offerings are so individualistic in character that it is almost impossible to present them over the air. Real estate board propaganda can be disseminated over the air advantageously and the public taught to consider the advantages of dealing with realtors. For the most part it remains for a new type of program to be invented that will make it worth while for realty brokers individually to benefit by spending their money for radio presentations.

Advertising via television, especially colored television, gives considerably greater promise of success. Through this medium an appeal can be made to the eye as well as the ear: A thirty-second spot of people moving in and out of your open house, for instance, may be not only profitable but economical in view of the fact that TV advertising costs are dropping as a result of competition.

Bus advertising is another type that has never held much promise for realty brokers. A subdivider can use it sparingly on routes operating out to and past his property but it has never been conspicuously successful in attracting attention to broker offerings. The same applies to billboards. These can be used advantageously by a subdivider but are of practically no use for brokerage activities. Single large billboards on important properties are the exception. Here the sign can be used to outline the size, conditions and terms of sale in an appealing manner. Agency signs on the back of local taxicabs have also been effective.

Calendars, ball point pens, small novelties of glass or plastic, year books and similar things should be used judiciously, if at all, for the building up of brokerage good will. They cost money and often it is impossible to trace anything that is gained by their distribution. Seasoned brokers refuse to consider them.

In the preparation of advertising copy there are a few basic principles which apply equally as well to real estate copy as to any other kind. Experts in this field urge the use of ample white space in advertisements—as contrasted to closely set copy which covers the entire space available. This is a matter of good judgment and must be learned from experience. Classified ads may be cleverly worded and set with sufficient white space to stand out in a sea of closely set copy. The same applies to display copy. Sometimes the advocate of white space goes to extremes however and the ad lacks interest and appeal.

In issuing circulars every effort should be made to illustrate them with attractive photographs. These are easy to get and to reproduce and have a strong appeal to the average reader, and they should be used whenever possible.

In considering a budget for operating a real estate office, an advertising appropriation should be provided for. This should be from 5 to 10 per cent of estimated income in most instances. A small broker working in a neighborhood office will probably not spend that much. Advertising expense, like rent, is relative. If it can be depended on to bring back a relative mass return, there seems no limit to what can be appropriated for it. The judgment of the broker must prevail here.

A survey made by one real estate publication among leading real estate firms of the way their advertising dollar was spent resulted as follows:

Newspaper classified	61.57%
Newspaper display	21.70%
Outdoor signs	6.53%
Circulars to a list	3.76%
Radio and TV	1.35%
Handbills	.75%

Window displays .... .26%
Building shows .... .20%
Other forms 3.88%

The consensus among seasoned real estate men the country over is that the best advertising results can be obtained from:

1. Classified real estate ads.
2. Display ads.
3. Signs.
4. Circulars, briefs, catalogs, and so on.

Advertising itself is but a phase of the wider field of *publicity*, which can be said to cover all types of promotional work in which the written, printed, spoken, and televised word is used.

In distinct contrast with paid advertisements are the publicity stories which appear from week to week in the news columns of newspapers and local magazines. In most of the larger cities, in the Sunday editions of daily newspapers, real estate pages are conducted by editors who circulate around the real estate offices looking for news concerning important sales and new building developments of interest generally. Real estate sections are not conducted entirely for the benefit of real estate men but for the genuine value of the news stories as well. Real estate editors, however, are glad to have stories sent to them about the completion of interesting deals, the placing of a new subdivision on the market, new building projects, such as condominiums, and anything having news value. It is useful for a broker to have his name appear in print occasionally, as it identifies him with the realty business and indicates that he is successfully engaged in it. If a broker does have a sale of interest, it is a good idea for him to write out a complete account of it and mail it to the real estate editor, who can check back if important details are lacking. If you hear of an important deal that has been completed, call the real estate editor of your local paper and tip him off. He will appreciate it and may do something for you sometime. Don't fail to take advantage of every possible opportunity to secure good, dignified publicity on the real estate page or news columns of local papers.

Some large real estate offices maintain their own advertising and publicity departments, in the charge of ex-newspapermen or advertising experts who prepare copy for daily and Sunday advertisements and, when the occasion permits, relay news stories to the real estate editors who always welcome and use them. In advertising real estate:

Be truthful.
Use few media.
Keep repeating.
Use interesting slogans.
Use human-interest pictures.
Use short, well-chosen words.
Promise less than you give.
Always advertise your best buys.
Make copy descriptive, not boring.
Facts are what readers want given them.
Observe simplicity, directness, and dignity.
For institutional advertising, use display columns.

Careful study of advertising methods and techniques will repay the realty broker for all the time spent doing it. It is one of the prime creative forces that make the real estate business possible and profitable.

CHAPTER 33

How FHA Can

Help the Broker

BACK IN THE DAYS OF THE DEPRESSION following the first World War the building industry was at a standstill. Lending institutions had practically ceased making real estate loans and had borrowed all they could on the choicest loans in their portfolios. In every part of the country property owners were crying for relief from intolerable conditions. Did no one have a solution for the riddle of frozen mortgages?

Then like a voice from the wilderness came the word in 1934 that Congress had enacted the National Housing Act. A most interesting piece of financial engineering had been created. By having the federal government insure or guarantee payment of loans made on real estate by private lending institutions, through the medium of the Federal Housing Administration, the building industry was gradually restored to normalcy, and with it the real estate and mortgage businesses. Insured mortgages became liquid assets and, in bank statements, were treated the same as cash or government bonds. The outmoded short-term real estate loan, always technically in default, combined with a high-interest-bearing second mortgage, was replaced by the long-term, non-callable, high-percentage monthly payment loan, and no second mortgage.

Thus it became possible through the FHA plan to buy or build an attractive modern property on a sound economic basis, with a small down payment, and to pay for it out of a moderate income, the loan being amortized in monthly installments about equal to rent to suit the family income. Each convenient monthly payment reduces the principal of the loan and also includes a portion of the interest, taxes, mortgage and hazard insurance, and other fixed charges. It is usually a long-term loan extending over a convenient period of years, made by a bank, by a savings and loan association, or by a life insurance, mortgage, or finance company, or by some other qualified lending institution, on limited financing rates. Advance is made by the lender of a large part of the total value as determined by FHA's own standardized appraisal, from 80 to 100 per cent, depending on the purpose and type of construction.

With FHA financing available, the broker's problem of meeting sales resistance is greatly simplified. Sales need never be lost because the seller wants all of his equity in cash, or because the purchaser cannot pay all cash. The FHA plan calls for a single mortgage only, usually a high percentage of loan to value, and no secondary financing is permissible.

The first step in making a sale is to qualify the purchaser. Can he afford to live in the property under consideration, and does he have sufficient cash to swing the deal? Without a definite plan of action it may be a ticklish procedure to find this out, and rebuffs frequently follow any effort to probe into the prospective purchaser's personal affairs. But the resourceful broker approaches the problem from the standpoint of rendering helpful, intelligent service to both buyer and seller by working out the necessary financing arrangements, in advance if possible, and making it easy for the buyer to buy and the seller to sell.

The policy of the Federal Housing Administration is such that no opinion is rendered about the eligibility of a mortgage transaction except as a direct result of a formal application through an approved lending institution willing to make the loan. Either a conditional commitment or a firm commitment may be applied for.

Conditional commitments are issued as the result of an application describing a property, either existing or contemplated residential construction, by which it is proposed to secure a mortgage given by a mortgagor as yet unnamed. FHA makes the usual examination of the property and assumes an unknown but satisfactory borrower in determining the eligibility of the proposed loan.

After issuance of the conditional commitment, the broker has a definite proposition to offer in negotiations for the sale of the property. The time between signing the sale agreement and closing the deal can be shortened because, after submission of a borrower, the administration is able to render its decision with a minimum of delay, examination of the property having already been completed. A minimum fee is charged, which is credited toward the regular fee when the application of a known borrower is submitted for a firm commitment. Rejection of the borrower does not invalidate the conditional commitment. When purchasers are carefully selected by the broker, the procedure is almost automatic.

Firm commitments are issued as a result of applications describing a mortgage transaction in which the borrower is named, and may involve either new or existing residential construction.

If a broker has arranged for the issuance of a conditional commitment prior to entering negotiations with the purchaser, he can map out a definite plan of procedure, know exactly how much cash is required, and have a definite value established by a disinterested governmental agency to present to a seller, who may be asking an inflated price for his property. FHA values are usually made on a stabilized basis, rather than in conformity with prices paid because of abnormal market conditions governed by conditions of unusual supply or demand. In an ascending market, valuations would therefore lag somewhat behind prices being currently paid. In a declining market, the reverse would apply. Insured mortgage financing, therefore, has a generally stabilizing influence on the whole real estate market. The pattern of appraisal procedure and nomenclature established by FHA has unconsciously influenced the methods and thinking of lenders very generally throughout the country.

If a broker uses the two kinds of FHA application forms as regular tools of trade, encourages his customer to take the lending institution into his confidence, and offers his intelligent, helpful guidance in filling out application forms, he will quickly find that he has almost automatically been able to qualify his customer and eliminate the perennial time-consuming shopper who never does anything but waste gasoline and time, which are the broker's stock in trade.

FHA offers the broker a complete service ranging all the way from the insuring of short-term personal loans for modernization and repair, home purchase, and construction, to high-rise or garden-type apartment developments having mortgages up to $25,000,000. Any broker will find himself richly rewarded by giving a few hours' intelligent study to the workings of this government agency. Offices are established in all of the principal cities, and helpful assistance is available for the asking from qualified members of the underwriting staffs.

CHAPTER 34

Escrows and Titles

ESCROWING REAL ESTATE TRANSAC-
tions has become a fixed practice in most large cities and
is rapidly spreading to other sections.

Escrow departments are usually conducted under the auspices of title or abstract companies, banks, and building and
loan associations, or under private auspices by companies organized for that purpose. A seller about to transfer a property
to a purchaser, either directly or through a broker, agrees to
escrow his deal with such an office, deposit his deed, furnish
a title, and make delivery, the purchaser at the same time
agreeing to desposit his funds with the escrow office with the
understanding that they will be conveyed to the seller when
good title is created in him, as the buyer. Both agree to pay a
portion of the escrow expense.

The function of an escrow holder is, in effect, to act as a stakeholder.
To illustrate this function, a simple transaction would be to take the
case of two boys who make a swap, subject to certain conditions. They
appoint a third boy to act as a stakeholder to hold the articles to be
exchanged. When the conditions have been met, the stakeholder will
then turn over the articles which have been deposited with him.[1]

In contrast to the transaction referred to, present-day escrow services have been expanded to cover numerous and complex transactions,
and have imposed upon the stakeholder, actually the "escrow holder,"
a multitude of duties and obligations.

[1] The author of this volume is indebted to Gordon E. Sanborn, of Los
Angeles, for the outline of escrow and title proceedings found here.

The buyer and the seller, and the lender, if one is involved, deposit their documents, papers and money in the escrow department of some bank, escrow company, loan company, or land title company, which is called the "escrow holder." While the documents, papers and money are in the custody of this escrow holder, the real estate transaction is referred to as being "in escrow." The documents, papers and money are handed to an employee or officer of the escrow holder, who is called the "escrow man."

When you think of an escrow, keep in mind that it is but an arrangement created to safeguard the interests of all persons involved. When you buy real estate, the thing you want to be assured of is that you acquire a valid or legal ownership, free and clear of all liens or encumbrances except those to which you agree your property shall be subject. Naturally, until you are assured of such acquisition of ownership, you will not want to turn over to the seller the purchase price involved in the buying of this real estate. It is to bridge this gap that the services of an escrow holder are employed.

By the use of an escrow, the seller, or his real estate broker, hands to the escrow holder the seller's deed, fire insurance policies, and other supporting papers relating to the property involved, directing the escrow holder, in writing, to deliver the deed, fire insurance policies and other supporting papers to the purchaser—when he, the escrow holder, is in a position to deliver to the seller the purchase price involved.

The buyer, or his real estate broker, hands to the escrow holder the money to purchase the property. He will direct the escrow holder, in writing, to deliver the money to the seller when the escrow holder is able to obtain, from a title company, an evidence of title which will show the title vested in the buyer, subject only to such liens and encumbrances as the buyer has agreed to take the title subject to.

These written instructions, signed by both the buyer and the seller, are called the "escrow instructions."

In contrast with the simple duty of the boy who acted as stakeholder in the illustration, the duties and obligations of an escrow holder in the modern escrow are numerous and—many times—complex.

Generally, the escrow man will list the various things he must do or which he must have others perform, pursuant to the escrow instructions. One of the first steps will be for the escrow man to order a title company to make a search of the title of the real estate being transferred. When this search is completed, the title company will send to the escrow holder a report as to the present condition of the title to the property. When the escrow is in a position to be closed, the escrow holder will then instruct the title company to record the deed, subject only to liens and encumbrances which have been approved by the buyer. The escrow man will also make arrangements for the transfer to the buyer of existing fire or other insurance policies.

If there is an existing mortgage or deed of trust against the property, the escrow man, on request, will obtain a paper called an "offset statement" from the mortgagee or lender. This offset statement will show the present unpaid principal balance of the debt, and whether any delinquencies exist in the payments of principal or interest thereon.

If rents are coming in from the property being purchased, the seller and the buyer generally will instruct the escrow man to adjust, or, as it is termed in escrow language, to "prorate" the rentals, as of the date the transaction is closed. The escrow man will determine the amount of the current year's taxes, and will prorate the taxes. Proration is also generally made of the premiums paid for fire and other types of insurance policies, based upon the used-up portion of the term of such policies.

When the escrow man is in a position to comply with all of the instructions of the seller and buyer, and the lender if one is involved, he will then instruct the title company to record, in the office of the county recorder, the deed and other supporting documents necessary to convey ownership from the seller to the buyer.

The title company, upon receipt of these instructions from the escrow holder, will then so record the deed and other supporting documents subject only to such liens and encumbrances as the buyer has approved.

When the title company has advised the escrow holder of the recording of the deed and other supporting documents, the escrow holder will thereupon turn over to the seller, the purchase price being paid for the property. The escrow holder will, at the same time, turn over to the buyer the documents and papers which he, as buyer, is entitled to. The escrow holder also will turn over to the lender, if a lender is involved in assisting in the purchase of the property, supporting loan documents and papers. In due course, the buyer will receive, from the county recorder's office, the seller's deed, which the title company has recorded.

Thus it may be seen that the present-day use of an escrow is that of a clearing house, facilitating the transfer of real estate from a seller to a buyer. It is this service of an escrow holder and—the protection afforded by a sound title—that help make real estate a safe and sound investment.

When you have selected the home site on which you wish to build, you will then want to arrange for the protection of the title to that land. Quite properly, at this point, you may ask, "What is this thing called 'title' that I am to acquire? All I want is to own that land."

There are at least forty-eight distinct usages of the word *title*, such as "the title of a book," "the title role in a play," "the title of Duke," and "deciding the heavyweight title." And even as applied to real estate, the term has been used with a variety of meanings. But, as most often used in speaking of land, title is ownership.

However, land ownership usually is subject to many kinds of interests, rights, claims and liens of others, in and to the same parcel of land. Before you purchase land, you want to know what rights you will have to the use and possession of that land—for others already may have certain superior rights or interests in that same land.

In other words, ownership of land consists of a number of legal rights and interests, like so many sticks in a bundle. For example, the federal, state, county and municipal governments possess certain of these sticks, such as the right of taxation, which rights may and do become charges against the land, as tax assessments and liens.

Others than governmental bodies may, and usually do, hold one or more of the sticks in this bundle, such as rights and interests created by contract with the owners; for example, a mortgage or deed of trust; an agreement of purchase; a lease; and others. Then, too, there are rights or interests created by operation of law, as, for example: The rights or interests of the trustee and creditors when the owner of land becomes bankrupt; the rights or interests of heirs or others who succeed to the property when the owner of land dies; the rights or interests of a wife in community property; and so on.

The problem, then, is to know the extent of ownership and right to use, possession, and enjoyment of the land purchased. Now, the title to that land involves not only yourself and the person from whom you buy. It goes way back through the years to the date when that land was first granted, or sold, and includes all sales or other transactions that have taken place during that time. You want to know that all those sales and other transactions were valid, and what liens, encumbrances, defects, or other matters, if any, affect that land today.

Your next question could properly be, "What things or factors contribute to or make a title invalid; and how am I to ascertain what liens, encumbrances, defects, or other matters, if any, affect that land today?" The answer to those questions requires the consideration of three problems:

1. *The public records system;*
2. *Facts, rights, interests and claims determined by an inspection and survey of the land;*
3. *Hazards not revealed by either the public records or by an inspection or survey of the land.*

Consider first *the public records system*, and the liens, encumbrances, defects, or other matters, if any, disclosed by an examination and interpretation thereof. This will require an examination of all records to be found in the recorder's office of the county in which the property is located. Here will be found copies of all instruments that have been filed and that directly affect the property under consideration.

In addition, records in other public offices must also be investigated, such as those in county and city offices, for taxes, tax sales, bonds and assessments. Federal court, superior court, and municipal court records also must be searched for actions, orders and decrees; and if any are found affecting your land, they must be examined as to their validity and effect.

If you had the time to spend weeks, or in many cases months, in making this examination, you might do the job yourself. But when you finished you still would have no positive assurance that you had examined all instruments, documents or proceedings, or that you had correctly analyzed or construed their validity and effect, or that some of those which you did examine had not been improperly executed or forged. A title company, however, will do all this work and for a fraction of the cost, and in a fraction of the time, it would take you to do the same job.

In many cities there have come into existence companies that provide titles to land and in addition insure a landholder against loss should a defect in a title appear. This is what is known as title insurance. An insured title policy is actually a contract of indemnity and is the holder's protection against loss to the extent of the full value of a property that has been insured if the extent of title or ownership as defined in the policy is not as represented at the date of the policy.

There are, however, in the ordinary standard form of policy, certain exceptions as to which no insurance is undertaken. This leads to a consideration of: *Facts, rights, interests, or claims determined by an inspection and survey of the land.* These matters are not covered in the standard form of policy. But since these matters relate to things which you, as a home buyer, can find out for yourself, there are but few cases where you would need to go to additional expense of having a title company do that work for you.

These exceptions in the standard form policy relate, generally, to things that can be determined by investigating the property and by having it surveyed.

The survey will determine the boundary lines, and whether buildings or improvements on adjoining lands encroach upon your parcel. Or, if you are buying "improved" property—that is, *built upon* property— whether the buildings or improvements on your property encroach upon your neighbor's land. The survey will also disclose the location of easements, such as utility easements.

By inspecting the land, you can determine who is in possession, and the nature of their possessory rights; also whether building and other restrictions, if any, have been, or would be violated—and, if so, whether any right to declare a reversion or forfeiture of title exists or would arise by reason of such violation.

There is another problem: *Hazards not revealed by the public records or by an inspection or survey of the land.* Thus a title may be invalid or illegal by reason of: A statute or statutes enacted by the state legislature; a rule of law established in some court decision; insanity or incompetency of a former owner; minority; an unauthorized exercise of power by someone acting under a power of attorney, or by an agent or trustee; forgery or false personation.

Land titles are like a chain. They may be only as strong as their weakest link. If any link in the chain is defective, title may then be defective from that point on.

Brokers should always see to it that their clients are protected by having a proper search of title made for every property transferred.

As reported above, title companies will inspect the validity of a title and will issue an insured title which, in effect, guarantees remuneration to the buyer in case the title subsequently proves to be faulty. In cases where, for one reason or another, the insured title is unavailable or deemed unsatisfactory, the title examination should be placed in the hands of a competent attorney who will, for a fee, render an opinion of the title.

It is often true that a title company will pass over some small flaw and be willing to take the calculated risk that no trouble will ever arise. But where expensive buildings are to be erected, the insurance available under the insured title may be almost inconsequential compared to the possible loss that could be suffered. So, in many cases, an attorney should be called upon to render his opinion, even though there may be an insured title.

CHAPTER 35

A "Policy" Book —
an Office Asset

IN THE CONDUCT OF A MODERN REAL estate office it will be found that many problems arise from time to time that directly concern the policies placed in effect by the owner or manager. The relations between the head of the office and his salesmen and among the salesmen themselves often become quite complex and need interpretation. Almost every office establishes rules of conduct, but many an office makes little effort to put them in writing.

When a new man joins an organization it is necessary to inform him of the rules and practices of the office. This is done by the owner, the office manager, or the sales manager, or the new salesman must find out about them himself, probably stumbling headlong into trouble while doing so.

It was to obviate this situation that the author many years ago began to compile a policy book for his office. The rules and regulations were written whereby salesmen were to conduct their relationships with the office and with each other. Division of commissions, the way listings are filed by salesmen and the reward for getting them, dealings with other offices, and many other matters of interest are set forth in such a policy book. New rulings may be entered when new situations come into being.

When a new man enters the employ of a company as a salesmen, the first thing he is required to do is to sit down and thoroughly digest the policy book. After doing so he is required to sign it, agreeing to abide by all of its provisions and procedures. If he is found breaking the rules, it can easily be shown that he has done so with his eyes open, for the policy book will clearly outline the principles and regulations under which the office is conducted.

Anyone can make up a policy book. The one presented here simply suggests some of the items that may be covered.

Policy Book

This book is designed to contain a record of certain definite policies and rulings adopted by............................for the conduct of its business.

From time to time there arise more or less puzzling problems relative to procedure to be followed in the real estate business. These questions frequently come up at staff meetings, at which time an effort is made to solve them and decide upon a definite practice. To record these rulings permanently and also for the purpose of presenting general matters of policy to new members of the sales department, it is intended herein to maintain a careful record of them.

This book is also intended to become a repository for useful information which may be referred to from time to time by those who desire to know just what principles rule the conduct of this office.

There are two important things which need to be observed to make one a successful real estate salesman. One is "be square" and the other is "work hard." Every salesman in this organization must have the former quality inherently, and if he does not already have the latter, he must quickly acquire it in order to continue with us.

It is the purpose of the Policy Book to guide and direct him intelligently in good business practices, showing him how to "be square" and to furnish him in concentrated form the experience of the entire organization to serve as a help and incentive to show him *how* to "work hard."

Everyone connected with this organization is invited to submit matters or suggest rules or policies which may be helpful in following out a comprehensive and effective sales plan.

Commissions

This organization is a member of The .... Real Estate Board and is bound to adhere to the board schedule of commissions, a copy of which is contained herein.

It is a fixed and definite policy of this office that property be not accepted on a net listing basis. In other words, if a client states that he wants $20,000 for a property net to him, the property should be listed in the office files at $21,000, which is the net listing price plus the regular board commission for the sale of the same.

Commissions of The .... Real Estate Board are the recommended commissions. No agent operating in this office is authorized at any time to alter a commission charge without consulting with the head of the office.

Commissions are earned when the minds of the parties have met, as evidenced by a written contract and a down payment in money.

Commissions are collectible under the usual procedure at the time the deal is closed and papers signed. Defects in title do not relieve a client from paying commission on the sale of a property, if he is unable to deilver it.

Division of Commissions to Salesmen

Division of commissions in this office is made upon the following basis:

1. Except as specified below, and as provided for elsewhere herein, all commissions collected will be divided 50% to the salesman and 50% to the office.

2. This office recognizes the fact that a property well listed is half sold, and wishes to encourage the listing of property by salesmen. Whenever a property is sold by a salesman other than the one who turned in the listing, a listing fee of 10% of the commission collected will be paid, one-half out of the commission of the salesman making the sale and one-half by the office.

Selling salesman	45%
Listing salesman	10%
Office	45%
	100%

No listing fee is paid where a salesman sells one of his own listings. (See section 1, above.)

3. No listing fee is imposed on listings made by members of the firm and the manager. The salesman selling such listings receives the full 50% of the commission collected.

4. Where two salesmen list a property together, both of their names will go on the listing card, and they will share the listing fee equally, unless one of them sells the listed property, in which event the selling salesman receives no part of the listing fee, but receives his full 50% of

the gross commission collected; and the other salesman receives one-half of the listing fee or 5% of the gross commission collected and the office receives 45% of the gross commission collected.

Division of Commissions with Other Brokers

The matter of dividing commissions in so-called "split" deals is rather difficult to make a definite ruling on, because it is usually subject to negotiation.

It is a general practice for members of the local real estate board to split 60-40 (60 per cent to the selling broker, 40 per cent to the listing broker) on deals which are listed in one office but for which a buyer is secured through an outside office.

Divisions of Commissions Where Trades or Exchanges Are Effected

The matter of compensation in the way of commission to a real estate firm where trades or exchanges are made is definitely settled by rules and procedure of the Real Estate Board to which we adhere, which reads:

In exchange of property, mortgages or equities each party is to pay the full commission herein provided, based on the sale price, and should be so advised.

Failure to advise both parties that you are collecting commission from each of them may seriously affect a broker's ability to collect commissions, so that the statement should be made frankly to each party that in making the deal each party will be required to pay the full regular commission on the sale value of his property.

Trades or exchanges are profitable deals to work upon, as the task of making an exchange is seldom greater than that of making a straight sale for one party, while the compensation is often double that received for making a single sale.

Prospects Referred by One Salesman to Another

Frequently a salesman learns of someone on the East Side who wants to buy property on the West Side. The salesman should refer such a prospect to an office associate working in the territory where the property is wanted. No commission division is acknowledged, as one salesman is likely to have good prospects referred to him as often as he refers prospects to another. By the law of averages this arrangement should prove equitable.

Regarding Checks Posted on Deals

All checks received by salesmen as deposits on deals are to be deposited immediately upon receipt with the head of the office, instead of being carried about in pocketbooks or kept in the salesman's desk. Loss of a check of this sort might prove a very serious matter. This rule must be rigidly observed.

Sale of Businesses

When this office is instrumental in selling a business, such as a restaurant, the commission on the business brokerage deal is 10% of the value of the property transferred. If a new lease is negotiated by us, the office is entitled to the regular commission on that as well. (Note: It is assumed that the office is licensed to sell businesses as well as real estate.)

Arbitration of Disputes

In order to promote harmony among associates of this office, it is agreed by everyone who subscribes to this policy book that, in the event of a dispute of any kind arising between salesmen or between salesmen and the office, all such matters will be submitted to arbitration. Such action shall be taken by all employees of the organization assembled for that purpose. A chairman of the arbitration proceedings shall be appointed and shall have full control. After hearings of both sides of the dispute there shall be a vote taken and the majority of such votes shall prevail. Associates of the organization whose signatures appear herein faithfully agree to abide by such decisions.

Listing Property

In listing a property always secure full details, giving particular attention to the matter of financing. Secure information relative to the amount of mortgages, to whom given, when they expire, rate of interest throughout mortgage term, monthly payments, if any, and whether they include interest or not when interest is payable. These are details which must be learned before a deal can be consummated and it is easier to find them out when listing the property, thus avoiding the possibility of a seller raising the price or changing the terms just when a deal is ready to close. Also, be sure to inquire how much cash is required and what best terms the seller will make.

Always inquire seller's reason for selling, whether it is because he wants to make a profit, is leaving the city, is in straightened circumstances, needs the money in his business, has had sickness, to close an estate, etc. Such information makes valuable selling talk.

When listing residence property, particularly in high grade localities, inquire who the neighbors are. Many sales are made to neighbors or their friends.

Have it clearly understood by the seller what the rate of commission is and what he will be expected to pay in the event of a sale. Require him to quote a price to include commission and not a net price. If he is endeavoring to sell the property himself, require him to agree to quote the same price we are quoting in order to avoid putting us in an embarrassing position by being underquoted.

Remember always that "a property well listed is half sold."

Unless a property is so priced, or so strategically located that you are certain of selling it within a given time, do not take an exclusive listing, unless the seller is not in a hurry about selling.

Keep circulating. Remember that everyone you meet carries some kind of real estate information. If he is not in the market himself, he knows someone who either wants to buy or wants to sell. Everybody is interested in real estate. Start talking real estate and then be a good listener. If you are clever enough to keep him talking, you will get information which you can cash into dollars.

Adjustment of Taxes, Insurance, etc.

It is a policy of this office that contracts providing for the sale or purchase of property shall stipulate that all taxes, assessments, water rents, insurance charges, and other permiums are to be prorated, as of the date of actual transfer of property.

In drawing contracts it is imperative that it be clearly stated that there must be furnished by the seller "a merchantable title free and clear of all encumbrances whatever, including liens, clouds, and dower rights." Care in the handling of this matter will avoid much confusion and difficulty.

Insurance

This office is a duly qualified member of the local fire insurance exchange. For all insurance premiums written through this office, the regular commission is paid. Any member of this organization who has any insurance of his own, except life insurance, or who through solicitation obtains authority to write policies, is entitled to the regular salesman's commission on policies written through this office. Members of the organization are urged to turn in as much insurance as they can obtain, as they make a commission on it, or save that much in the event that they insure their own real estate or automobiles through this office. The same commission is paid on renewals.

Earnest Money

It is customary in selling a piece of property for a down payment of from $200 to $500 to accompany the offer to purchase.

Further, it is a rule of this office that down payments shall be accepted and will be held by this company in a trustee account, pending completion of the transaction.

The only deviation to this rule is when the transaction is placed in escrow with a professional escrow agent or company held by it pending completion of the deal and payment of the commission. In such a case, a clause must be inserted in the escrow letter that the amount of the regular commission is to be paid this company by the escrow agent on behalf of the seller for services rendered, payment to be made at time papers are executed and transfer made. Whenever question is raised by the seller about turning over the deposit to him, the head of the office must be consulted at once.

All deposits made as earnest money are placed in a special trustee bank account and are not banked with office funds, but are ready to turn over immediately when a deal is consummated.

A Salesman's Rights to Prospects

One of the most puzzling problems confronting us is the handling of prospects by salesmen. It is a well-recognized fact in all selling organizations that no one factor contributes more toward harmony and a spirit of coöperation than a definite policy regarding a salesman's right to the fruits of his labor. A policy of fairness and absolute impartiality upon the part of the office is a wonderful incentive to greater production and efficiency, and naturally breeds loyalty. A salesman does his best work when he is filled with a spirit of enthusiasm and loyalty to the organization.

To promote such an atmosphere of square dealing is the purpose of the following definite policy regarding right to prospects:

Office prospects. An "office prospect" is a prospect secured through general office advertising, or one who comes into or telephones the office personally, or who writes to the office of his own accord, or one whom the manager himself secures, with whom no negotiations are pending as evidenced by the prospect file mentioned hereafter, or an "individual prospect" who through failure on the part of a salesman to report has become an "office prospect," as provided in paragraph 3.

Individual prospect. An "individual prospect" is a prospect secured by a salesman through his own efforts, either personally or through advertising bearing a reference to such salesman, and with whom no negotiations are pending, as evidenced by the prospect file mentioned hereafter.

(1) An office prospect not retained by the manager will be assigned by him, or the salesmanager in charge of the office, impartially to such salesman as he believes can best handle such prospect.

(2) When a salesman secures an individual prospect or is assigned an office prospect he shall be required after his first interview to report to the office upon a prospect card as hereafter provided, the results of his call and such card in the prospect file shall constitute notice to every other member of the organization of his exclusive right (subject to exceptions hereafter provided) to canvass said prospect for a period of 30 days from the date of the report on the prospect card. The date on the prospect card shall be the date of the call. Prospect cards before being filed must show at least one call within one week of filing same. Each salesman will be expected at least once a week to make a report on his progress on all prospects on which he is actively working.

(3) When a subsequent call is reported and entered on the prospect card, the salesman's right to canvass the prospect shall be automatically extended for another 30-day period from the date of said reported call. If no report is turned in before the 30-day period has elapsed the prospect shall automatically become an "office prospect" and may be assigned to any other salesman by the salesmanager. Notice of such assignment must be given by the salesmanager to the salesman from whom the prospect is withdrawn, so that he will cease negotiations until the prospect is reassigned to him. A notation of the reassignment and date of same will be made on the prospect card by the salesmanager at the time of such assignment.

(4) The salesmanager shall have the right at any time to withdraw a prospect, either "office" or "individual," from a salesman, if he believes such prospect is being neglected or improperly handled.

(5) Prospects originated from general office advertising are "office" prospects and shall be assigned by the salesmanager. If a salesman originates an advertisement bearing a reference to such salesman, or sign, and a prospect is secured, such prospect is to be regarded as an "individual prospect" of such salesman and shall be governed by the rules covering that classification.

(6) The head of the firm reserves the right at any time to submit property to prospects who have previously come to him directly. If there is a prospect card already in the file on such a prospect, on which the 30-day limit has not expired, he will notify the holder of such prospect before any property is submitted by him.

(7) Generally speaking, it shall be the policy of this office to leave prospects in the hands of the salesman to whom they are first assigned, providing the salesman displays due diligence and judgment in handling

them. Salesmen should co-operate with the office in these matters
and realize that these rules are as fair to one salesman as to another.

(8) It is well recognized by most offices that when two or more
salesmen are trying at the same time to sell the same prospect, they
usually block each other's sales and place the office in a bad light
with the customer. From time to time problems along this line may
come up which are not covered by these rules. Such cases will be
decided by the salesmanager impartially after hearing both sides of
the case and if a matter of precedent is established, notations shall
be made in the policy book from time to time as to new rules governing
the problems involved.

When A Listing Is Earned

Claim to a listing fee may be made when a listing card has been
turned in to the office on a property not previously listed and before
such property is sold.

When two salesmen go out together to list, they shall enter both
of their names on the listing cards and shall share listing fees equally.
But if they go out together to list a specific property known to one
of the salesmen, and not to the other, then the first salesman shall
file the listing and receive full credit for it.

If one salesman gives information to another salesman regarding
a property (unlisted), for the purpose of enabling the other salesman
to make a listing, then both of their names shall be placed on the
listing card and the listing fee shall be shared equally.

As soon as a listing is made it becomes the property of the office,
even before a listing card is turned in. Every other salesman shall
have the same right as the listing salesman when it comes to selling
the property listed, and the salesman first reporting to the office that
he has a bona fide written and signed offer, accompanied by earnest
money from his purchaser, shall have the right, with the approval
of the office, first to present his offer to the owner for acceptance.

A listing may be held out by a salesman only by securing the
manager's written permission, with a definite date, on the listing card.

When a salesman leaves the organization he shall forfeit all rights
to listing fees on sales, and his listings shall become office listings.

Salesmen's listings not revised for over one year become office listings and may then be claimed by any salesman who checks them up.

Commission Due One Salesman from Another for Securing a Prospect

Where one salesman voluntarily turns over one of his own prospects to another salesman, who succeeds in selling said prospect, the
salesman who refers the prospect shall be entitled to 10% of any
commission earned, and the balance of the commission shall be divided

equally between the selling salesman and the office, subject to the rules already provided governing listing fees and division of commissions.

In the event the salesman who makes the reference of the prospect happens also to have listed the property which is sold, he shall be entitled to both the listing fee on the property, amounting to 10%, and also to the 10% fee for the prospect, a total of 20%, and the remaining 80% shall be divided equally between the selling salesman and the office.

Salesmen Buying or Selling Property

This office has no objection to its salesmen investing in real estate, either individually or as members of a syndicate, provided property is bought and sold and a commission paid to this office in the regular way. When a salesman is buying individually, he must reveal the fact to the person selling the property, and reach an agreement for the payment of commission to the office. In selling property, the regular commission shall be paid the office, as in the case of buying. Any commission paid shall be divided between office and salesman in the regular way, according to rules found elsewhere herein.

Conditions Relating to Salesmen When They Leave the Organization

It is natural that salesmen will, from time to time, decide to leave the organization, either to affiliate with other offices, to go into business for themselves, or for other good and sufficient reasons.

The following conditions are specifically understood and agreed upon by salesmen becoming associated with this organization:

1. In establishing relations with the organization a salesman accepts the conditions of employment as set forth in this policy book. It is therefore consistent that he abide by all of the rules and regulations so set forth when he decides to sever his relations with the office. To this end, therefore, all such conditions contained herein shall be observed in settling any deals or other affairs at the time a salesman departs.

2. A salesman contemplating leaving should notify the office at least 30 days in advance of so doing, fully stating his future intentions and, in the meantime, should make every effort to close pending deals in which he is interested. If he closes such a deal or deals just before departing, any commission due him will be paid just as soon as it is received, out of escrow, by the office. The same applies to any deal which may be closed at any time after leaving the office, provided the salesman has been instrumental in closing it or has any

interest in it. Any deferred commissions due salesmen will likewise be paid promptly by the office upon receipt.

3. It is agreed that all real estate listings accumulated by and/or assigned to the salesman during his term of service are the sole property of the office and that all listing cards are to be surrendered by the salesman without copying for the purpose of later contacting prospects or property owners. No salesman's right to contact shall be abridged, but he must make such contact after leaving the employ of this organization.

4. Data sheets, cards, set-ups, and statements regarding any properties assigned to or worked on by the salesman are likewise to be surrendered before leaving.

5. All prospect cards on which the names and addresses of real estate prospects or buyers are inscribed and which have come into possession of the salesman shall be turned in to the office before leaving.

6. The real estate act of this state, under which salesmen operate, requires a broker to report unethical conduct on the part of any salesman who leaves the office, and it is likewise necessary for the salesman to secure an authorized release and transfer signature from this office before he departs in order that he may submit it to the department before joining any other office force.

7. Any deals in progress or being worked upon at the time the salesman leaves are to be considered office deals and are to be closed and commissions divided under regular office rules as outlined in this policy book.

8. Any deal started or revived through other organization salesmen with office prospects after a salesman has left this office are to be considered new deals, and the departing salesman will have no interest in them and agrees not to make any claim to commissions in the event such commissions are earned subsequently to his leaving the office. He likewise agrees not to interfere in any manner with the closing of such deals after he leaves the office.

9. The salesman, upon leaving, shall have delivered to him by the office his salesman's certificate, which the Real Estate Commissioner requires to be displayed in any brokerage office where he becomes employed.

In conclusion, it is the genuine desire of the head of this office that all salesmen leave it under friendly circumstances. Great care is taken in qualifying salesmen before they become affiliated with this office, and the honor and integrity of the office lies largely in the hands of those associated with it. Leaving any office under a cloud of discord or suspicion, or any unfriendly circumstances, invariably hurts the salesman most. A salesman should, therefore, be most careful in his conduct when making up his mind to establish new affiliations. Loose or unethical actions at such a critical time are dangerous and may later lead to unpleasant difficulties for the salesman involved.

Very seldom in the past has anyone left this office under other than the most friendly conditions, and this has been due entirely to the complete understanding which has existed between the office and those affiliated with it, by reason of this policy book and the mutual conditions it outlines.

Name .... Date .... Date ....

Name .... Date .... Date ....

Name .... Date .... Date ....

When a salesman has read the policy book, he should be asked if he understands it thoroughly and is ready to agree to abide by its rulings. If so, he signs it and writes the dates of his entry as a salesman in the organization. When he leaves, his date of departure may be inscribed opposite his name. This gives a complete record of his term of service.

The use of a policy book in any office will be found valuable. It pins the employees down to a mode of procedure and enables the manager to show a salesman where he has erred if he breaks any of its rules. It proves most useful for the salesman himself, for it explains to him many of the procedures under which an up-to-date office operates.

CHAPTER 36

Behavior

and Ethics

SQUARE DEALING CONSTITUTES THE very foundation of the real estate business. No broker or salesman ever carried on his calling successfully if he did not conduct his operations honestly and to the advantage of the seller, the purchaser, and himself. That "honesty is the best policy" has been demonstrated in a thousand lines of endeavor, and especially in the real estate field.

The realty business has suffered severely in the past from the questionable practices of men who have taken a fling at it, engaged in crooked or, to say the least, doubtful operations, and then, like the Arab, folded their tents and disappeared. They may have prospered for a brief time but the invariable result is that they lost everything in the long run.

The National Association of Real Estate Boards, consisting of over 1,500 boards and over 82,600 realtors, has for many years subscribed to a code of ethics on behalf of its entire membership. It is strictly enforced, committees of individual boards being charged to see that rules are not violated. If they are, suitable penalties are assessed. The code, as most recently amended and revised, consists of three sections, one dealing with professional relations, a second having to do with relations with clients, the third covering relations with customers and the public. Let the code speak for itself:

292

Preamble

Under all is the land. Upon its wise utilization and widely allocated ownership depend the survival and growth of free institutions and of our civilization. The Realtor is the instrumentality through which the land resource of the nation reaches its highest use and through which land ownership attains its widest distribution. He is a creator of homes, a builder of cities, a developer of industries and productive farms.

Such functions impose obligations beyond those of ordinary commerce; they impose grave social responsibility and a patriotic duty to which the Realtor should dedicate himself, and for which he should be diligent in preparing himself. The Realtor, therefore, is zealous to maintain and improve the standards of his calling and shares with his fellow-Realtors a common responsibility for its integrity and honor.

In the interpretation of his obligations, he can take no safer guide than that which has been handed down through twenty centuries, embodied in the Golden Rule:

"Whatsoever ye would that men should do to you, do ye even so to them."

Accepting this standard as his own, every Realtor pledges himself to observe its spirit in all his activities and to conduct his business in accordance with the following Code of Ethics:

Part I

Relations to the Public

Article 1. The Realtor should keep himself informed as to movements affecting real estate in his community, state, and the nation, so that he may be able to contribute to public thinking on matters of taxation, legislation, land use, city planning, and other questions affecting property interests.

Article 2. It is the duty of the Realtor to be well informed on current market conditions in order to be in a position to advise his clients as to the fair market price.

Article 3. It is the duty of the Realtor to protect the public against fraud, misrepresentation, or unethical practices in the real estate field. He should endeavor to eliminate in his community any practices which could be damaging to the public or to the dignity and integrity of the real estate profession. The Realtor should assist the board or commission charged with regulating the practices of brokers and salesmen in his state.

Article 4. The Realtor should ascertain all pertinent facts concerning every property for which he accepts the agency, so that he may fulfill his obligation to avoid error, exaggeration, misrepresentation, or concealment of pertinent facts.

Article 5. The Realtor should not be instrumental in introducing into a neighborhood a character of property or use which will clearly be detrimental to property values in that neighborhood.

Article 6. The Realtor should not be a party to the naming of a false consideration in any document, unless it be the naming of an obviously nominal consideration.

Article 7. The Realtor should not engage in activities that constitute the practice of law and should recommend that title be examined and legal counsel be obtained when the interest of either party requires it.

Article 8. The Realtor should keep in a special bank account, separated from his own funds, monies coming into his possession in trust for other persons, such as escrows, trust funds, client's monies, and other like items.

Article 9. The Realtor in his advertising should be especially careful to present a true picture and should neither advertise without disclosing his name, nor permit his salesmen to use individual names or telephone numbers, unless the salesman's connection with the Realtor is obvious in the advertisement.

Article 10. The Realtor, for the protection of all parties with whom he deals, should see that financial obligations and commitments regarding real estate transactions are in writing, expressing the exact agreement of the parties; and that copies of such agreements, at the time they are executed, are placed in the hands of all parties involved.

Part II

Relations to the Client

Article 11. In accepting employment as an agent, the Realtor pledges himself to protect and promote the interests of the client. This obligation of absolute fidelity to the client's interest is primary, but it does not relieve the Realtor from the obligation of dealing fairly with all parties to the transaction.

Article 12. In justice to those who place their interests in his care, the Realtor should endeavor always to be informed regarding laws, proposed legislation, governmental orders, and other essential information and public policies which affect those interests.

Article 13. Since the Realtor is representing one or another party to a transaction, he should not accept compensation from more than one party without the full knowledge of all parties to the transaction.

Article 14. The Realtor should not acquire an interest in, or buy for himself, any member of his immediate family, his firm or any member thereof, or any entity in which he has a substantial ownership interest, property listed with him, or his firm, without making the true position known to the listing owner, and in selling property owned by him, or in which he has such interest, the facts should be revealed to the purchaser.

Article 15. The exclusive listing of property should be urged and practiced by the Realtor as a means of preventing dissension and misunderstanding and of assuring better service to the owner.

Article 16. When acting as agent in the management of property, the Realtor should not accept any commission, rebate or profit on expenditures made for an owner, without the owner's knowledge and consent.

Article 17. The Realtor should not undertake to make an appraisal that is outside the field of his experience unless he obtains the assistance of an authority on such types of property, or unless the facts are fully disclosed to the client. In such circumstances, the authority so engaged should be so identified and his contribution to the assignment should be clearly set forth.

Article 18. When asked to make a formal appraisal of real property, the Realtor should not render an opinion without careful and thorough analysis and interpretation of all factors affecting the value of the property. His counsel constitutes a professional service. The Realtor should not undertake to make an appraisal or render an opinion of value on any property where he has a present or contemplated interest unless such interest is specifically disclosed in the appraisal report. Under no circumstances should he undertake to make a formal appraisal when his employment or fee is contingent upon the amount of his appraisal.

Article 19. The Realtor should not submit or advertise property without authority, and in any offering the price quoted should not be other than that agreed upon with the owners as the offering price.

Article 20. In that event that more than one formal written offer on a specific property is made before the owner has accepted an offer, any other formal written offer presented to the Realtor, whether by a prospective purchaser or another broker, should be transmitted to the owner for his decision.

Part III

Relations to His Fellow-Realtors

Article 21. The Realtor should seek no unfair advantage over his fellow-Realtors and should willingly share with them the lessons of his experience and study.

Article 22. The Realtor should so conduct his business as to avoid controversies with his fellow-Realtors. In the event of a controversy between Realtors who are members of the same local board, such controversy should be arbitrated in accordance with regulations of their board rather than litigated.

Article 23. Controversies between Realtors who are not members of the same local board should be submitted to an arbitration board consisting of one arbitrator chosen by each Realtor from the real estate board to which he belongs or chosen in accordance with the regulations of the respective boards. One other member, or a sufficient number of members to make an odd number, should be selected by the arbitrators thus chosen.

Article 24. When the Realtor is charged with unethical practice, he should place all pertinent facts before the proper tribunal of the member board of which he is a member for investigation and judgment.

Article 25. The Realtor should not voluntarily disparage the business practice of a competitor, nor volunteer an opinion of a competitor's transaction. If his opinion is sought it should be rendered with strict professional integrity and courtesy.

Article 26. The agency of a Realtor who holds an exclusive listing should be respected. A Realtor cooperating with a listing broker should not invite the cooperation of a third broker without the consent of the listing broker.

Article 27. The Realtor should cooperate with other brokers on property listed by him exclusively whenever it is in the interest of the client, sharing commissions on a previously agreed basis. Negotiations concerning property listed exclusively with one broker should be carried on with the listing broker, not with the owner, except with the consent of the listing broker.

Article 28. The Realtor should not solicit the services of an employee or salesman in the organization of a fellow-Realtor without the knowledge of the employer.

Article 29. Signs giving notice of property for sale, rent, lease, or exchange should not be placed on any property by more than one Realtor, and then only if authorized by the owner, except as the property is listed with and authorization given to more than one Realtor.

Article 30. In the best interest of society, of his associates and of his own business, the Realtor should be loyal to the real estate board of his community and active in its work.

Conclusion

The term *Realtor* has come to connote competence, fair dealing, and high integrity resulting from adherence to a lofty ideal of moral conduct in business relations. No inducement of profit and no instructions from clients ever can justify departure from this ideal, or from the injunctions of this Code.

Code of Professional Ethics for
Institute of Real Estate Management

Preamble

The objective of this Professional Code is the continuing enhancement of professional performance by Certified Property Managers through acceptance and conformance with those procedures that are the necessary elements of a mutually beneficial relationship between the Certified Property Manager, his fellow CPMs, his fellow Realtors, his clients, his employers, and the public at large.

A CPM shall be bound by the following professional Pledge:

"I pledge myself to the advancement of professional property management through the mutual efforts of members of the Institute of Real Estate Management and by any other proper means available to me.

"I pledge myself to seek and maintain an equitable, honorable and cooperative association with fellow members of the Institute and with all others who may become a part of my business and professional life.

"I pledge myself to place honesty, integrity and industriousness above all else; to pursue my gainful efforts with diligent study and dedication to the end that service to my clients shall always be maintained at the highest possible level.

"I pledge myself to comply with the principles and declarations of the Institute of Real Estate Management as set forth in its Bylaws, Regulations and this Code of Professional Ethics."

Article 1. The Code of Ethics of the National Association of Real Estate Boards as in effect from time to time is incorporated into this code by reference.

Article 2. A CPM shall not use or permit the use of the CPM designation in any manner that shall adversely affect the objectives or high purposes of the Institute of Real Estate Management.

Article 3. A CPM shall not make, or authorize, or otherwise encourage any oral or written statements of a derogatory nature concerning another CPM or of his business practices.

Article 4. **Section 1:** A CPM shall neither in his own behalf nor for others solicit the services of any employee known to be under the supervision of another CPM without prior knowledge by the other member. **Section 2:** A CPM shall not offer his services to the client of another CPM whose services have heretofore been satisfactory, by basing his solicitation on the inducement of a reduced management fee.

Article 5. A CPM shall not accept association with or employment by an individual, partnership, group or other organization unless, to the best of his knowledge and belief, such organization complies with all applicable governmental laws, ordinances, rules and regulations and with this code of professional ethics.

Article 6. A CPM shall at all times be loyal to his clients, and shall be diligent in the maintenance and protection of their reputations and properties.

Article 7. A CPM shall not represent divergent or conflicting interests, nor engage in any activity reasonably calculated to be contrary to the best interests of his client or client's property unless the clients have been previously notified.

Article 8. A CPM shall not receive directly or indirectly any rebate, fee commission, discount or other benefit, whether monetary or otherwise, without the full knowledge and prior consent of the client concerned.

Article 9. A CPM shall not disclose to a third party confidential information concerning the business or personal affairs of his clients without prior authorization, except upon legal demands by competent governmental authority.

Article 10. A CPM shall keep his clients currently advised in all matters concerning their respective properties or welfare. A CPM shall cause to be furnished to each client at agreed intervals a complete regular accounting in respect to the operation of that client's properties.

Article 11. A CPM shall exert due diligence for the protection of client's funds against all foreseeable contingencies. The deposit of such funds in account with a reputable banking institute shall constitute due diligence.

Article 12. A CPM shall at all times keep and maintain accurate accounting records, properly marked for identification concerning the properties managed for each client, and such records shall be available for inspection at all reasonable times by each respective client.

Article 13. The interpretation of compliance with this professional code is the responsibility of the Ethics and Discipline Committee of the Institute of Real Estate Management. Disciplinary action for violation of any portion of this code shall be instituted by the Governing Council of

IREM in accordance with rules and regulations established by that Governing Council and approved by the membership.

American Institute of Real Estate Appraisers

Code of Ethics

Land is the basic source of all wealth. Real estate wisely used and widely allocated in private ownership is essential to our national well-being. Upon its intelligent and proper evaluation depend the investments and lifetime savings of our people and their confidence in the economy which sustains our free institutions.

The functions of the real estate appraiser are strictly professional in character; he is charged with solemn business, civic, and social responsibilities.

Recognizing these obligations, we mutually pledge to each other our knowledge, our experience, and our sacred honor. Each Member of the American Institute of Real Estate Appraisers agrees that he will:

1. Conduct his professional activities in a manner that will reflect credit upon himself, other real estate appraisers, and the American Institute of of Real Estate Appraisers.
2. Protect the professional reputation and prospects of other real estate appraisers who subscribe to and abide by this Code of Ethics.
3. Acknowledge the contributions of others who participate professionally with him in an appraisal.
4. Secure appraisal assignments by referral and through recognition of his professional competence without unprofessional solicitation or advertisement, without payment or acceptance of commission, without unprofessional fee bidding, and without contingencies dependent upon findings, conclusions, or value reported.
5. Accept only those appraisal assignments relating to which he has no current or prospective unrevealed personal interest or bias and which he is qualified to undertake and complete without his professional standing or integrity being placed in jeopardy.
6. Preserve a professional, confidential relationship with his client, revealing or reporting only to his client his conclusions and valuation.
7. Render properly and adequately developed valuations without advocacy for accommodation of any particular interests, being factual, objective, unbiased, and honest in presenting his oral or written analyses, conclusions, and opinions.
8. Cooperate with the Institute and its officers in all matters, including investigation, censure, discipline, or dismissal of members who, by their conduct, prejudice their professional status or the reputation of the Institute.

9. Conform in all respects to the Code of Ethics and to the Standards of Professional Conduct adopted by the American Institute of Real Estate Appraisers as the same may be amended from time to time.

Regulation 10—Standards of Professional Conduct

Relations with Clients

10.101   It is unethical for an appraiser to reveal the findings and results of his appraisal to anyone other than his client until authorized by the client to do so, or until he is required to do so by due process of law, or until he be released from this obligation by having publicly testified as to such findings.

10.102   It is unethical for an appraiser to render an improperly and inadequately developed opinion of value.

10.103   It is unethical for an appraiser to accept employment to appraise a property in which or relating to which he has any current or prospective direct or indirect personal interest or bias unless such is understood by his client prior to his employment and is explicitly and prominently set forth in his report or testimony, if any.

10.104   It is unethical for an appraiser to make any incorrect oral or written statement with reference to his affiliation with the Institute.

10.105   It is unethical for an appraiser to accept or claim any commission, favor, or emolument in connection with the appraisal of a property other than a fair professional fee for the responsibility entailed and the work and expense involved.

10.106   It is unethical for an appraiser to accept an appraisal assignment without either having had previous exxperience or having or acquiring knowledge of such character as to qualify him to accept such an assignment unless either:

a. He has associated with him in the making of the appraisal an appraiser who has had experience in the valuation of the type of property under appraisement, or

b. Unless the facts are fully disclosed to the client.

10.107   It is recommended that an appraiser include the following in his appraisal report.

a. An unequivocal and reasonably complete description of the property appraised.

b. A clear statement of any contingent conditions upon which the appraisal has been based. For example: (1) The validity of legal, engineering, or auditing opinions used; (2) the completion of projected public or private improvements; (3) that management is assumed to be competent and the ownership to be in responsible hands.

c. The date or time at which the value obtains.

d. The amount of the value.

e. A statement that the appraiser has no present or contemplated future interest in the property appraised; or a statement disclosing all such interests which the appraiser may have in the property appraised.

f. In case the property appraised is a fractional part of the property, a statement that the value reported is invalidated if used in making a summation appraisal of the property as a whole unless conditions and limitations of the use of the report are clearly stated.

10.108 It is recommended that each appraisal report should contain a statement or certificate, substantially in the following form:

"I (we) the undersigned do hereby certify that to the best of my (our) knowledge and belief the statements contained in this appraisal, and upon which the opinions expressed herein are based, are correct, subject to the limiting conditions herein set forth; also, that this appraisal has been made in conformity with the professional standards of the American Institute of Real Estate Appraisers of the National Association of Real Estate Appraisers of the National Association of Real Estate Boards.

Relations with the Public

10.201 It is unethical for an appraiser to accept employment to appraise a property if the employment is contingent upon his reporting a predetermined amount of value or is otherwise contingent upon any predetermined finding to be reported.

10.202 It is unethical for an appraiser, retained in cases where monetary damages are involved, to accept such assignments on condition that his compensation will be a percentage of the damages which may be agreed upon or finally decreed.

10.203 It is unethical for an appraiser to fix his compensation as a percentage of the amount of his value estimate.

10.204 It is unethical for an appraiser to render an appraisal deviating from an unbiased and objective opinion of value, whether to accommodate the interests of his client or for any other reason.

10.205 It is unethical for an appraiser to issue an appraisal report in which the reported valuation is based upon predicted rentals and expenses unless he describes in detail in his report the basis for his prediction. In particular, it is unethical for an appraiser to certify a valuation predicated upon assumed rentals and expenses which he does not demonstrate as certain or highly probable of achievement under ordinary competent management.

10.206 It is unethical for an appraiser to issue an unqualified appraisal report on an investment property which does not reflect the effects of existing leases upon the value of the property.

10.207 It is unethical for an appraiser to issue an appraisal report in which the reported value is based upon the completion of public or private improvements which are not assured unless he clearly states that the appraisal is made on that hypothesis. In any event, he must state in his report the conditions with regard to such improvements which he assumes in estimating the value reported.

10.208 It is unethical for an appraiser to issue an appraisal report in which the reported value is based upon the assumed absence of any legal restriction unless such assumption is reasonable or in accord with legal opinion accepted by the appraiser, and unless the legal authority and opinion are quoted in the appraisal certificate, and it is expressly stated that the validity of the valuation is contingent on such lawful restriction being changed or absent in accordance with the assumption.

10.209* It is unethical for an appraiser to issue an appraisal report on only a part of a whole property unless he specifically states that it is a fractional appraisal and as such can be used only in a manner consistent with such limitations.

10.210* In appraising the security for a loan it is unethical for an appraiser to issue a certificate covering anything less than all of the property designated as security for the loan unless conditions and limitations of the use of the report are clearly stated.

10.211* In appraising the security for a leasehold loan, it is unethical for an appraiser to issue a certificate of value of the improvement only, omitting the value of the leasehold, which latter may be positive, zero, or negative.

10.212* It is unethical for an appraiser to issue an appraisal report on a property in which the total reported value is derived by adding together the values of fractional parts of the property unless the limitations are clearly stated or other and conclusive evidence is given that this result equals the total value of the property considered as a whole.

10.213 It is unethical for an appraiser to issue an appraisal report giving his opinion of value based solely upon the cost approach unless his reasons and justification are clearly and explicitly set forth in the appraisal report.

* It is not intended that anything in these Sections shall be construed to prevent an appraiser from preparing and presenting fractional appraisals or summation appraisals where such appraisals are required for rate making, cost accounting, and other special purposes where the concept of cost independent from value may be appropriately involved.

10.214 It is unethical for an appraiser to issue an appraisal report on a construction project which does not give the appraiser's estimate of the reasonably expected earnings of the project and his opinion on the economic soundness thereof, together with an opinion as to the reasonable time required to attain normal occupancy.

Relations with Fellow-Members

10.301 It is unethical for a member falsely or maliciously to injure, directly or indirectly, the professional reputation of another member, candidate, or applicant for candidacy.

10.302 It is unethical for a member to enter into competitive bidding for appraisal assignments when the member has reason to believe that the work is to be awarded to the lowest bidder. Nothing herein shall, however, be construed as forbidding an appraiser to quote a maximum or a minimum fee, or both, the amount thereof to be later determined by the time involved, data furnished, and other circumstances surrounding an assignment, nor to forbid an appraiser from quoting the amount of a fee to a client or prospective client when the appraiser has no reason to believe that such quotation is to be used in the nature of a competitive bid against the quotation of another appraiser.

10.303 It is unethical for a member to pay or claim a fee or commission for the purpose of obtaining or referring employment.

Relations with the Institute

10.401 It is unethical for a member to conduct himself in such manner as to prejudice his professional status or the reputation of the Institute.

10.402 It is unethical for a member of the Institute to solicit appraisal assignments or to advertise his professional attainments or services except in a dignified manner in keeping with high professional standards. Public notices preferably should be limited to an advertisement of the name, professional titles including M.A.I. (Member of the American Institute of Real Estate Appraisers of the National Association of Real Estate Boards), class of service, and address of the advertiser without any other qualifying word or letters, or in the case of the announcements of change of address, the plain statement of the fact for the publication of which the announcement purports to be made. Cards permitted by this rule, when appearing in newspapers, shall not exceed two columns in width and three inches in depth; when appearing in magazines, directories, and similar publications, cards shall not exceed one fourth of a page in size. This rule shall not be construed to inhibit the proper and professional dissemination of impersonal information among a member's own clients or personal associates or the properly restricted circulation of bulletins containing professional information.

It is ethical, however, for an appraiser of the Institute to carry an announcement in a classified directory, as follows: "JOHN DOE, M.A.I. *Address, Telephone Number*" under the subdivision REAL ESTATE APPRAISALS.

10.403   It is unethical for a member to claim qualifications in reports, testimony, or elsewhere which are not factual or which may be subject to erroneous interpretation.

10.404   Before testifying in court or before any public commission or other tribunal as an appraiser, an appraisal report or a complete memorandum, containing data, reasoning, and conclusions upon which the testimony is based, shall be prepared by the appraiser and shall be preserved and made available to the Governing Council or the President of the Institute upon request, to justify the testimony given in the case, if such testimony is widely divergent from the testimony of another member of the Institute in the same case. Since the testimony of the appraiser shall have made his conclusions public, the provisions of Section 10.101 shall no longer be applicable.

10.405   If widely divergent testimony, unethical practices, or other acts by members or candidates are such as to discredit the Institute or to lower the prestige of membership therein, it is the duty of each member to report such facts and circumstances to the Ethics Committee or to the President of the Institute.

CHAPTER 37

Land Booms

and Depressions

EVERY SINCERE STUDENT OF REAL ES-
tate will make it his business to investigate the subject of
business cycles and the recurrent real estate booms and depressions resulting therefrom. In the past, at least, the country no sooner got over a real estate boom than it was plunged
into what seemed to be an inevitable depression. With the
greatly expanded interest of the federal government in keeping close watch over the economy, and with its increasing
ability to control the economy to at least some extent, there
are those who feel that a depression such as that of the 1930's
is no longer inevitable.

Nevertheless, while the hills and valleys may have been
rounded off, most economists would agree that the general
business cycle is still with us. An upward economic trend for
a decade or so will be followed by a downward trend, perhaps of shorter duration. Hence, the cycle is still worth studying.

When a boom starts, the upward trend is gradual at first,
shoots up feverishly for the next several years, and finally
levels off for a year or two. Overproduction of all kinds of
buildings takes place, employment falls off in the building
trades, rents begin to sag downward, and a depression is

then under way. The course of a depression is about the same as a boom but in the opposite direction.

There are four characteristic phases of business cycles. These are, in their regular order: prosperity, recession, depression, and recovery. Depressions as such are usually characterized by economists as major or minor ones. The great depression of the 1930's was doubtless the most severe in American history as well as the longest. It was finally cut short by the advent of World War II. Straightway the picture changed into a rosy one and a full-fledged boom got under way.

American land booms originated in Atlantic coast states a century or two ago when they were first attempting to expand and care for the rapidly increasing population which was rushing in from the countries of Europe. Most large Eastern cities, and territories surrounding them, experienced land booms, but because of the lack of transportation facilities for the most part, they seldom reached sizes proportionate with those encountered in recent times.

New York, Albany, Syracuse, Rochester, and Buffalo all had land booms when the Erie Canal was opened in 1825. Cleveland also had its first and greatest boom about that time when lake shipping in sail boats was inaugurated. Chicago had a boom when it first gave evidence of becoming a great railroad center, and later another boom when elevated railroads were introduced. Still another followed with the general advent of the automobile.

Many cities experienced land booms between 1910 and 1925 through a realization that the automobile could build up urban centers far beyond the old limits set by the use of horse cars and, later, interurban cars. Remember one vital fact, and that is, *that distance is measured in minutes and not in miles!* More miles were annihilated by the modern automobile than by all other forms of so-called rapid transit, except aircraft.

Principal cities in California, all the way from San Diego to San Francisco, were founded about missions in the early days. California had scarcely any population growth until the late 1840's. Then came the discovery of gold at Sutter's Mill near Sacramento in 1848, and within a year a great rush had started from Eastern states, overland, via the Isthmus of Panama, and even around Cape Horn, in a wild scramble to reach the gold fields. San Francisco and northern California benefited most through that particular boom, though it is interesting to know that the first gold actually found in California was at Saugus, just a few miles north of Los Angeles, several years before the gold boom of '49.

The long, frosty trek to Alaska's Klondike in 1897 was the occasion for a boom in Seattle and neighboring areas. The quest in the far north was not for free land but for gold. How that ended everyone knows. Today some Alaskan cities that formerly had 30,000 to 50,000 inhabitants have but a few hundreds, or even scores left, if they are not deserted entirely. Statehood for Alaska is helping to reverse this trend to some extent.

The building of railroads to the Pacific coast created booms for every town at "the end of rails." Omaha, Denver, Salt Lake City, and Oakland were only a few that experienced them. They were first heard of as the railroad boom rolled across the great plains and mountain areas towards the setting sun. The earliest boom was from 1868 to 1874, followed by another throughout the great Middle West when between 1880 and 1893 there was a phenomenal expansion of interlacing railroad and river vessel lines. Oil discoveries in Oklahoma and Texas later brought their booms and the rapid building of cities. Space installations in Texas and Florida are today doing the same thing.

Some realty booms are what are known as "work" booms— that is, free land offers opportunities for settlers to acquire cheap homes. The Florida and California booms were combined "work and play" booms. Marvelously rich resources were exploited together with the climate, which attracted so many to these natural paradises. Many came to play but remained to labor, fitting themselves snugly into the business picture and becoming good citizens.

Roger Babson, the well-known economist, once pointed out

that during the complete turn of a cycle of business activities there is a distinct sequence of events. Invariably, he declared, business passes through ten periods from the beginning of one cycle to its end and these are fundamental:

1. Period of increasing money rates.
2. Period of declining bond prices.
3. Period of declining stock prices.
4. Period of declining commodity prices.
5. Period of declining real estate prices.
6. Period of low money rates.
7. Period of increasing bond prices.
8. Period of increasing stock prices.
9. Period of increasing commodity prices.
10. Period of increasing real estate prices.

It is interesting, in the study of business cycles, to note that real estate is always the last commodity to go down in price and, by the same token, the last to come up in price when a period of prosperity impends. Some time after a business crisis appears, credit contracts and business assumes an attitude of fear, and the market for real estate likewise contracts. Prices may remain firm for a time, but then demand slackens and, finally, vacant real estate "freezes up," and there is scarcely a market for it at any price. Income property, still paying a return, remains attractive for a time for investment purposes, but finally even in this class fear leaps into the saddle and, as rents decline, it is found almost impossible to sell even improved property.

Then follows a period of several years until the business cycle again swings into ascendancy. This is about the only phase of the cycle that can actually be said to be static.

Is there any way to detect when a real estate boom is drawing to a close? The average real estate man will sense in his business when the demand is slackening. It is usually after a period of over-production of houses, apartments, and stores. Vacancies begin to appear. Building laborers accept lower wages to enable them to keep at work. Speculation in vacant property begins to lag.

The wise broker will advise his clients not to be caught with vacant property on their hands when a depression is about to ensue. Vacant property earns nothing, and at an interest rate of about 6 per cent, plus taxes, it eats itself up in eight to ten years. Since most depressions last nearly as many years, one stands a chance to have his entire investment wiped out! If you must carry property during a depression, see that it is improved property able to earn an income, or at least that it may serve as shelter for owner or tenant.

The wise broker or investor will keep a close weather eye on a period of real estate activity as it develops beyond boom stages. He will gauge his market to ascertain if it is being oversupplied with vacant lots and with buildings of various kinds. As long as there is a shortage the boom probably will not end but will continue until such a time as an excess has been built up. The early years of a boom are the time to engage in speculative buying of real estate, as it is then comparatively safe to hold property until it ripens before reselling it at a profit.

When it does appear that the end is in sight and sometimes well before that time, a wise broker should advise his clients to set their houses in order, to improve vacant property, or to sell it to someone who will do so. The broker should be careful what he offers his clients at this time, despite the fact that apparent bargains in vacant property may appear on the market. Some properties, at this time, may not be worth buying at any price.

Should a real estate salesman or broker, during a boom period, engage in the buying and selling of property which he owns outright? Provided he is careful to observe the ethics of the realty business, there is no reason why a real estate man should not make money by buying and selling the commodity in which he deals, if he has the funds and the inclination to do so. He should not take advantage of the fact that he sometimes comes in contact with owners who ask his advice about values and buy from such persons at figures below the market values of the properties concerned. Nor should he hide the fact from an owner that he is buying for his own account. Most brokers, as a matter of fact, make their purchases through other brokers and very often, indeed, make their sales through the same agencies.

The upward swing of a boom in real estate usually takes place quite slowly. It may be several years in developing momentum. The decline, however, often comes with speed and suddenness. One scarcely realizes that a boom is actually developing, but there is no mistaking the manner in which a depression sweeps down upon unsuspecting land owners. Vast fortunes have been made by speculators in real estate booms, but by the same token vast amounts have been lost in equities that have melted like snow before a hot wind.

Much money is legitimately earned during real estate booms. Apart from the increase in prices and values which real estate assumes, it inspires many promoters to erect buildings and projects such as amusement parks, resorts, new subdivisions, industrial developments, theaters, bus and air terminals, and other things that are sound and logical improvements greatly appreciated by those who patronize them.

Should one buy real estate in boom or in depression times? The answer is, *buy real estate when you need it!* In boom times prices are soaring and you perhaps pay more for it, but you get more income from it. In periods of depression, prices are lower, but so is the income from it. Leaving the element of speculation out of the question, properly priced real estate is a good buy at any turn of the cycle, particularly if it is a home which you can use for housing your own family. Certainly, if you buy in a depression when the outlook for real estate looks less rosy, you can at least hold the property until boom times come, when you can realize your profit if you desire to take it.

The fact that a wise investor should not carry over into a depression with vacant property on his hands applies equally to the subdivider who is marketing home sites. He, too, should study his market and not find himself at the end of the prosperity cycle with a quantity of lots on his hands, with expensive improvements to be paid for and with little prospect of selling them. There is nothing so dead as a dead subdivision!

Grass grows in the street, sidewalks and pavements disintegrate, and it looks like a graveyard that doesn't even boast perpetual care. If a subdivider is loaded with land, he should market it in comparatively small parcels, installing just the necessary improvements to do so. Then he can carry his land through on a basis of acreage and can probably persuade the tax assessor to do likewise.

Can booms and depressions be avoided? While the answer to that question must remain uncertain, we have already noted that there are those who believe that federal controls will make it almost impossible for a severe depression to overtake us again. They will also point to the general upward trend of business for several decades since the end of World War II as evidence of the effectiveness of government policies. It will, of course, take much longer to prove the case, but let us hope they are right. And if some further measures will need to be taken, it would seem strange if, advanced as this country is in every branch of economics, some solution to this vast problem cannot be found. If the answer eventually is found, it will mean stabilization of values that will result in vast savings, which will benefit every resident of the land.

CHAPTER 38

Women's Role
in Real Estate

THE ENTRY OF WOMEN INTO GENERAL business activities in recent years extended their contacts with the real estate business. Many women are associated with brokerage and subdivision offices and are proving successful in various branches of realty activity. Women establish contact:

1. As office help—in the capacity of stenographers, bookkeepers, telephone operators, and clerks.
2. As rental and management department employees.
3. As selling agents in subdivisions.
4. As hostesses in houses kept open for sale.
5. As members of the sales departments of brokerage offices.
6. As brokers, either operating independently or associated with husbands, relatives, or partners.
7. As operators and promoters, buying, selling, and building houses, and occasionally business properties.

Women as office help have excelled in real estate offices for many years. They are indispensable as stenographers and clerks and in positions where attention to detail is important. Many women in such positions gradually become acquainted with the sales activities of offices and graduate to sales departments, and frequently become quite successful. Some have even gone further, becoming full-fledged brokers and opening their own offices.

It has been a practice in many cities to employ a woman as a so called "hostess" when a new house is opened for sale. She acts as a receptionist to persons calling to inspect the premises, showing them about and, if possible, getting the names and addresses of visitors who may become prospects for this or other properties. In some states it is necessary that such a hostess have a saleman's license, but for the most part any attractive woman who knows how to meet people can do this work. It, too, is a job that often leads to membership on a sales staff. A hostess as such simply points out the advantages of a residence and seeks to place some sales representative in touch with visitors who seem interested. A hostess may be paid a salary for her work or may receive a share of the commission if the place is sold to someone she has contacted and reported.

An increasing number of women have joined the sales staff of real estate offices, particularly in the larger cities, in recent years. Most states now require all members of sales staffs to be licensed, including women who come in direct contact with customers to whom they submit properties either for rental or for sale.

It has been found, in most realty offices, that women are most successful in two endeavors: in renting houses and selling them. A rental department is where many saleswomen start. Armed with printed records, they go out into the field and solicit all kinds of rental properties. These are offered on bulletin boards or advertised in newspapers, and contacts are established. If a rental is for a considerable length of time, a regular realty board leasing commission schedule prevails. For a rental on a monthly basis, the compensation collected is one-fourth to one-half of the first month's rental, according to the practice in the particular city where the deal is made. This is divided one-half to the office and one-half to the rental agent.

Women know how to sell houses. They understand the feminine psychology better than men, in most cases, and are able to point out the advantages and disadvantages of a property listed with them and offered for sale. Most women in the real estate business operate in the house-selling departments, and make excellent incomes from their efforts.

It has been found that women who are really successful in real estate are the ones who devote their entire time to the business. There is a feeling on the part of some women that they would like to take a "fling" at real estate, secure a license and then spend only two or three hours a day at the work, remaining at their housewifely tasks the rest of the time. This seems to offer a nice way to add to their incomes, but actually it is seldom successful. If a woman makes up her mind to enter the field, she should plan to devote full time to the work.

Women must realize that in joining sales staffs they must expect to be treated just as other salesmen are treated. They cannot take advantage of their sex and expect to receive preferential treatment or favors of any kind. They are "on their own" just as every other salesman is. Competition is keen, and they must expect to abide by the rules of the office in every respect; otherwise they will not last very long.

Women must be aggressive but *not too aggressive* in their dealings with prospects. Women prospects will resent it and men certainly will. Indeed, many saleswomen do not get along well with male clients. Men like to deal with their own sex, if possible. Women who have tact, who have good breeding, and who are adequately educated can succeed in the sales field, particularly in their dealings with other women who are prospective buyers of homes—and women buy most of the homes that are sold, their husbands merely paying for them in most cases. A woman broker will do well, however, not to ignore the husband even if the wife has been sold, for sometimes he may be found difficult to handle. Here is where skill and diplomacy shine out as the leading attributes of a woman sales agent.

Occasionally a woman is so successful at selling that she decides to qualify for a broker's license and open her own office. Here her problems multiply and she is in direct competition with all other real estate offices in the community. It will require her full time and all of her energies to carry on.

It sometimes happens that the wife of a realty broker gets interested in the business, secures her license as a salesman or a broker, and joins with her husband in handling sales, particularly of houses, in the neighborhood where their office is located. Husband and wife teams of this sort are common in many cities, operating successfully throughout the years. Occasionally a couple of women team up to conduct an office, operating as a partnership and sharing expenses and profits.

Women in some cities have developed into operators— buying houses, remodeling them, and reselling them at a profit. Some have even engaged in building new houses, installing ideas of their own which have often made such places exceptionally attractive, to be sold upon completion. Some women have made a specialty of buying houses, remodeling them artistically, furnishing them completely, and selling them to newcomers, reaping a handsome profit from the operation.

In one Western city, a woman promoter made quite a success of apartment-house building, units of which she furnished and sold to investors. Sometimes completely furnished apartment houses are leased to women, who operate them at excellent profits over the rentals they have to pay under the basic leases.

Most women in the real estate business, however, concentrate on the selling of houses. They think in the same language as other women and are able to point out quickly and unerringly the things that women like to find in houses, much more so than most men can ever hope to do.

Some women get prospects from sources that few men would ever contact. This may be through women's clubs, or neighborhood acquaintances, or "through a friend of a friend." These prospects are usually not of the "shopper" type and are exclusive for the most part, seldom ever going to other brokers for offerings. Properly handled, such a prospect frequently purchases through the woman broker who first establishes a contact.

Since women brokers deal largely with a feminine clientele, they should make themselves familiar with the rights that women have in property which they acquire either individually or with their husbands. Rights of dower in each particular state should be fully investigated.

Personality is an important factor in the success of a woman who seeks to make her living selling real estate. Whether she can secure attractive listings of property may depend in part upon her approach and the manner in which she seeks to influence the owner of real estate to give her a listing. The way she impresses an owner on the first interview may spell the success or failure of her effort to sell the property. By the same token, personality plays a powerful part in her dealings with clients she is seeking to influence to buy her listings. Her appearance and the general impression she creates will have much to do with the manner in which her deal will progress. Neatness, dependability, and honesty of motive must make their presence felt as the approach is made and the successive steps of the sale unfold. Too much scent, an untidy hair-do, or slovenly dress may be quite as much of an obstacle for a women to overcome as an alcohol-flavored breath, dirty linen, and an unshaven face may be for a man.

The management of good-sized apartment properties offers opportunities to women attracted to the real estate field. In the larger cities there are scores of such apartments, most of them presided over by women managers who receive good salaries and also have their living quarters provided. Their duties call for the exercise of executive ability, the overseeing of the necessary help, collection of rentals, payment of bills, and the rendering of regular reports to the owners. The maintenance of the building also comes under their care as well as the distribution of laundry and the replacement of dishes, furniture, and so on, which have to be made from time to time.

Besides having charge of rental departments in larger offices, women sometimes qualify as managers of insurance departments. Such a person must have had extensive training in the insurance field before assuming charge of such an office department. She may have been associated with it in some capacity for a considerable time to become familiar with its operations.

A woman with the proper qualifications, a pleasant personality, and a liking for sales work and the contacts that it brings, can readily succeed in the real estate field if she applies herself seriously to the tasks that must be faced and earnestly and studiously seeks to make good.

CHAPTER 39

Hiring and

Training Salesmen

WHEN A BROKER FINDS HIS OFFICE AT-
tracting customers and sales are brisk, he begins to consider
expanding and adding a salesman or two to his staff. This is
the natural way for a real estate business to develop, but many
problems must be encountered and solved.

Not every broker has executive ability and is prepared to
hire and manage men. Frequently a broker can do more business and make more money operating alone than by spending
his time running around after careless and incompetent salesmen, trying to get them to produce. The position of the real
estate cycle has a good deal to do with whether it is wise to
expand and hire salesmen or to proceed on a more conservative
scale. When business is active, salesmen succeed. When it is
dull, they are sometimes more of a handicap than an advantage.

The task of building a sales organization is not an easy one.
Competent, successful salesmen with backgrounds of creditable
real estate experience are hard to find. Usually a broker must
start from scratch and build his own organization. In the long
run this is the most satisfactory method because it enables him
to obtain that most valuable business asset—loyalty to his
organization—that can seldom, if ever, be got from the clever
but unstable salesmen who float from office to office.

It is usually wise to employ young men with little or no real estate experience. Then it is not necessary for the new man to "unlearn" old tricks and practices or to overcome old prejudices he may have because things were done differently in his former office. If possible, hire a home-town product, a local man who knows the community and the people in it. He has a decided advantage over an outsider, who must learn all of the things the home-towm boy has already absorbed.

Don't select a man with too many responsibilities. A man whose head is full of other contacts or financial worries cannot give his best. Since a real estate salesman talks to clients in terms of thousands of dollars, he cannot inspire confidence if he looks worried or his appearance is slightly "seedy." A certain amount of responsibility is desirable, however, for it may keep a man on the job, and such a man is preferable to one whose thoughts are not on his work. If a new man feels it necessary to start earning substantial commissions at once, without training and establishing contacts, a real estate office is not the place for him. Such men quickly become dissatisfied and cause a high turnover in the sales force.

When interviewing a prospective salesman, get a line on him by asking just why he wants to sell real estate and why he thinks he can make a success of it. In other words, ask the man to sell himself! The hazards of the business should be explained to him. Point out that he may have to go some weeks before hoping to collect any compensation, because of the way the real estate business operates. Watch his reactions closely. He may quit dead, or he may explain that he is prepared to carry on for a reasonable time and really wants to learn the business and make good.

Years ago a clever insurance man put the proposition this way when a job seeker inquired what kind of money he could make in the insurance business: "Insurance," he said, "will pay better for *extremely* hard work than practically any other business. It won't pay a nickel for any other kind of work."

After the applicant has thought a bit, ask him if he is still interested and why. A salesman applicant should sell his personality to you, at the same time grinning over the shattering of his first golden dream. Every applicant has dreams of vast success when he first applies. He is going to make a thousand dollars on his first deal and he hopes to close it tomorrow!

It is really difficult to find men who possess the ability to sell. If they have that ability and know it and can demonstrate it, in all likelihood they will set themselves up as brokers and not want jobs as salesmen at all!

Having engaged a new salesman, when he comes to work explain to him the character of the business being conducted and how things work. When he has familiarized himself with operations, send him out "cold turkey" to get listings of both rentals and properties for sale. Have him go from house to house punching doorbells and inquiring of the occupants if they want to sell or rent their holdings. This will give him a chance to meet people and overcome tendencies to shyness. He will soon indicate his sales ability.

Next, take a new man along when working on deals and let him see how the minds of both the broker and the prospect work. Have him present when a deal is closed and placed in escrow. Seeing a deal closed will excite and interest him and make him eager to do it himself. Proceed to train the new man in every angle of the business, for without this he will fail to know the ropes when he gets a prospect in hand and attempts to make a sale.

All during the training period, have the new man spend some of his time soliciting property listings. If one or more of these are sold by others in the office, he should be given listing commissions for having obtained them. Teach him the necessity for having a balanced work schedule. He must have a plan that allots time for seeking new listings and new prospects, and time to devote to actual selling. He cannot depend upon the office for all his listings. If everyone did so there would be no listings, except those left at the offices by owners, and those are few indeed. A man who has no schedule to work by will overlook the necessity of constantly seeking new merchandise to sell, and when he gets through with one deal he will have to start out all over again to get a new stock of goods.

Have a salesman report every morning and spend at least

thirty minutes discussing new listings or additional information
the other men have picked up. All the men in the office should
have all the information the office can produce. Salesmen,
however, should never be permitted to cut in on other men's
deals.

When a man seems ready to do so, let him begin to interview new prospects and try his hand at selling them. The
sooner he gets experience the sooner he will become a productive unit in the office. Require him to submit a daily or weekly
written account of how he has spent his time each day, indicating the condition of each deal he has worked on. Check those
reports carefully to see if he is using his time wisely and if the
various deals are being properly serviced. Opportunities will
be afforded to correct wrong selling ideas or techniques and to
give much valuable advice which he may otherwise have to
learn through difficult experiences.

Careful and intelligent supervision of a salesman will produce dividends in the way of new deals. Encourage him not
to waste or misapply his time. Check to see that he is doing a
sufficient amount of work each day to uncover new listings,
new prospects, and new approaches to prospects who have previously turned cold.

Treat a new man fairly, impress him with your desire to
help him become efficient, and don't play favorites. Back him
to the extent of going to court, if necessary, to protect his and
your interests. If he knows you will stand behind him when
he does right, he will give you all his loyalty and best efforts to
the limit of his ability.

It is a good idea not to hire a salesman on the first interview.
The new man comes to the office and expresses a desire to
join it. There is no telling where he got the inspiration to enter
the real estate business, whether he has had the idea for a considerable length of time or whether it just came to him as
the result of hearing about a deal in which a broker or salesman made a nice commission. Talk the matter over with the
young man, find out all that you can about him, and suggest
that he come back in a day or two to talk things over again.
In many cases the applicant does not turn up again. It was a

momentary inspiration and he would not have stuck if he had been hired on the first interview. Given time to think things over, he decides that there are too many hazards in the realty business. He simply is not the man who would make good anyway, and it is much wiser to find this out *before* he joins an office staff than some days or weeks later when he proves himself a failure.

When a man seeks to join an office in a sales capacity, always ask for references. A broker should do this to protect himself, for there is no way of knowing what the background of a newcomer may be. In states where license laws prevail there are usually regulations dealing with the way salesmen may operate. Before a man can ever take a salesman's license examination in some states he must have made an arrangement with some real estate office to employ him as a salesman when he qualifies as such. If the new salesman is not successful in the first office he joins, he may go to another, but he must have a clearance approved from one office to the other, and the license exchange must be filed with the state realty commission. A check is thus kept on drifters, many of whom were the kind that got into trouble and gave the business a bad name in former days.

Many men get the queer idea that they can join up with a real estate office and in a few weeks begin to produce fabulous commissions. This is particularly so in an active real estate market. Some men do become big producers in short periods of time, but they are the unusual cases, and they would probably succeed in any other sales field they entered. It takes patience, time, and effort for a salesman to become proficient at selling real estate. When a man makes an application for a job, he must be impressed with the fact that he will have to study, work hard, and learn through experience the things that seasoned salesmen and brokers know.

Some real estate offices, particularly those engaged in the sale of subdivision property, have made it a practice in active times to hire any salesman who asks to go on the office roll.

This is done on the assumption that he has a few relatives or friends whom he might interest in property, make a sale or two, and then drop out and be heard from no more. The turn-over among this type of salesmen is excessive, and the con-tacts seldom do the office or the salesmen any good. Sales-men should join an office staff determined that they are going to make good, and the office itself should give the salesmen every help in doing so. No man, however, should be encouraged with the idea that he is going to turn a fine deal in a few days and make a big commission. Frequently it takes a man several months to establish his connection, get a deal going, and close it before he can collect his compensation.

In a well-organized real estate office, even when a sales-manager is in charge of the selling force, the hiring of new men is done by the head of the firm. He wants to know who is representing him in the field and does not even leave it to the salesmanager to select the men, although he may help. There should always be a close and friendly contact between the head of the firm and all the men employed in a sales capacity. If a man is going to conduct a business in which he is asking other men to work for him, he should keep in close touch with his sales force at all times, know what each man is doing, and how he is getting along. Frequently a little per-sonal help and encouragement from the head man will make a salesman produce a volume of work he never before felt him-self capable of.

While enthusiasm is a necessary asset in a real estate sales-man, there is the danger that a man who is too enthusiastic will develop into a high-pressure salesman who, instead of selling a property on its merits, often forces his personality into the deal and persuades a buyer to buy unwisely, often ex-tending himself more than he should. In interviewing sales-men, it is always wise to watch for this type. Perhaps such a man can be controlled and developed into a valuable asset in the business, but he should never be permitted to run wild and simply make a record of sales at the expense of the good name of an office.

Beware of the young man who has an independent income and wants to go into the real estate business simply for the purpose of impressing his friends with the idea that he is engaged in some kind of business. Poor boys make better salesmen than well-to-do youngsters because they *have* to get out and hustle for their daily bread. The man who has independent means may occasionally develop into a good salesman, but the chances are that he will not attend to business the way the young fellow who really has to make a living will do.

Some brokers who themselve have been excellent salesmen have occasionally made the mistake of becoming executives over a sales staff when they did not have the ability to handle such a responsibility. One must study the question seriously to determine whether he is fitted to be head of an office, or whether it is better to proceed slowly and operate alone on a smaller scale. The responsibilities of being the head of an office are different from those of being a salesman or a broker. A certain amount of experience is needed to qualify in this field, so that it is well to make the transition slowly and with care if at all.

Frequently a broker makes up his mind to expand his office and does so, only to find that he seldom has time to make a deal himself, although he may be the best qualified man in the office to do so. Realizing this and still desiring to operate a sales force, he engages a sales manager to direct sales activities. A good sales manager is hard to get, for if he is a good producer he prefers straight selling to managing the activities of others. Occasionally a man with executive ability in handling men and organizing sales work prefers that type of work, only occasionally making a deal himself.

What are the qualifications a man must have to handle a sales force? Here are several:[1]

1. A pleasing and sympathetic personality.
2. A desire and an ability to perform hard work.
3. A capacity for arousing enthusiasm and inspiring men.
4. A natural gift for leadership.
5. A thorough knowledge of fundamentals underlying the

[1] From *Selling Real Estate*, 3rd Ed., by Stanley McMichael (Englewood Cliffs, N. J.: Prentice-Hall, Inc.)

development of scientific sales methods and their application to the real estate business.

The salesmanager must be, above all things, a manager of his men. Closing sales comes easy if he knows how to direct the activities of a salesmen. Salesmen expect from their salesmanager:

1. Cordial individual supervision and coöperation.
2. A capacity for analyzing the strong and the weak points of each salesman so there may be brought into play the latent abilities possessed by every man.
3. Fair and unbiased treatment.
4. Complete willingness to devote individual attention to the problems of salesmen as they present themselves.
5. Willingness to tell what he possesses in knowledge and experience.

A successful salesmanager must have been a successful salesman before graduating to his executive job. If he does not know his stuff, he soon loses the loyalty and coöperation of his men. He must win and retain their respect and allegiance if he is to direct them effectively.

Sometimes a broker who is enjoying a good business is lured into a partnership with another broker. Partnerships occasionally prove successful, but usually it is found that one horse in the team pulls harder and faster than the other and carries more of the load, while the other seems to shirk and lags behind. Consider the question very seriously before forming a partnership, for hazards may be encountered that will prove unpleasant later when an attempt is made to dissolve the partnership. It takes unusual qualities in two men to team up and pull together successfully throughout the years. It was Emerson who said, "Every business is the lengthened shadow of a man." Most offices were created from the inspiration of *one* man!

Study the essentials of good real estate salesmanship. In interviewing men seeking to enter the business, make sure that they show inclinations to meet the requirements demanded of them.

CHAPTER 40

Rehabilitating

Property for Sale

THE REALTY BROKER OR SALESMAN SHOULD always take a keen interest in property that owners desire to list with him, and should help them to put it in the most presentable condition possible before offering it for sale.

It is a well-established fact that most buyers of homes—and women buy most of them—want brand new houses. They frown on old, run-down dwellings just as they would resent having to buy and wear second-hand clothing.

Many fine improvements have appeared in new houses in the past few years that have outmoded the older structures and placed upon many of them a pall of obsolescence that makes it difficult to find buyers for them, unless they are overhauled and brought up to date.

To stimulate the demand for and sale of old houses is certainly the duty of the real estate fraternity. There are about 59,000,000 housing units in the United States, of which approximately 20,000,000 are in central cities, 17,000,000 in metropolitan areas outside the cities, and 22,000,000 outside standard metropolitan areas. Millions more are going to be erected in the coming years. About 60% of the homes in the country are inhabited by their owners. The others are rented to tenants of high and low degree. About 46.5% of the 59,000,-000 housing units are more than 30 years old. Most of them

325

lack the latest developments to be found in kitchens and bath-rooms, as well as in lighting, heating, and air-conditioning equipment. In many cases the architecture is old-fashioned and requires modernization.

When a broker is offered a house as a listing, he should do several things:

1. Refrain from setting a price on it or accepting a price from the owner until the broker knows something about it.

2. Visit the property and inspect it carefully.

3. Confer with the owner and persuade him to make the place as presentable as his means will afford.

4. Having agreed on a price, try to get an exclusive sales contract so that the broker can freely advertise it without starting on a free-for-all battle with every other real estate man in town.

The presentability of a house has much to do with the ease with which it can be sold as well as the price received for it. When a structure is 20 or 25 years old it is usually ready for a thorough overhauling. In many cases it should have a com-plete rebuilding job done, including, for instance:

1. Changing roof lines to make them more attractive and modern.

2. Wrecking old porches that are out of date eyesores and are seldom if ever used.

3. Re-doing the electrical system, adding more outlets, better lighting and 220 volt outlets for equipment like air-conditioners and dryers.

4. Installation of new bathroom outfits, including plumb-ing, fixtures, tiling, and vanity units.

5. Tearing out old out-of-date kitchens, installing new stoves, sinks, refrigerators, coolers, and other modern equip-ment. Include new linoleum, exhaust fans, enlargement of windows, and bring the washer and dryer out of the basement.

6. Provide another bedroom or two, *with bath* if needed.

7. Overhaul the basement and install a new economical

heating and air-conditioning plant with outlets in various rooms, where needed, before decorating is done.

8. Sand and varnish floors where needed, overlaying old wood floors with carpets, tile, or vinyl.

9. Add garage space. Some day every adult member of the family will own and operate an automobile.

10. Take a look over the grounds, eliminate or trim srubbery and trees, and clean up the entire premises.

11. Paint the building outside or install aluminum siding, and redecorate it inside.

Not all of these things will have to be done to every house, but many houses will require all or most of them. It costs money to do this work, but every dollar spent will add *at least two dollars in value to the premises*. And it is the broker who will be called upon for preliminary advice and suggestions in most cases.

Having a bright idea about rebuilding a house and proceeding to do it are two entirely separate things. Yet it is not difficult to finance the work—at one time the big stumbling block. The United States Federal Housing Administration, which operates throughout the nation, cooperates in guaranteeing any loan a financial institution is willing to advance to accomplish such work. Under Title I, §2, and Title II, §§203(k) and 220(h), the FHA has a broad program for insuring lenders against losses on loans that are used to pay for alterations, repairs, and improvements upon existing structures. Application to any bank, mortgage company, or savings and loan association will promptly be considered and, if accepted, will be submitted to FHA for its loan guarantee. Work can then proceed. FHA merely guarantees the loans; financial institutions actually make them.

It is necessary for a property owner to have a sketch of his dwelling to show what improvements he contemplates. It need not be an elaborate drawing. It can easily be worked into shape by a draftsman. The sketch permits the securing of a building permit so the work may be done under departmental rules and regulations.

The maximum loan to be insured varies with the Title under which it is obtained. Thus, the maximum loan under Title I for Class 1(a) loan (single-family residential dwelling, is $3,500. Under Title II the maximum loan on such a dwelling would be the lesser of (a) the FHA's estimate of the cost of improvements, or (b) $10,000. (However, these Title II amounts may be increased up to 45 per cent in high-cost areas.) Loan maturities are generally shorter under Title I than under Title II.

Competent building craftsmen can be found in most communities to do rehabilitation work. However, most architects and building contractors unfortunately are averse to small remodeling jobs, preferring new construction jobs at higher contract figures.

To old neglected houses can be directly traced the running down of neighborhoods in American cities, the speedy deterioration of residential buildings, and the breeding of slums.

The federal government, recognizing the problem, has started to attack it, as, for example, in the Urban Renewal Program. But much more remains, and will remain, to be done. Apart from the federal programs, few communities are making any concerted effort to do much about it. Speculators occasionally will buy old houses, rebuild them, and sell them at a profit. But much more could be done if real estate brokers made the owners of old homes aware of the desirability of placing their premises in good physical condition before offering them for sale.

The grim spectre of obsolescence is constantly stalking throughout the land. Every time a new building gadget or device is invented and used generally in new homes, every old structure without such a gadget immediately suffers in sales appeal. Over a period of years so many new things have been invented and installed on a wide scale that a dwelling 20 years old, which usually has none of them, is scarcely presentable for sale. The thing to do, in most cases, is to take an old house apart and put it together again, installing all types of new improvements, many of which cost very little but add greatly to the value of the new dwelling when offered for sale. And often it is merely some new, attractive gadget that clinches a sale!

Take an old house worth, say, $16,000, situated in an old but fine residential district, in an average city or town, near a main thoroughfare where there is a bus line. It is not far from a school, a church, a library, and stores. This well-built old structure has an attractive living-room with an old-fashioned fireplace, a dining-room with outmoded, built-in glass cabinets, a library, and a kitchen. On the back porch is a toilet. Upstairs are four or five bedrooms and *one* bath. Here is what might be done with this old dwelling:

1. Modernize the fireplace in the living room by installing a new mantel.

2. Tear out the old-fashioned built-in cabinets in the dining-room. Eliminate gingerbread trellis in arch and do away with beamed ceiling.

3. Overhaul the old library and convert it to a modern den.

4. Go into the kitchen and replace the old plumbing. Install a new sink, a stove, refrigerator, ventilating system, and floor coverings. Convert one corner into an attractive breakfast compartment.

5. Look over window arrangement, eliminate some of them, and greatly enlarge some of the other windows.

6. Upstairs, completely overhaul the old bathroom and install new tile walls, plumbing, and fixtures.

7. Cut in and install another bathroom between two of the bedrooms.

8. Install more windows to allow cross-ventilation and more light.

9. If you must keep the big porch, build a place on its roof for sun baths.

10. Double or treble the size of the one-car garage.

11. Redecorate inside and out.

This complete job, in most communities, would probably cost up to $10,000 or $12,000, most of which could be financed through FHA. Total cost of the property would then be about

$28,000, but it could be sold, in all probability, for $35,000, and probably could not be reproduced new for less than $40,000. And it would be in a prime residential location and not ten miles out in the suburbs where it takes 30 minutes in an automobile to come and go, mornings and evenings.

The next few years will doubtless see even higher building costs in most cities. In many cases it might be cheaper and more desirable to rehabilitate old and rundown homes rather than build new ones. And it should be the duty of every real estate broker and salesman to help in this work. He should be throughly familiar with building and remodeling costs and be able to recommend builders who are willing to accept and execute such work. Doubtless this will be a field in which many small but expert builders will specialize.

Buying old houses, remodeling, and reselling them is a profitable sideline for real estate brokers themselves and a thoroughly legitimate one, for they are the men who know how to do it, who appreciate the need for such work, and who can resell them to buyers who are as well served as if they purchased brand new dwellings.

Even if complete remodeling cannot be done on a dwelling, for various reasons, no property should be offered for sale by a broker or salesman which is not at least in a clean and presentable condition. Even a coat of paint on the outside and some decorating inside will make a dwelling much more attractive than the shape it was in when vacated. New lighting fixtures cost very little but do much to tone up the rooms in which they are located. Carpeting floors is not an expensive operation but pays big dividends in the price obtainable.

What has been said heretofore about the necessity for rehabilitating old houses applies equally as well to store properties, thousands of which will require "face-lifting" operations during the next few years. Stores need new fronts periodically just as women need new dresses. Beyond exterior and interior decorating there is not much one can do to a store. Every broker or salesman who lists property should keep in mind the need and desirability of overhauling it and the probable new values such work will create

CHAPTER 41

Compensation for

Brokers and Salesmen

IT IS GENERALLY KNOWN THAT THE REAL estate business is operated on a commission basis, brokers and salesmen drawing as their compensation a percentage of the total selling price of the properties they dispose of.

Through the years commission rates have been fixed in each community by the local real estate board, or, if no board exists, through a long-standing agreement among the brokers involved. Broadly speaking, the rate for selling property is about 6 per cent of the selling price in most parts of the United States and Canada.

Commissions are considered earned by a broker when he secures the names of buyer and seller on a written contract and consequently has achieved a "meeting of the minds." It is usually collected at the time title passes from seller to buyer, at the close of escrow, when the buyer gets his deed and the funds representing the sale price are turned over to the seller, less the commission and transfer expenses of the deal.

All real estate boards have regular schedules of commissions for most types of deals and contingencies. A newcomer to the business should immediately get in touch with his nearest board, secure a copy of the commission schedule, and abide by it.

The compensation due to a broker, acting independently as such, is not a difficult thing to establish. It is when compensation is to be paid a salesman that problems arise. It is a very general practice, in most cities, to make a 50–50 division of commissions between an employed salesman and the office for which he works. If a house is listed and sold for $20,000 by a salesman, a gross commission of $1200 is collected, of which the salesman gets $600 and the office $600.[1]

Salesmen work under varying conditions in different offices in different parts of the country. No standardization of commissions has ever been considered feasible or desirable. There are varying arrangements under which salesmen work, also. For instance, one large Chicago office has three distinct arrangements, as follows:

1. Salesmen working on a salary basis (which is unusual).

2. Salesmen working on a drawing-account basis (which is seldom done).

3. Salesmen working on a straight-commission basis (which is usual).

In some offices an arrangement is made with a salesman who has a reputation for good production to grant him 60 per cent of all commissions on deals he closes up to a certain volume of business, 40 per cent going to the office as its compensation for overhead and management.

Then there is the sliding scale arrangement that some offices use. In the Chicago office mentioned above, an arrangement was reached with salesmen to increase the proportion of their commissions as their total income for the year increased. To do this the following schedule was adopted:

Gross Commissions	Salesman	Office
Up to $7,500	50%	50%
$7,501 and under $10,000 .... $\begin{cases} 50\% \text{ on 1st} & \$ \ 7,500 \\ 55 \ \ \text{ on next} & 2,500 \end{cases}$		50% 45

[1] See Chapter 35, "A Policy Book an Office Asset," for a discussion of various ways of dividing commissions with salesmen.

$10,000 and under $25,000	50% on 1st $ 7,500 55 on next 2,500 60 on over 10,000	50% 45 40	

$25,000 and up	50% on 1st $ 7,500 55 on next 2,500 60 on next 15,000 65 on over 25,000	50% 45 40 35	

Example

$ 7,500 per year	$ 3,750	$ 3,750
10,000 per year	5,125	4,875
20,000 per year	11,125	8,875
25,000 per year	14,125	10,875
50,000 per year	30,375	19,625

When salesmen have demonstrated their ability to earn consistently they are sometimes granted drawing accounts to tide them over dull periods, these amounts being charged against their commission accounts as deals are closed. For men receiving drawing accounts, the following schedule might be used:

Gross Commissions	Salesman	Office
Up to $7,500	47½%	52½%
$7,501 and under $10,000	47½% on 1st $ 7,500 52½% on next 2,500	52½% 47½
10,000 and up	47½% on 1st $ 7,500 52½ on next 2,500 57½ on over 10,000	52½% 47½ 42½
$25,000 and up	47½% on 1st $ 7,500 52½ on next 2,500 57½ on next 15,000 62½ on over 25,000	52½% 47½ 42½ 37½

Example

$ 7,500 per year	$ 3,562.50	$ 3,937.50
10,000 per year	4,875.00	5,125.00
20,000 per year	10,625.00	9,375.00
25,000 per year	13,500.00	11,500.00
50,000 per year	29,125.00	20,875.00

A salesman may choose to drop his drawing account and go back on the regular schedule. But while he is in debt to the company he works on the schedule for salesmen on drawing accounts. If a salesman manages to get out of debt to the firm at the end of three months or six months, his commissions are figured pro rata on the basis of a salesman financing himself for the pro rata part of the year in which he actually does finance himself.

Salesmen who occasionally operate on a salary basis usually receive 25 per cent of the gross commissions earned on deals they negotiate.

To encourage listing of properties by salesmen, many offices allow a 10 per cent commission to the listing salesman. When a sale is made, the salesman negotiating the deal gets 45 per cent, the office 45 per cent, and the listing salesman gets the other 10 per cent. This is the practice in most offices, although in some the listing fee paid is only 5 per cent and that comes out of the 50 per cent paid to the negotiating salesman. Out of the 50 per cent going to the office, all advertising, overhead, and other expenses are paid.

Heads of offices, including officers of companies, reserve the right to make deals in any territories in which listings are held. The commissions received from such deals are not divided with salesmen, except that the person who has brought in a good listing that is sold gets his commission for it.

Salesmen in well-conducted offices are not permitted to deviate from board schedules of commissions. If they do so, the amount of the reduction is charged against that portion to be received by the salesman who allowed such reduction.

Offices generally have a rule that no salesman can collect a commission on the sale of a listing of any property if the sale is made after the salesman has left the employ of the company. If a contract of sale is signed prior to his leaving, however, he is considered to have earned his commission.

Commissions on short-term leases are computed on the total rental for the term of the lease.

Rental commissions vary throughout the country. When a

month-to-month rental is made, one-half of the first month's rental is usually assessed as the commission. When 5 per cent of the total rental is larger than that, then that sum is charged. In some rental departments the commission on commercial property on a lease basis is 6 per cent. Property managers usually retain 5 per cent of the monthly rentals they collect as a management charge.

Many real estate offices operate insurance departments where salesmen may receive one-half of the regular commissions earned on the policies they are instrumental in obtaining for the office.

Competent brokers, after years of study, often develop into appraisers, in which capacity they are called upon to make valuations for property owners and for public utilities, towns, cities, counties, and school boards. Compensation for appraising differs in different parts of the country and according to the quality and type of service rendered.

Many brokers who had never had appraisal experience gained valuable knowledge and contacts during the time the Home Owners Loan Corporation was functioning. Hundreds of valuators were needed and a standardized form of appraisal was created and used, for which the appraisers got $5 each at the outset, later being required to give additional service and a more extended report for which they received $20 for each assignment. The Federal Housing Administration at the outset used what were known as "fee appraisers," that is, regular brokers who accepted assignments but did not give all of their time to the work. For the most part FHA now uses its own staff members who are on a monthly salary. The Veterans Administration uses many appraisers. It, too, uses a standardized form and pays about $25 for an appraisal.

Fees for appraisal work will vary widely, depending upon the type of property being evaluated, the amount of work involved, and the qualifications of the appraiser. (As noted earlier in Chapter 36, it is unethical for a member of the American Institute of Real Estate Appraisers to fix his compensation at a percentage of his valuation estimate). Typical fees for a member of the Institute (M.A.I.) would be $50 for a residential appraisal, $150 for a gasoline station, and $500 to $2,000 for an apartment building.

Most members of the American Institute of Real Estate Appraisers ask and receive $75 to $100 a day for court appearances at which they testify as to valuations they have made of property under court consideration, usually for condemnations in connection with street openings and similar purposes. These men are the top rankers in the business.

Special assignments that require an appraiser to leave the city call for higher compensation, since the valuator must go into a territory with which he is not familiar and a condition exists which calls for close and intensive study of the district in which he is asked to value a property. For out-of-town calls the valuator gets his hotel and traveling expenses in addition to whatever fee is agreed upon.

There is a tendency for realty boards to standardize their commission charges and make them fairly uniform throughout the country. Eventually this may be accomplished. In times of advancing prices, when wage earners are clamoring for higher returns in their pay envelopes, the real estate broker does not worry much, for such conditions stiffen property prices and, when a sale occurs, the commission paid to a broker is correspondingly higher and in keeping with prevailing price levels.

A real estate broker or a salesman is well or poorly paid according to the volume of business he is able to do from month to month and from year to year. Clever, well-grounded individuals who work hard frequently pile up large commissions, while men poorly adapted to do the work and who are sluggish in their actions earn little and soon retire.

The question often arises whether a broker should confine himself solely to selling property for others, receiving his compensation entirely from commissions earned. It is a fact that those real estate men who have really made money for themselves have conducted their brokerage business honestly and in the interest of their customers, but have at the same time bought and sold properties on their own account. There seems to be no reason why a broker should not do this, provided he advises an owner that he is buying a property listed with him. In such a case it should be clearly understood that the broker is buying direct from the owner, with no commission to be charged the owner on the transaction, and at a price satisfactory to the owner.

CHAPTER 42

Selling Real Estate

As A Vocation

MANY DIFFERENT MOTIVES DOUBTLESS prompt men and women to engage in the real estate business. Some are attracted because it promises to be a good way to make large commissions with relatively little effort. Others are attracted through an acquaintanceship with a broker or developer who suggests taking up the occupation. The ones who really are the most successful are those who perceive opportunities to serve in an environment rich with possibilities of constructive effort in dealing in the world's most extensive commodity—land—and the fascinating work of improving it in many different ways.

Most men who have entered real estate work in the past have had little opportunity to realize its vast possibilities. But now the importance of real estate education has been recognized by institutions of higher learning. The University of Wisconsin was the first to establish a full-time four-year course in real estate, and it was followed by various other large colleges and universities throughout the country. In many night-school departments of high school systems throughout the country regular courses on real estate now have their place and are extensively patronized.

Real estate appraising has become recognized as an established science under the sponsorship of the American Institute of Real Estate Appraisers, which embraces in its membership all of the leading appraisers of the country. Extensive courses in appraising are now directed by this organization, presided over by the most experienced valuators in the business. While real estate appraising is a profession in itself, it is nevertheless a subject in which every man or woman who expects to succeed in the business must be well versed. Without an accurate knowledge of how to establish values, a broker is simply at sea. Ability to appraise is the foundation of real estate education.

There is so much to know about real estate and it takes such a long time to secure a thorough working knowledge of it that many state real estate commissions require applicants seeking licenses to operate as salesmen and to take courses of study so they can pass examinations to become brokers.

The real estate business presents golden opportunities to serve in the handling of deals involving many millions of dollars annually in each community as well as many millions more as represented in the mortgage encumbrances associated with such transactions. If a man fails to make good, it can almost always be traced to the fact that he has failed to prepare himself properly for the work undertaken, or that he is not mentally or physically qualified to engage in this calling.

Just what are the necessary qualifications of a person who will make good in the real estate business? Here are only a few:

1. A genuine liking for people, and an eagerness to mingle with and be interested in them.

2. A reasonable amount of enthusiasm in the opportunities afforded in real estate, so that one will seek to qualify himself to serve.

3. A willingness to study and continually seek out and learn new things about real estate, and the business of selling and improving it.

4. Absolute honesty of purpose and a background of good conduct in all lines of endeavors formerly engaged in.

5. Good health.

6. An alert imagination, which can be quickened and made to function when coming in contact with many phases of the business. This attribute leads to promotional selling and developing, the most profitable of all lines of real estate activity.

7. Rugged steadfastness and perseverance to carry on against discouraging odds which sometimes engulf even the most earnest worker.

8. Patience—*infinite patience!*

9. A personality that enables one to influence others favorably.

10. A willingness to work. Few good real estate brokers observe a forty-hour work week. It's a business to make good in if you *work hard!*

A real estate man gets out of his business just what he puts into it in the way of preparation and attention. To the degree that he is qualified will he be able to earn good commissions. It is a calling of tremendous scope, and few become expert in all of its branches.

Genuine opportunities exist for the man who will earnestly seek to become proficient in real estate. There are commissions to be earned and also chances to buy and sell property on one's own account at substantial profits, at a later time when he has accumulated capital with which to operate. For the first few months he must regard himself as an apprentice who is learning the trade. He is of comparatively little value to his firm even if he is earning his way. It is when he has gained experience and can go out and turn good deals on a large scale that he becomes valuable to his office and is ready to earn good compensation for his own services.

Few men are sufficiently qualified to enter the real estate brokerage field without some preliminary training in an established office, even if they do hold broker's licenses. For their own benefit and to widen the horizons of their own knowledge and experience, it will be wise for them to team up with an operating broker or office where they can learn the ropes without being forced to learn the business the hard way, and by making mistakes which might otherwise be avoided.

The real estate business offers much and at the same time it demands much. For the man who is suited to carry on the work there are ample financial rewards and chances to become wealthy through operating and building. It is an interesting, dignified business that enables one to use to the highest advantage whatever intellect, physical charm and personality, and moral and physical courage one has. All of these qualifications welded into a dynamic individaul spell the highest degree of success in this fascinating field of human endeavor.

The real estate business as a vocation may be entered at almost any period of one's life. Many men who have been sucessful in other lines have been attracted to it in middle life, have studied earnestly until they became familiar with most of the fundamentals, and then often have made an outstanding success of their efforts. One should not wait until he is too old, however, to make up his mind to join the ranks of realtors, for physical stamina is required to carry on. It is no business for broken-down members of other businesses or professions to seek a haven when they have failed elsewhere.

There never was a more wonderful period in history in which to go into the real estate business! Vast housing and business facilities are needed in towns and cities throughout the country. While the last fifty years have seen miracles, the next fifty years will see them eclipsed in a manner no one can even imagine now. The use of plastics and other new materials will be woven into real estate promotions. Transportation facilities will be improved and added to immeasurably. With great increases in the use of machinery to do the heavy work, leisure time for all will be increased. Five hours a day five days a week may shortly be all the work the average working man may be called upon to do. This will broaden opportunities for enjoyment of outdoor life, travel, and activities about one's home.

There never was such a period of time in which to live! We never before knew so much or could do so much! Never before have we managed to live in such comfort, among conditions of such magnificence. With the unfolding of a period of great building expansion the outlook for success in real estate definitely brightens. There *are* opportunities to succeed in the real estate business. More men of real capacity *can* make good. Can you?

IT IS UP TO YOU!

INDEX